The
History
of
ORT

The History of

By Leon Shapiro

ORT

A Jewish Movement
for Social Change

Schocken Books · New York

First published by Schocken Books 1980
10 9 8 7 6 5 4 3 2 1   80 81 82 83
Copyright © 1980 by World ORT Union

Library of Congress Cataloging in Publication Data

Shapiro, Leon.
    The history of ORT.

    1. World ORT Union—History.   2. Occupational
training—Jews—History.   I. Title.
HD5715.S5   331.2'592   79-22379

Design by Sidney Solomon
Production by Publishers Creative Services

Manufactured in the United States of America

Acknowledgments

It is my pleasant duty to acknowledge with many thanks support given me by the World ORT Union in preparation of this volume.

In the course of my work I used the library of the Institute for Jewish Research in New York, as well as the National Library in Jerusalem. I wish to express my sincere thanks to the YIVO Librarian, Ms. Dina Abramovicz, and to Mr. Abram Wolfson and Ms. Inna Apanovskaja of the Jerusalem National Library, who were very helpful in locating material on the early Tsarist period of ORT.

Special thanks are due to Ms. Sara Bramson, who put at the disposal of ORT, much material left by her father, the late Dr. Leon Bramson. Mr. Sussya Goldmann, who knows ORT from its Berlin days, and whose memoirs on ORT represent an important contribution to the ORT archives, helped me to locate documentation related to ORT in its European period. He was most gracious in assisting my research in the archives of the World ORT Union. Mr. Joseph Neville, Director of the ICA, was very generous in putting at my disposal the important ICA archives. Mr. Jacob Oleiski shared with me his thorough knowledge of ORT and, more particularly, of the DP period.

I am indebted to many colleagues and friends who read parts of the manuscript and gave me the benefit of their comments and suggestions. As the continuous reader of the manuscript in the course of its preparation, Jack Rader deserves special mention and special thanks. He has given generously of his time to assure the successful outcome of the project.

May I add a word of caution addressed to the men and women in ORT with whom I had conversations, consulted, or interviewed in the course of writing this book. Some of them might be disappointed in not finding direct reference to our sometimes lengthy and significant discussions. They should not be disappointed. Their contribution to my understanding of ORT and its activities was significant. I could not, however, quote or refer to all my oral research work on ORT; it would take us beyond the limits of this volume and, perhaps, interrupt the natural flow of the narrative.

I do wish, however, to express my sincere gratitude to the following men and women who were particularly helpful in the elucidation of many problems encountered in the preparation of the manuscript: Max Braude, Director General of the World ORT Union; Vladimir Halperin, Director of the World ORT Union; Dr. William Haber, President of the World ORT Union; Daniel Mayer, Chairman of the World ORT Union Executive Committee; Harold Friedman, formerly President, and now Chairman of the Executive Committee, of the American ORT Federation; John F. Davidson, American ORT Federation; Paul Bernick, Executive Director, American ORT Federation; Nathan Gould, Executive Vice President of Women's American ORT; Messrs. Edward Sard and Louis Walinsky, formerly with ORT; Herman Benson, American ORT Federation; Samuel Milman, Executive Secretary, American Labor ORT.

I wish to record my gratitude to Mrs. Mowshovitz and

Mr. Mark Wolf of British ORT, who have given me the benefit of their thorough knowledge of the beginnings of ORT in Western Europe; also to Cecily Zimmerman, whose knowledge of ORT work in England was very helpful, and to Morton Creeger, ORT Director in England.

I wish also to express my thanks to the late Feivel Schrager who gave me the benefit of his views on ORT, its history, and its significance. Special thanks are due to Georges Melamed, formerly the Director of ORT-France, whose knowledge of French ORT and whose generous assistance I appreciate. Mr. Bernard Wand-Polak was helpful in providing an insight into ORT in Latin America.

Mr. Joseph Harmatz, the Director General of ORT-Israel, introduced me to the widespread activities of ORT in Israel. For many days we travelled around the country, studying the ORT schools and installations; therefore, my gratitude to him, both for the information provided and for his hospitality. Thanks are owed, as well, to Michael Avitzour, Deputy Director, who gave me unsparingly of his time and his knowledge of ORT in Israel. I am indebted to Joshua Fliedel for his explanations of the school system in Israel. Rene Weil was very helpful in his discussion of the ORT position in Israel.

My appreciation to the staff of the World ORT Union in Geneva and to the staff of the American ORT Federation in New York, who dealt with the unglamourous, but essential, task of typing the manuscript; and to Mrs. Tillie Klorman who helped me in the technical preparation of the manuscript. I am grateful to Ms. Adrian Mann and to Ms. Susan Fletcher for many courtesies and for making my work so much easier. I appreciate Sidney Solomon's attention to the design of the volume and Emanuel Geltman's close reading of the manuscript. My wife, Luba, was not only the first reader of the manuscript, but she endured with me the tiresome task of reading and checking all these pages. Her patience and encouragement were of inestimable help.

I wish to add that I alone am responsible for the selection of the material and for the views expressed in this book.

Preface

Reconstructing the chronicle of ORT, an organization that was born in Russia a century ago and which survived two World Wars and the ravages of revolution, presents innumerable difficulties. Losses of documents and records reflect these harsh events, thus creating obstacles to the historian. Other losses must have occurred during the early European period, the Nazi era, and the period of the Holocaust. Important archives exist, but they are unevenly distributed in terms of period and country.

Established, as we have said, in 1880 in Imperial Russia, ORT proceeded, after World War I, to spread its organizing activities to many countries. By the end of World War II, coordinated and stimulated by the World ORT Union, which came into existence in 1921, it had succeeded in extending its work to countries on all five continents. The historian, then, has to cope with an additional problem: the relationship between ORT programs in different places and the ORT organization as a whole.

Does a history of ORT call for a summary description of the activities carried on in separate countries, or does it call for this and something more?

I believe that a history of ORT, while embracing activities at different periods and in different countries, must above all investigate the development of the idea central to all local ORT manifestations. I shall not presume to follow all the small tracks into the past in all their multi-colored details.

Proper space will of course be given to the labors performed in separate countries, but these programs will be brought into focus, giving them a rational shape in the coordinating principle of ORT as it operates through the instrument of the World ORT Union.

This history of ORT will therefore be viewed from a three-layered perspective: (1) stable elements visible throughout its development; (2) moving patterns appearing here and there, depending on time; and (3) adaptation and readjustment to meet changing needs.

The meaning of ORT, the only Jewish organization of Russian origin to attain its 100th year, will be viewed against the broader background of Jewish life with its continuing interplay of social and political environment and the inevitable clash between ideas and practical necessity. Those events that played a crucial role and contributed to a coherent picture of the development of ORT will be given their proper weight.

There are methodological difficulties involved in an inquiry that would attempt to answer such questions about a phenomenon of the past of which we are the heirs and at a point in a continuing flux. To devise a critical framework within which it would be possible, without too much misreading, to pinpoint positive and or negative aspects we must return to the distant past so that we may see things as they were then.

The periodization will reflect significant changes crucial to ORT's evolution, providing, as it were, natural frontiers in time and space. My methodological approach is to show how the central ORT idea projected itself into the multitude of Jewish communities which strove and still strive to meet the compelling needs of the Jewish people.

Contents

The
History
of
ORT

Chapter 1

The Setting

Anti-Jewish restrictions in Russia are as old as the Russian state itself. The Charter of Iaroslav, successor to St. Vladimir, promulgated in the 11th century, placed severe limitations on Jewish inhabitants of Kievan Russ, and this was also true during the latter period of Moscow Russia. The "Jewish question" in its various manifestations, however, appeared in Imperial Russia only toward the end of the 18th century when, after three successive partitions of Poland (1772, 1793, and 1795) large, formerly Polish territories were incorporated into Russia.

With these territories Russia also acquired a considerable Jewish population, estimated by many reliable sources to have numbered 600,000 to 700,000. Initially, following the annexations, some promises of liberalization were made by Catherine II (1762-1796), but the Russian government, unprepared to deal with large masses of a distinctly different people and unable to depart from centuries-old anti-Jewish bias, soon instituted a policy of exceptional laws and restrictions. For the new Jewish inhabitants of Russia everything was taboo unless permitted by special laws.

By a decree of 1794 the Jews of Russia were confined

1

to a specified geographic area which they were not permitted to leave and in which they could engage only in certain occupations. Thus was created the Pale of Settlement which for some 120 years placed the Jews of Russia in a "special situation."

The same 1794 law that established the Pale imposed a special discriminatory status on Jews who wished to better themselves by entering the class of merchants or citizen burghers, who were compelled to pay double the tax imposed on non-Jews.

Soon, the "liberal" Empress decreed that Jews residing in villages be registered in and transferred to towns "for their own benefit." There followed a series of expulsions from the villages that deprived settled Jewish families of their livelihood and relegated most Russian Jews to the bottom of the Russian social structure, reduced to living from day to day.[1]

An Early Study

The critical situation of the Jewish masses came somewhat indirectly to the attention of the Russian authorities during the reign of Catherine II's successor, Tsar Paul (1796-1801). In the course of investigating conditions in the former Polish lands now part of Russia, the not very knowledgeable Russian bureaucrats also looked into the status of the Jewish population. Toward the end of Paul's short reign, Gavrila Derzhavin, a celebrated Russian poet of the early period, was entrusted with the mission of investigating the situation of the Jews in the area of their concentration and to suggest remedies conforming to the interests of the Crown.

Derzhavin's mission culminated in a complex report under the title "Opinion of Senator Derzhavin Concerning Curbing the Avaricious Pursuits of the Jews and Concerning Their Re-education and Other Matters." The "Opinion" makes the Jews the scapegoat for the continuing impoverishment of the Russian peasants, the serfs of the rich and often absentee Russian and Polish landlords. We shall not go into all of the details, but some aspects of the "Opinion" are of immediate concern to our present investigation.

While discriminatory suggestions, offensive statements, and evidence of ignorance in the "Opinion" are plentiful, the document nevertheless contained a number of interesting suggestions. According to Dubnow,[2] Derzhavin used ideas proposed to him by two "enlightened" Jews. One idea apparently came from Nota Shklower,[3] a rich merchant of St. Petersburg, a Russian Court Jew who had connections in various ministries and was something of a Jewish *shtadlan*. Shklower proposed to attract Jews to agriculture by settling them in the area of the Black Sea. He also proposed the establishment of factories where young Jews could learn crafts which, he believed, would bring Jews into productive labor, an idea dear to the *maskilim* (the enlightened) in both Eastern and Western Europe.

We do not need to know what use was made by Derzhavin of suggestions coming from Jewish *maskilim*. It is sufficient to record that already in the 18th century the idea of Jewish productive labor was becoming an important element of many projects aimed at the amelioration of the economic conditions of Jewish life in the Pale. Jacob Girsh submitted in 1783 a memorandum to the authorities in St. Petersburg suggesting the establishment of a network of schools in Belorussia, where Jewish children would receive general education and vocational training.

Much later, Isaac Ber-Levinson (1788-1860), an early Russian *maskil* with connections in St. Petersburg ruling circles, in his treatise, *Teuda be-Israel* (Instruction in Israel), published in Vilna in 1828, pleaded for the promotion and extension of productive labor which would reduce the number of Jews employed in commerce and, most important, the number of those without occupations, *luftmenchn*.

Appeals to bring productivization to the Jewish Pale came not only from the *maskilim*; similar ideas were expressed within Jewish religious circles, where Hasidic opposition to rabbinic Judaism created considerable dissension and questioning of many aspects of Jewish social life. Rabbi Menashe Ilier (1767-1831), a Talmudic scholar (not a Hasid), who was called to account by the rabbinical authorities for his philosophic volume, *Alfe Menashe*, was also the author of a plan propagandizing physical labor as a means of overcoming the structural shortcomings of Jewish social life.

At the same time, Rabbi Shneur-Zalman (1747-1812), a founder of Habad, counseled Jews to go into manual work, and even established a fund for agricultural settlement. There were many others on both sides of Jewish society in the 19th century,[4] among *maskilim* and among the rabbis, and of course among the St. Petersburg Tsarist bureaucracy who, unwilling to grant the Jews civil equality, frequently proposed various and not always practical schemes of productivization.[5]

Tradition and History

It is ironic to observe this combination of Jewish dreams and Imperial Russian projects aimed at returning the Jewish masses to productive labor, particularly so for a Jewish historian whose purpose is to record the Jewish past. After all, labor as a concept and its place in the life of the Jew were recognized at the very inception of our history and are an essential part of the Jewish tradition. Physical labor was, indeed, a life pattern, and early Jewish history gives unmistakable indication of its place in the life of Jews of all classes.

Jacob and his sons were shepherds, as, later, were Moses and David. Can one imagine a greater evidence of respect for labor than the blessing with which workers tilling the soil were greeted in Psalms 128, 2; 129, 8; and Judges 6, 11-12? The sages of the Talmud emphasized the importance of work; the laws on labor, particularly agricultural labor, constitute a considerable part of the Mishna. Many hundreds of the great Talmudic sages earned their livelihood in menial occupations.

The Christianization of Europe from the 4th and 5th centuries on, which often led to the outlawing of Judaism, increased the limitations on Jewish labor, along with all sorts of restrictions in other social areas. Following persistent denunciations by the Church Fathers, Jews were, in effect, segregated within a number of peripheral occupations. Thrown out of agriculture, deprived of their land, facing discrimination in professional crafts corporations, without legal security of residence, they were gradually forced to adapt their socio-economic structure to new conditions, concentrating in certain areas of commerce, money, finance, and some crafts in which it was possible for them to engage despite legal and social restrictions.

The Jewish communities of the Diaspora suffered a long period of exclusion and restrictions imposed by the host countries to arrive at the unenviable status of not being free to choose their occupations and to be forcibly divorced from labor.[6] The effects of this cruel process of social discrimination have been felt throughout Jewish history encouraging self-perpetuating difficulties in the Jewish communities in the various countries. It was only the great changes that came during a century of revolutionary enlightenment that brought the realization of how urgent was the need for reform to the outside society and to the closed Russian Jewish community.

We shall discuss in the next chapter the beginnings of an organized effort at "return to labor," begun in Imperial Russia as a means of solving the difficult social and economic problems confronting Russian Jewry toward the end of the 19th century, an effort destined to spread to other countries on all continents.

Chapter II

A Backward Glance

Tsar Aleksandr II (1855-1881) is remembered in Russia as *Tsar Osvoboditel* (The Liberator). He succeeded Tsar Nikolai I (1825-1855), a primitive, narrow-minded man who liked to think of himself as an honest Russian army officer and who governed the country in the way a strong disciplinarian would command a provincial regiment. At Nikolai's death, Russia was engaged in the Crimean War, the tragic outcome of which deeply hurt the Russian people.

There was rebellion in the air; Russians clamored for a change. With the advent of the new regime, Russian society entered into a political springtime which saw the liberation of the serf, the reforms of *zemstvo* (rural self-government), judicial reforms, and proposals for the introduction of a constitution. Many of the measures initiated under Aleksandr II, however, were grossly inadequate to solve the grave problems facing Russia, and the Tsar continued to face bitter political opposition and a growing revolutionary movement.

The early years of the reign of Aleksandr II, however, brought some relief to the Jews of the Russian Pale of Settlement. The special law relating to Jewish military conscription was abolished; "cantonists" were no more; and the terrifying *khapers* (catchers) disappeared from Jewish towns and villages.[1] The Jews remembered these acts and called Aleksandr II *Tsar Chesed v'Emes*, "the righteous Tsar."

Against bureaucratic opposition, Aleksandr II, approved a law (1865) permitting Jewish artisans, merchants, and specialist-distillers, including apprentices, to reside in areas outside the Pale. Although there were some important qualifications in the law, such as the requirement that artisans be certified by both professional groups and the local police, the latter making its determinations on the basis of "good conduct," the measures afforded some economic relief for the Jews confined to the Pale.

Nevertheless, the liberal spirit of the early period of the new regime benefited only limited and special categories of the Jewish population. The masses of the Pale remained largely unaffected. In accordance with established Russian bureaucratic practice Jews were treated in a "special" way, the authorities consistently interpreting the new decrees in their own not very generous fashion, addressing themselves to details and half-measures instead of to the basic problems: the absence of legal equality and the limitations of the Pale.[2]

Economic Transformation

Partly as the result of the reforms introduced by Aleksandr II, Russia was undergoing a profound transformation. Slowly, the old regime, which had been based on serfdom and absolute state supremacy, was giving way to capitalist initiative. The new capitalist structure forced rapid economic development of the country.

Capitalism, it should be noted, did not come to Russia as it had earlier in Western Europe. In the Western countries capitalism was a natural product of gradual social development that organically transformed the old economic structure and introduced new technical methods of production. In Russia, it came about as a result of a decision to change the inefficient and unproductive old economy based on serfdom.

It was planned, as it were, by the authorities. A new industry sprang up from nowhere, created with the best available machinery of the time.[3]

Many foreigners with capital and know-how played an important role in the process of introducing industrialization. Some Jews who had capital to invest, including a number who had attained the status of Merchant of the First Guild, or who simply had entrepreneurial skills, greeted the new economic and social opportunities with enthusiasm.

The state bureaucracy apparently tolerated or accepted these offers by Jews and, perhaps, in St. Petersburg these Jews were considered to be on a par with foreigners. Outsiders managing to get inside is a fascinating subject beyond the limits of this study. But in this connection the reader should remember the names of the Rosenthals, the Fridlands, the Zaks, the Wavelbergs, the Brodskis, and the Poliakovs among the rising Jewish financiers and entrepreneurs. In a separate category, and for good reason, was the Baron Gunzburg family, which occupies a deserving place in the history of Russian Jewry.

The New Capitalism

These Jewish bankers and industrialists represented but a small minority of the Jewish population. The emancipation of the peasants and the abolition of serfdom had a negative impact on the economic condition of the mass of Russian Jews. The new regime took away from the landlord, the "Pan," a great part of his economic power. For the Jews this meant a loss of many professional occupations that they had filled on and around the estate of the landowner, including the alcohol business, from which Jews were now forced out by the authorities.

With the introduction of rail and steam facilities, many Jews who had made their living as innkeepers and coachmen, traditionally Jewish occupations, lost their source of livelihood. The liberated peasants who could not fulfill the financial obligations imposed by the laws of emancipation were forced to leave the villages for hamlets and small cities, thus increasing by hundreds of thousands the availability of cheap labor. Not only did Jewish peddlers lose their natural clientele in the villages, but the newcomers now competed for the small opportunities that existed for making a living.

Besides, the new capitalist form of production needed the services of a new type of worker, a factory worker, who required a different attitude, a different psychology, and a kind of training that was rare or non-existent in Jewish labor which was concentrated in a limited number of crafts.

Jewish Social Structure

Simultaneous with these economic changes, the Jewish population, enclosed within the walls of the Pale, experienced a rapid growth. In 1825 there were about 1,250,000 Jews in Imperial Russia; this total number had risen to some 4 million; and at the end of the century it had risen to 5 million. Over 30 percent of the gainfully employed Jews were in small businesses and trading, principally shopkeeping, markets, and peddling; some 30 percent were in innkeeping; and some 15 percent were in crafts or, specifically, in social groups most endangered by the new modes of economic life. It has been estimated (statistics of the period should be accepted with some reservation) that up to 25 percent of the Jews were *luftmenchn*, that is, persons without skills or specific occupations, living from day to day or on public charity. (See page 44 and note 12, Chapter III.)

Except for the rich and the chosen few the Jewish population, still locked in the Pale, were gasping for air in hopeless poverty.

The various schemes, some with the hesitant help of the government, to establish Jewish agricultural settlements, fell tragically short of their intended goals. The several thousand Jewish peasants benefitting from these schemes did not essentially affect the economic status of the multi-million Jewish population of Russia.[4] With the pauperization of the Pale gradually reaching critical proportions, little was being done to alleviate the misery of the Jewish masses.

Not only were the economic foundations of the Pale being destroyed but, under the increasing strain, the social and inner life of the Pale was undergoing a deep crisis. Theoretically, the government of Aleksandr II encouraged "fusion of the Jews with the original population." The officially instituted new crown schools and rabbinical schools of Vilna and Zhitomir succeeded in recruiting a number of Jewish children and youth whose parents saw this as an opening to a better future.

But, unlike the *maskilim*, the Jewish masses from the beginning rightly suspected the reasons behind official "enlightenment" and were hardly encouraged by the anti-Jewish mood palpable throughout Russian society. The tiny Jewish plutocracy, the new Jewish financiers, railroad builders, and even the few Jewish alumni of the secular schools in the professions and academia, created fear and jealousy among the Russian social classes affected by the emergence of Jews, however small their number, in positions of economic power and higher social status.

We cannot here go into the attitudes of Russian writers and intellectuals to the Jewish situation. We shall only point out that many of them considered Jews untrustworthy and alien, and some charged them with striving for world domination through their financial power.[5] Aleksandr Khomiakov (1804-1860), the founder of the Slavophile movement, who advocated the unity of Slavs, opposed "foreign ways" and included the Jews among the "foreigners" and "enemies" of Holy Russia, as did Ivan Aksakov, an influential Slavophile poet and writer (1823-1886), who even defended pogroms. Fyodor Dostoevsky (1821-1881), in addition to his great novels, produced many writings that deserve inclusion in an anthology of undiluted anti-Semitism.

Supported by government funds, the Russian press in many cities, and in St. Petersburg the semi-official *Novoe Vremia* (New Times), systematically published anti-Jewish material calling on the authorities to further enlarge legislation limiting Jewish rights within and outside the Pale. Strong anti-Jewish feelings were hardly confined to the slavophile or nationalist camps. Russian society paid little attention to the plight of the Jewish masses.

Lack of understanding of Jewish conditions complemented an outright anti-Jewish bias among the upcoming progressive Russian intelligentsia. After the famous murder trial in Kutaisi, Georgia (1878-1879), the liberal historian Nikolaii Kostomarov (1817-1885) defended the validity of the ritual murder accusation. Blind to the poverty and oppression prevailing in the Jewish Pale, even some revolutionary militants in the Populist movement accepted anti-Semitic propaganda and pogroms, with the idea that these might awaken the peasant masses and create the mood for a wider rebellion.

Some Jewish revolutionaries who joined the Populist movement shared the ignorance and arrogance of the Populists toward the Jewish masses. They worked for the salvation of the Russian people; for their own Jewish people, whom they viewed as "exploiters" and "the rich," they had only contempt.[6] Happily, they were only a small minority among emancipated Jews.

Rise of New Ideas

During this period Russian Jewry was not organized, and lacked resources for a systematic fight for Jewish rights. The only modern Jewish organization then in existence was the Society for the Diffusion of Enlightenment among the Jews, established in St. Petersburg in 1867. With Baron Evzel Gunzburg (1812-1878) among its founders, it aimed at disseminating secular knowledge and the Russian language among their brothers in the Pale. It was their hope that with education "[the Jews] shall all become fullfledged citizens of this country."[7] They were well aware that this was a long-term goal and not the answer to the immediate pressing needs of the Jewish Pale.

In the late 1860's Russia experienced one of its bad harvests. The natural calamity struck most severely in the area of the Jewish Pale in the northwest. There followed famine, epidemic, and internal migration of Jews looking for a safer abode but unable to penetrate areas outside the Pale.[8]

In this climate of hopelessness and poverty, ideas emerged among Jewish groups to relieve suffering in the Pale by radical methods and through emigration. But in influential Jewish circles, those with connections in the government, and in the recently established Jewish press, the search for a solution lay elsewhere. In 1862, a year after the liberation of the peasants, Baron Evzel Gunzburg presented a memorandum to the government suggesting a program of agricultural settlement as well as enlargement of the rights, and therefore of the economic opportunities of Jewish artisans.

The old idea of the productivization of the Jewish masses was taken up by the new Jewish press. In the absence of other Jewish social organizations, the press assumed a prominent role and was active in propagandizing the necessity of changing the social structure of the Pale.[9] Writers in Hebrew and Yiddish, in their tales, novels, and poetry, turned again and again to the subject of the educated and productive individual reconciling his traditional upbringing with science and industry. Many articles satirized the narrowmindedness of the old Jewish life-style.[10] These writings were perhaps also an unconscious reflection of the new economic order, writers being, as it were, harbingers among the Jews of the coming entrepreneurial capitalist society. The idea of productive labor, of men trained for the new tasks, self-reliant men proud of their work, was in the air. In the air to be sure, but the question remained: What was to be done and how to do it?

One might truthfully say that this was an idea in search of a man. And the man who knew how to achieve the "return to labor" and give it a practical framework was Nikolaii Bakst, a Russian Jewish intellectual, active in many fields, including the Society for Enlightenment. Bakst was undoubtedly the first theoretical exponent in the modern period of a coordinated effort toward productivization of the Jewish masses and, later, provided the organizational genius. He was, in short, the father, the originator, of ORT. Iulii Gessen, the author of a history of the Russian Jews, has clearly accepted Bakst as the initiator of the new effort. So too Genrikh Sliozberg (1863-1937), a St. Petersburg lawyer and a future ORT chairman, writing about ORT much later, states that "this initiative belongs to Professor Bakst," and that it was Bakst who attracted to it S. Poliakov.[11]

Early Steps

It was not simple, in Imperial Russia, to obtain the necessary permission for the organization of welfare societies or any kind of association with social goals. It required not only connections in the proper places, but an advocate who had standing in the eyes of the authorities. Bakst himself could originate ideas and work for them, but his profession of educator and journalist put him in less than good standing with the Russian police. Men with names, influence, and perhaps also money were needed. We know that Bakst enjoyed good relations with the Jewish financier and railroad builder Samuil Poliakov. Poliakov had connections in the "higher" spheres but was not particularly involved with Jewish interests. Bakst had served, in a way, as Poliakov's adviser on Jewish affairs.

In 1880, in celebration of the 25th anniversary of the Tsar's reign, Poliakov had donated 25,000 rubles for a student dormitory at the University of St. Petersburg. In accepting the provision in the rules which excluded Jewish students from the dormitory, he appears as less than an endearing figure; yet from the point of view of the Russian authorities this could have been a plus in his favor. It was Bakst who suggested to Poliakov that it would also be good, in honor of the Tsar's celebration, to create a fund for the establishment of a society to spread handicrafts and agricultural

Nikolaii Bakst (1842-1904)
Scientist and writer, one of the founders of ORT who was at its helm for its first quarter century.

Baron Horace Gunzburg (1833-1909)
Financier and industrialist, he was one of the most renowned Jewish
leaders of St. Petersburg, and a founder of ORT.

SAMUEL POLIAKOV
FOUNDER OF ORT 1880

HILLEL TUROK

Samuel Poliakov (1836-1888)
Financier and railroad builder, one of the founders of ORT.

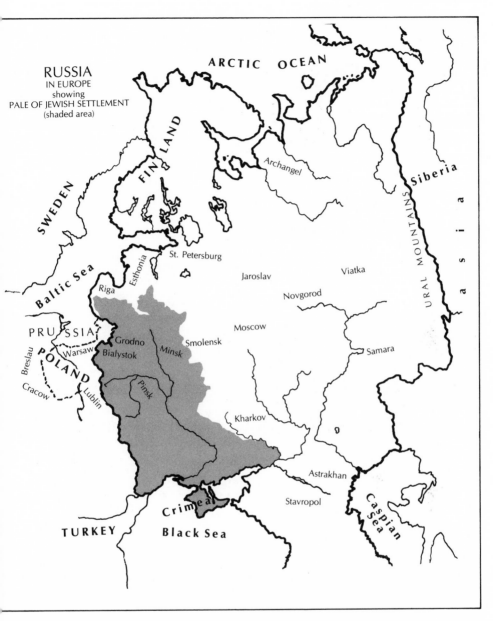

Map of the Jewish Pale of Settlement in Tsarist Russia.

Гъ II.   Вторникъ, 2 сентября 1880 г.   № 36

РУССКІЙ ЕВРЕЙ

ЕЖЕНЕДѢЛЬНОЕ ИЗДАНІЕ.

РЕДАКЦІЯ
(С.-Петербургъ, Измайл. просп., д. 12)

КОНТОРА
(С.-Петербургъ, Измайл. просп., д. 7, кв. 12)

№36.

Годъ II.   3 Іюля   1880

РАЗСВѢТЪ

ОРГАНЪ РУССКИХЪ ЕВРЕЕВЪ

ЕЖЕНЕДѢЛЬНОЕ ИЗДАНІЕ.

Выходитъ по Четвергамъ.

ПОДПИСНАЯ ЦѢНА:

РЕДАКЦІЯ ОТКРЫТА:

№ 27.

Адресъ редакціи: Новая ул., д. № 10, кв. № 106.

Адресъ конторы: Новая ул., д. № 10, кв. № 106.

Russkii Evreii of Sept. 2, 1880 (top), and *Rassvet* of July 3, 1880 (bottom), most prominent Russian-Jewish periodicals of the 1880's, expressing support of the newly created ORT.

ПРОТОКОЛЫ ЗАСѢДАНІЙ

ВРЕМЕННАГО КОМИТЕТА

ПО ОБРАЗОВАНІЮ ОБЩЕСТВА

ремесленнаго и земледѣльческаго труда среди евреевъ въ Россіи

ВЪ ПАМЯТЬ ДВАДЦАТИПЯТИЛѢТІЯ ЦАРСТВОВАНІЯ

ИМПЕРАТОРА АЛЕКСАНДРА II.

———————

Отъ 4-го ноября 1880 до 1-го августа 1882 г.

С.-ПЕТЕРБУРГЪ.
Англійская Набережная, д. 4.
1882.

Title page of book of minutes of the Provisional Committee for the establishment of ORT, covering the period November 4, 1880 to August 1, 1882

Most esteemed Sir,

One of those here undersigned, S. S. Poliakov, has petitioned to H.E. the Minister of Interior Affairs for his approval of the proposal of several Russian Jews to assemble from among their co-religionists, a fund for a public charitable purpose, in honor of the first Twenty-fifth Anniversary of the glorious reign of our beloved Monarch, His Most Illustrious Imperial Majesty, which will be held on February 19th of the year 1880. On that occasion, S. S. Poliakov contributed 25,000 Roubles toward that purpose. In reply to the petition, H. E. the Minister of Interior Affairs, on the 22nd March honoured S. S. Poliakov with a letter worded as follows:

"H. M. the Emperor having graciously heard my report on the proposal of the Russian Jews to collect in their midst a fund for charitable purposes, in honor of the 19th February 1880 and of the donation by your goodself for that purpose of 25,000 Roubles, expresses His Majesty's appreciation of Your Excellency's so considerable donation. I have humbly informed His Imperial Majesty that the contributions will be collected by your Excellency in a private manner and that the use of the funds will be accounted for subsequently."

Having received that letter, S. S. Poliakov applied to the undersigned, inviting a common action with regard to the collection of funds, as well as the determination of those publicly useful aims which should be materialized from the income of this capital.

The undersigned heard with sincere joy of the most gracious authorization of His Imperial Majesty to perpetuate the memory of the 19th February 1880 by a work of general use for our people. With regard to the future determination of the character of that charitable work, which will be materialized in memory of that day, the undersigned consider that among the numerous needs of the mass of our co-religionists in Russia, the first place is occupied by the needs of the artisanal and agricultural occupations. Nothing, in fact, could better ameliorate the position of the mass of our co-religionists, than a thorough and systematic development among that mass of artisanal and agricultural occupations.

In view thereof, the undersigned assume that the most generally useful work which could be achieved, would consist in the creation of a fund, the income from which could be used to the aid in the further development of already existing trade schools for Jews, for assistance towards the opening of new trade schools, for facilitating the movement of artisans from one place to another, and for assistance to Jewish agricultural colonies, the founding of such colonies, model farms and agricultural schools. The future determination of the use of the income from the capital for the purposes indicated above will be effected according to our proposals, by the Society, for the creation of which, upon the collection of a considerable part of the anticipated fund, we shall submit separately an application for the authorization of the Minister of Interior Affairs.

Though the scope of the aims for the materialisation of which the income from the expected capital will serve is wide, the undersigned apply to you, most esteemed Sir, with full confidence in the success of the work already begun. This assurance they draw from those joyous feelings which are evoked in each one of us by this good work. The need among the masses of our co-religionists is extreme, and we are convinced that that need could be alleviated only by the development among that mass of artisanal and agricultural knowledge and trades.

On this basis the undersigned hope that you, most esteemed Sir, will afford the work started every possible support both by personally participating in the subscription, as well as by inviting other persons to take part. The participation of as large a number of people as possible in that subscription is extremely dear to us, and the gift of a rouble by a poor man is not less dear to us than donations of tens of thousands!

We request you to send the money to St. Petersburg, in the name of Samuel Solomonovith Poliakov, who has already arranged for the deposit of all sums anticipated for this purpose in the State Bank. The names of donors will be published in due course.

This, our application, has the character of a private letter and it should not be attributed any publicity in periodical print.

Persons who will make their contribution not later than the 15th of July of this year will be considered as founding members of the proposed charitable institution.

Please accept, most esteemed Sir, our respectful greeting, and may God's blessing grace the work we have begun.

> S. S. Poliakov, Baron H. O. Gunzburg,
> A. I. Zak, L. M. Rosenthal,
> M. P. Friedland.

St. Petersburg, April 10th, 1880.

The first public announcement of the establishment of the fund, addressed to the Jewish communities throughout the Tsarist Empire, including an appeal for financial support to this new initiative.

ПРОТОКОЛЪ

I-го предварительнаго засѣданія лицъ, подписавшихъ циркулярное письмо отъ 10-го апрѣля 1880 г., по дѣлу образованія „Общества ремесленнаго и земледѣльческаго труда среди евреевъ въ Россіи", 4 ноября 1880 года.

Согласно Правиламъ для Временнаго Комитета, утвержденнымъ г. Министромъ Внутреннихъ Дѣлъ, лица, подписавшія циркулярное письмо отъ 10-го апрѣля 1880 г., приступили прежде всего къ выбору другихъ членовъ Временнаго Комитета. При этомъ оказались избранными: П. И. Бакстъ, Э. В. Банкъ, А. М. Варшавскій, Я. М. Гальперинъ, раввинъ А. Н. Драбкинъ и И. Н. Кауфманъ. Такимъ образомъ, согласно Правиламъ, Временный Комитетъ въ Петербургѣ состоитъ пока изъ слѣдующихъ лицъ: П. И. Бакста, Э. В. Банка, А. М. Варшавскаго, Я. М. Гальперина, бар. Г. О. Гинцбурга, раввина А. Н. Драбкина, А. И. Зака, И. Н. Кауфмана, С. С. Полякова, Л. М. Розенталя и М. П. Фридлянда.

Кромѣ того, въ томъ же засѣданіи рѣшено пригласить и нѣсколько иногороднихъ членовъ Временнаго Комитета, преимущественно въ главныхъ центрахъ осѣдлости евреевъ, для совѣщанія съ ними, какъ по выработкѣ главныхъ основаній устава Общества, такъ и вообще по дѣйствіямъ Временнаго Комитета. Имена избранныхъ при этомъ иногороднихъ членовъ Комитета будутъ опубликованы, по мѣрѣ полученія отъ этихъ лицъ письменныхъ извѣщеній объ ихъ согласіи на принятіе павшаго на нихъ выбора.

Затѣмъ рѣшено было приступить къ дальнѣйшимъ дѣйствіямъ Временнаго Комитета въ слѣдующемъ засѣданіи, 12-го ноября, по вступленіи въ этотъ Комитетъ вновь выбранныхъ шести членовъ, имена которыхъ перечислены выше.

Minutes of the preliminary meeting of the Fund's Provisional Committee held on November 4, 1880.

License issued to a Jewish artisan of Rostov by the local Bureau for artisans authorizing him to practice his trade as a mechanic, March 30, 1907.

§ 1. Капиталы для образованія „Общества ремесленнаго и земледѣльческаго труда среди евреевъ въ Россіи", донынѣ поступившіе, а равно и имѣющіе поступать, какъ въ видѣ единовременныхъ, такъ и въ видѣ годичныхъ взносовъ, вносятся на храненіе въ Государственный Банкъ, на имя Временнаго Комитета.

§ 2. Временный Комитетъ образуется изъ лицъ, за подписью коихъ было разослано первоначальное приглашеніе къ участію, а равно и изъ приглашенныхъ ими другихъ лицъ, принимавшихъ съ самаго начала близкое участіе въ осуществленіи дѣла „Общества ремесленнаго и земледѣльческаго труда среди евреевъ въ Россіи". Члены Комитета избираютъ изъ своей среды предсѣдателя. Въ случаѣ отсутствія предсѣдателя, мѣсто его занимаетъ одинъ изъ старшихъ членовъ Комитета. Кромѣ предсѣдателя, избирается дѣлопроизводитель и казначей Комитета.

§ 3. На обязанности Временнаго Комитета лежитъ: а) составленіе проекта устава „Общества ремесленнаго и земледѣльческаго труда среди евреевъ въ Россіи", для представленія онаго на утвержденіе Правительства, каковой проектъ устава имѣетъ быть представленъ по собраніи всѣхъ свѣдѣній и выработкѣ всѣхъ данныхъ, долженствующихъ служить основаніемъ для составленія подробнаго устава Общества, б) временное завѣдываніе какъ дальнѣйшимъ сборомъ, такъ и расходованіемъ процентовъ съ основного капитала и годовыхъ взносовъ, на основаніяхъ, изложенныхъ въ § 4,—и в) принятіе надлежащихъ мѣръ къ приглашенію возможно большаго числа членовъ и участниковъ въ „Обществѣ ремесленнаго и земледѣльческаго труда среди евреевъ въ Россіи"

§ 4. Временному Комитету предоставляется расходовать проценты съ основного капитала и годичные взносы, какъ уже поступившіе, такъ и имѣющіе еще поступать, на слѣдующіе предметы: „на вспомоществованіе и дальнѣйшее развитіе существующихъ уже для евреевъ ремесленныхъ училищъ, на содѣйствіе къ открытію новыхъ такихъ училищъ, на облегченіе переѣзда ремесленниковъ изъ одного мѣста въ другое и содѣйствіе къ открытію имъ правильныхъ ремесленныхъ

заведеній на вспомоществованіе еврейскимъ земледѣльческимъ колоніямъ и основаніе новыхъ такихъ колоній, образцовыхъ фермъ и земледѣльческихъ школъ.

§ 5. Комитету не предоставляется права расходовать капитала единовременныхъ пожертвованій.

§ 6. По утвержденіи устава Общества, назначается первое общее собраніе, которому Комитетъ представляетъ отчетъ о всѣхъ его дѣйствіяхъ, распоряженіяхъ и расходахъ изъ суммъ процентовъ и ежегодныхъ взносовъ. Засимъ, по избраніи общимъ собраніемъ Правленія Общества, на указанныхъ въ уставѣ основаніяхъ, Комитетъ передастъ въ вѣдѣніе и распоряженіе Правленія Общества всѣ собранныя суммы, всѣ книги и отчеты, словомъ все дѣлопроизводство, и прекращаетъ затѣмъ свою дѣятельность по этому предмету.

§ 7. Экземпляръ отчета Временнаго Комитета представляется Господину Министру Внутреннихъ Дѣлъ.

§ 8. О всѣхъ поступившихъ пожертвованіяхъ и сдѣланныхъ расходахъ Комитетъ доводитъ до свѣдѣнія Господина Министра Внутреннихъ Дѣлъ и публикуетъ во всеобщее свѣдѣніе не менѣе 2 разъ въ годъ.

Rules of procedure of the Provisional Committee approved by the Minister of Interior, September 30, 1880.

Approved by the Minister of the
Interior on 30 September, 1880,
under No. 3888

RULES OF PROCEDURE

*of the Provisional Committee for the establishment of a Society
for the Promotion of Handicrafts and Agricultural Work
among Jews in Russia*

In commemoration of the 25th
anniversary of the reign of
Tsar Alexander II.

(1) The funds to be used for the establishment of a Society for the promotion of handicrafts and agricultural work among Jews in Russia, whether they be collected now or in the future, and whether they be constituted by single donations or annual subscriptions—shall be deposited on the account of the Provisional Committee in the National Bank.

(2) Members of the Provisional Committee shall be the signers of the first appeal calling for participation in the projected organization, and persons who shall be coopted by these signers and who have shown, from the beginning, a keen interest in the establishment of a Society for the promotion of handicrafts and agricultural work among Jews in Russia.

Members of the Committee shall elect among themselves a chairman. In the absence of the latter the chair shall be occupied by one of the senior members of the Committee. In addition to a chairman, a secretary and a treasurer shall be elected.

(3) The Committee shall have the following duties:

a) To draw up a draft of statutes of the "Society for the Promotion of Handicrafts and Agricultural Work among Jews in Russia", to be submitted to the Government for approval; to draw up this draft in its minute details the Committee shall previously collect all the pertinent basic data.

Translation

b) To direct the collection of funds in the future and to ensure the rational utilization of interest on fixed capital and annual subscriptions in accordance with Article 4.

c) To take measures for the recruitment of the greatest possible number of members and of contributions to the "Society for the Promotion of Handicrafts and Agricultural Work among Jews in Russia".

(4) The Provisional Committee shall make all efforts to use the funds—already on hand and those to be collected in the future—for the achievement of the following aims:

to aid and develop existing Jewish vocational schools; to subsidize the establishment of new Jewish vocational schools; to facilitate the transportation and the re-establishment of Jewish craftsmen; to aid Jewish farm settlements, model farms and agricultural schools.

(5) The Committee shall not be authorized to spend the capital formed by single donations.

(6) The first General Assembly shall be convened after the approval of the Society's statutes. The Committee shall render to the Assembly a report on its activities and measures taken and shall render an account of the expenditure of interest on fixed capital and annual subscriptions. The Assembly shall then nominate an Administrative Council to which the Committee shall transfer all liquid assets and all accounts and reports; the Committee shall then resign from its functions.

(7) A copy of the report of the Provisional Committee shall be submitted to the Minister of the Interior.

(8) The Committee shall render an account to the Minister of the Interior of all the donations received and of all the monies spent; the Committee shall publish its accounts at least twice a year.

Ecole de Travail
pour les Jeunes Filles Israélites

Fondation Bischoffsheim.

3ᵉ Trimestre 1878.
2ᵉ Division.

Notes méritées par Mᵈᵉˡˡᵉ Henriette, Frank élève. Couturière

		Compositions.	
Conduite	Bien	Orthographe.	22.
Devoirs	Très - bien.	Grammaire et Analyse.	19.
Leçons	Bien	Calcul	22.
Propreté	Bien	Histoire	18
Ordre	Très - bien	Géographie	"
Politesse	Très - bien	Style	.
Place moyenne sur 24 élèves 9.		Récitation	11
Travail à l'Atelier Bien		Instruction religieuse	"
		Hébreu	16
		Anglais	"
		Comptabilité .	"

Paris, le 30 Septembre 1878

Le Directeur,

J. Bloch

Officier d'Académie

Report card of a pupil of a Jewish trade school in Paris, dated
September 30, 1878, in Fashion Design.

NOTE.

On the Jewish Population of Russia.

Russian statistics are in a very backward state. The results that are reached by the Imperial Statistical Bureau are very incomplete, and are rarely published in such a way as to be checked. This is specially the case with the statistics of Russian Jews, and a good deal of uncertainty exists as to their number, which is variously put down at three and at six millions.

The most recent figures that have been published are contained in a Report made to the Pahlen Commission in 1885, and professed to give the Jewish population of the Pale of Jewish Settlement of 1884. It is very doubtful whether this was the case, and it is more probable that the figures were extracted from the latest census of Russia, that of 1879. The figures are at best only a minimum, and should probably be increased about 30 per cent.

I.—Western Russia.

	Total Population	Jews	Percentage
Grodno,	1,163,525	229,574	19.7
Kovno,	1,419,493	269,399	19.0
Minsk,	1,410,754	283,194	20.1
Mohilev,	835,244	151,055	18.1
Podolia,	2,239,514	418,858	18.7
Vilna,	1,191,992	175,996	14.8
Vitebsk,	1,037,892	133,785	12.9
Volhynia,	1,946,438	289,820	14.9

II.—The Ukraine (Little Russia).

	Total Population	Jews	Percentage
Kiev,	2,332,421	339,557	14.6
Poltava,	2,399,400	84,041	3.5
Tchernigov,	1,896,450	83,117	4.4
Charkov,	2,160,203	8,474*	0.4

*This number must refer to artisans, etc., who have right of residence outside the Pale, as Charkov is not included within it.

An estimate of Jewish population of the Pale during the last quarter of the 19th century. Reprinted from "The Persecution of the Jews in Russia," issued by the Russo-Jewish Committee of London, Jewish Publication Society, Philadelphia, 1897.

III.—South Russia.

	Total Population	Jews	Percentage
Bessarabia, ...	1,385,743	267,827	12.1
Cherson, ...	1,479,303	140,162	9.5
Ekaterinoslav, ...	1,459,066	47,304	3.2
Taurida, ...	898,945	21,197	2.5
Odessa, Kertsch, and Sebastopol, ...	265,813	77,279	29.1
Total, ...	25,481,896	2,920,639	11.5

To this total of 2,920,639 has to be added (a) the Jews of Poland, reckoned to number 1,079,000, or 14.4 per cent of the population; (b) the Jews outside the Pale, probably numbering 750,000. This would raise the total number of Jews in the Russian Empire in 1884 (? 1879) to 4,748,640. There can be little doubt, therefore, that they amount to more than five million at the present time, even though their infant mortality must have been increased by the May Laws, and such large numbers, say 200,000 in the six years, have emigrated.

Some interesting details were given to the Pahlen Commission of the proportion of Jews in the towns of the Pale. In four towns they were over 80 per cent.; in fourteen from 70 to 80 per cent.; in no less than sixty-eight from 50 to 70 per cent.; in twenty-eight they were from 20 to 40 per cent. These 114 towns probably include the whole of the towns and "townlets" within which Jews are now allowed to reside.

labor among Jews. Several moves were made, following Bakst's initiative, which involved a group of men who became the real founders of ORT, and in effect supplied the leadership for the organization, then being born, for two generations. We do know that early in the year 1880, Poliakov, in the name of a group of well-established Jews, petitioned the Minister of the Interior of Imperial Russia for approval of a project for a Jewish charitable public fund in honor of the forthcoming 25th anniversary (February 19, 1880), and that, on the occasion, he contributed 25,000 rubles. Baron Horace Gunzburg (1833-1909), always active in Jewish causes, participated in the initial steps and was instrumental in helping to obtain a favorable response from the authorities.[12]

Permission to proceed was granted on March 22, 1880. In accepting the proposal, the Minister of the Interior informed Poliakov that collection of funds would have to be made in a "private" manner and that, at a later date, the specific goals of the fund and the manner in which it would be used were to be determined and reported to the authorities.

Immediately after receiving the government's approval, a small group of outstanding St. Petersburg Jews—the petitioner Samuil Poliakov, Baron Horace Gunzburg, Abram Zak, Leon Rosenthal, and Meer Fridland—met to plan the implementation of the project. These five men signed the original letter of appeal. All were residents of St. Petersburg and all were financiers and businessmen.

The Jewish intelligentsia, individuals in the professions and academia, did not, at this time, usually take part in "practical" Jewish projects, Bakst being a notable exception. Most of them were trying to integrate into Russian society. If they were concerned with the Jews at all, it was merely as a part of their political commitment to the general improvement of conditions in Russia. In time there were to be changes in this attitude, as there were to be changes in the composition of the leading group destined to initiate the future ORT.

The earliest documents surviving from this period show

that the request submitted to the Tsar was carefully couched in vague and general terms. It simply suggested that the Jewish group intended to create a "charitable fund for a useful purpose" in honor of the Tsar's anniversary. Notwithstanding, the originator of the proposal (Bakst?), the first group of founders, or both or some of them in concert, did indeed have a plan; only 18 days after permission had been granted they spelled it out in a "private" appeal initiating the collection of funds. The vagueness of the original request created some problems later, when the men responsible for the project were confronted with the day-to-day work of distributing the funds, but we will come to this when we discuss the evolution of the fund and its use.[13]

The Appeal

The "private" appeal, inviting contributions to the fund, was sent out on April 10, 1880, to members of Jewish communities in Russia. The appeal was more than a letter; it presented a program. It pointed out that among the ways of meeting the numerous needs of the masses of their co-religionists, nothing would be more useful and helpful than the systematic development among these masses of handicrafts and agricultural labor.

Russian Jews were asked to help in the establishment of a considerable fund, the income of which would be used for assistance and further development of existing Jewish trade schools and for assistance in opening new schools. They were also asked to facilitate the movement of artisans from one city to another, and to support Jewish agricultural colonies, and the establishment of new colonies, model farms, and agricultural schools.[14]

Within a short time over 10,000 letters were sent to Jews throughout Russia. The response exceeded all expectations. As of October 30, 1880, 12,457 individuals residing in 407 localities of the Russian Empire had contributed some 204,000 rubles, not including membership dues.[15] In addition to this sum and the contribution made initially by Poliakov, Baron Horace Gunzburg donated 25,000 rubles. Contributions were also made by Zak, Rosenthal, and Fridland. The appeal had been eminently successful.

An instrument, a responsible body, had to be created to manage the fund and elaborate rules for its administration. On September 30, 1880, the authorities gave permission for the creation of such a body, a Provisional Committee for the Establishment of a Society for Handicrafts and Agricultural Work among the Jews of Russia.

On the same day, the Minister of the Interior approved a set of specific rules governing the activities of the Provisional Committee. The rules included a stipulation (Rule No. 3) that bylaws of the new society would be prepared by the Provisional Committee and presented to the government for approval before the society could begin to function. Another rule required that a report of the activities of the Provisional Committee be presented in due course to the Minister of the Interior.[16]

The first meeting of the signers of the April 10th appeal took place, in accordance with the approved rules, on November 4, 1880. At this meeting the group constituted itself the Provisional Committee for the Establishment of the Society for Handicrafts and Agricultural Work among the Jews of Russia.[17] Six additional members—Nikolaii Bakst, Emanuil Bank (1840-1897), Abram Drabkin (1833-1917), Jacob Galpern (1840-1914), Abram Warshavskii (1821-1888), and I. Kaufman (?)—were elected to the Committee, bringing its total membership to 11. In addition, in order to create a broader base, it was decided to invite a number of well-known Jews from outside St. Peterburg, particularly Jews from the important centers of the Jewish Pale, to join the Committee.

While the Society sought to enlarge its framework, some doubts apparently existed as to the compatibility of the views of the St. Petersburg group with those of representatives from the Pale. This can be seen in the record of the Committee's second meeting, on November 12, 1880. The question of the rights and obligations of the "out-of-the-city" members was an item on the agenda.

Here it should be borne in mind that the founders of ORT were socially apart from the bulk of the Jews of the Pale who made up 95 percent of the Jewish population of Russia. Their concern for avoiding ideological quarrels or any controversy that might endanger the newly created initiative was probably a reasonable one. Perhaps, also, the founders were not psychologically prepared to hear their views debated, possibly rejected, by men of a different social class.

In any event, it was decided that out-of-the-city members, if present in the capital, could participate in all meetings and be accorded equal rights with St. Petersburg representatives. It was made clear, however, that reponsibility for the direction of the Society would remain in St. Petersburg and that all projects and suggestions emanating from out-of-the-city members would have to be approved by the Committee in St. Petersburg.

At the November 12th meeting the Committee elected the following as its officers: President, Samuil Poliakov; Senior Member, Baron Horace Gunzburg; Treasurer, Abram Zak. Nikolaii Bakst was elected Chief Executive (*deloproizvoditel*), since it was required that this post be filled by a member of the Committee. A secretary and a clerk were engaged to perform the technical work. At this meeting also a special committee, consisting of Bank, Galpern and Kaufman, with the ad hoc participation of Bakst, was formed to prepare a draft of the bylaws of the future society.[18] Bakst continued as chief day-to-day planner and executive until his death in 1904.

So began the work of the small Provisional Committee, which at that time was known as *Remeslennyii Fond*, or Handicrafts Fund.

The Founders

We have no Jewish Balzac, no Jewish Stendhal, and no literature describing the coming into their own of a group of men, and families, whose work and destinies in the not too friendly Russian surroundings are intriguing ingredients of Russian Jewish history. The October, 1917 Revolution destroyed, at its beginnings, Jewish social research, except for works conforming to the Party line. October was a time for glorification of the future, and there was no interest in the Jewish past, which, in any event, was to be obliterated. This is not the place, nor is it our task, to go fully into this important matter. Nevertheless, some description, however incomplete, of the men who initiated the idea and made possible the development of ORT may provide some additional social and perhaps psychological dimensions to our inquiry.

Nikolaii Bakst (1842-1904), the originator of the ORT idea, was born in the small town of Mir in the region of Minsk, renowned for its great yeshiva. He studied at the newly established rabbinical school in Zhitomir,[19] where his father, a Talmudic scholar, was a teacher. He was reared in an enlightened but deeply religious family and he remained until his death a committed Jew.

After graduating from St. Petersburg University he was sent to Germany to continue, in Heidelberg, his studies in zoology, comparative anatomy, and physiology. Upon returning to Russia, he taught and worked in the field of physiology at the St. Petersburg University and later at the Medical School for Women. Because of his reputation as a scholarly researcher, recognized both in Russia and abroad, he was one of the first of the few Jews admitted with the status of professor to a Russian school of higher learning or university.

In the 1870's Bakst joined the Society for the Diffusion of Enlightenment among the Jews, and was thinking about the establishment of a Jewish theological academy which would provide Russian Jews with modern rabbis and religious guides expert not only in Jewish religious tradition but also adequately educated in the secular sciences and speaking the Russian language. At the same time he supported many yeshivas and in fact maintained contact with the outstanding Russian rabbis of his day.

Like all the *maskilim* of his generation he was convinced

that education was the road to salvation. He believed also that, along with education, the development of productive labor and training for practical occupations was a necessity for the survival of Russian Jewry. Hence, his interest in the creation of the organization which ultimately became ORT.

Bakst did not believe in emigration and viewed with scepticism the ideas preached by Pinsker and the Hovevei-Zion movement. Later he was a consistent opponent of Herzl's Zionism. A man of great intellect and dedication, he was active in many areas—research, writing, and teaching. He was the author, among other works, of a scholarly volume on the ritual murder libel, so much a part of the anti-Semitic propaganda. (The book was destroyed by the authorities.)

For a time he was close to the Russian nationalist writer Katkov [20] with whom he shared an interest in matters of education and in whose publications he occasionally collaborated. He was invited to participate in the Academic Committee of the Ministry of Public Instruction (1886), of which he later became a member. Earlier, he had been appointed as an expert to the High Commission for the Revision of Current Laws Concerning Jews, the so-called Count Palen Commission. [21] A sworn enemy of Russian liberalism, or of what he called "fashionable trends," he frequently accused some well known liberal journalists of hidden anti-Semitism. His association with Katkov, who was anathema to progressive groups, and, perhaps, his conservative views were never forgiven by the Russian Jewish militants. This attitude toward Bakst was later reflected in ORT debates.

Among the five signatories of the April 10th letter of appeal, Baron Horace Gunzburg (1833-1909) requires special mention. A scion of a celebrated Jewish family, he continued the tradition inherited from his father, Baron Evzel, who emphasized social duty. The *mitzvah* of assistance to the needy was not only a humane and natural expression, it was organically associated with Jewish religious precepts. Throughout his life, Baron Horace Gunzburg was the unofficial representative of Russian Jewry.

Under three Russian regimes—Aleksandr II, Aleksandr

III, and part of Nikolai II—it was the Gunzburg family that was most responsible for bringing the privations of the Jewish population to the attention of the authorities. There were those who criticized the Gunzburgs for their self-appointed role of *shtadlonim*. Nevertheless, Horace Gunzburg, successful banker, active in Russian industrialization projects, and accepted in the higher circles of St. Petersburg society, was a generous, committed Jew who participated in all the Jewish initiatives of his time. He was the builder of the Jewish community in St. Petersburg. The well known St. Petersburg synagogue was erected and opened in 1892 through his efforts. He was an advocate of Jewish schools in which the language of instruction would be Russian.

He believed that Russian Jews should fight to improve the conditions of their life in their own country. Herzlian Zionism was alien to him. To him, as to Bakst, ORT, representing a social restructuring of the conditions of life of the Jewish masses in Russia proper, was more than a practical task; today we would call it an ideological stand.[22]

Samuil Poliakov (1836-1888), who, following the counsel of Bakst, petitioned the Tsar for permission to initiate the Jewish charitable fund, was one of the most successful Jewish industrial promoters of his time. Born in Orcha, he became, early in his career, a railroad contractor, eventually taking over the construction and management of the most important railroad system in Imperial Russia. The Russian government accorded him a status corresponding in civilian life to army general, a confidential counselor (*taiinyi sovetnik*). His Jewish interests, Jewish activities and Jewish charitable works were limited, and his Jewish connections in general were few. With Bakst, however, he maintained a close relationship. He rarely participated in the numerous Jewish actions initiated or sponsored by Baron Horace Gunzburg, one of which was ORT.

Leon Rosenthal (1817-1887) was a well known *maskil* who up to his death was the treasurer of the Society for the Diffusion of Enlightenment among the Jews. A financier and businessman of great means, he was in close contact with writers and maintained an active correspondence with Khaim Slonimski and Osip Rabinovitch. He also had contact with Montefiore during the latter's visit to Russia. His interest in the new Society was a natural extension of his Jewish preoccupations.

Among the small group of founders of ORT two men, Abram Zak and Meer Fridland, were connected, through business, with the Gunzburgs. Zak (?-1893) was a former employee of the Gunzburg bank, and later became the chairman and director of the St. Petersburg Discount Bank, one of the most prestigious financial houses of Russia. He was offered and refused high government posts if he would accept conversion to Greek Orthodoxy. He participated in St. Petersburg communal work and was active in the Society for the Diffusion of Enlightenment. Known as a supporter of musical life in the capital city, he was friendly with many persons in Russian society interested in cultural pursuits. He was a follower of Gunzburg in the small circle that established the new Society.[23]

Meer Fridland, a wealthy army contractor, born in Minsk, was well known as an orthodox Jew. He was particularly interested in Jewish youth coming to the capital from the Pale and did much to help Jewish students in need, devoting special attention to those of traditional Jewish background who often felt uprooted in the absence of Jewish surroundings. His brother, Lev, was a generous contributor to Jewish institutions and supported, in St. Petersburg, an orphanage which provided training in handicrafts.

It was a homogeneous group that seconded Bakst in the cause of the new project, and a powerful one, tied by business and personal and family relations. Their natural allies were men or families of similar standing residing in Moscow, Kiev, Odessa, Warsaw and other large cities.

This first generation of the founders of ORT were upper-class Jews with essentially conservative views, rich men whose life style in many ways resembled members of their class in the non-Jewish Russian society. Aside from the general *zeitgeist*, what motivated them, what led them to give of their time, money and effort to a Jewish cause which from its beginning was more than a customary Jewish charity? Did they have feelings of guilt toward their less fortunate brothers in the Pale? Under the impact of the Enlightenment, did they feel a duty, akin to the Russian *Narodnichestvo*, to go to the people, in their case, the Jewish people? Or was their scheme simply one devised to alleviate the difficult economic conditions of the Pale because, beneath the glitter of high life in St. Petersburg, the fear persisted that a common fate awaited all Jews, rich and poor.[24]

While all were "enlightened," some more, some less, they were not assimilationists, and in this they stood apart from the majority of the progressive Jewish intelligentsia, who at that time, as we have noted, were removed from the Jewish masses and Jewish goals.[25]

We shall not try at this point to analyze the available data to locate a systematic design in the motivations and activities of these men. With the benefit of hindsight, it is reasonable to assume that all the elements mentioned above, in varying degrees, played a role in directing the original founders to create ORT. If they perceived the far-reaching significance of their actions at all, they perceived it only dimly.

Chapter III

First Stages
Provisional Committee: 1880-1906

That there was a feeling of urgency among the initiators of the new society is apparent from the fact that at its second meeting (November 12, 1880), in addition to electing officers and arranging for other organizational matters, the Provisional Committee approved a set of fundamental rules designed to guide its work. The minutes, prepared or approved by Bakst in his official capacity as *deloproizvoditel*, are brief, but that there was a definite plan is evident. Was it Bakst who prepared this plan? We do not know.

According to the plan, assistance was to be provided on two levels: vocational training for persons desiring to acquire specialization in crafts or agriculture, and direct support to individuals and families then in or preparing to enter an artisan profession or agricultural settlement.

In the first category it was proposed to provide grants for new handicraft and agricultural training programs to be conducted by already functioning Jewish elementary schools (*uchilishche*).[1] A one-time grant of 100 rubles (1 ruble = $.50) for initiation costs and a per capita grant of 5 to 10 rubles for each student was provided for. Newly established, government approved Jewish schools for handicrafts and agricul-

39

tural training would receive one-time grants of 200 rubles in addition to the 5 to 10 rubles per capita to meet costs.

In the category of direct assistance, provision was made for travel expense of from 50 to 100 rubles for Jewish artisans who, following the 1865 law, were permitted to change their place of residence and go to areas heretofore closed to Jews. Such individuals were to receive, in addition, 200 rubles toward the costs connected with establishment of new shops. The grants to artisans moving to new locations were given not as charity but as loans to be repaid within eight years at an annual interest of 3 percent beginning with the fourth year, the first three years being interest free.

The Committee also undertook to purchase small parcels of land (about 10 desiatin: 27 acres) for families desiring to settle in agriculture and to provide loans to help with initial costs. Beneficiaries under this program were to repay the purchase price of the land and the loan within three years according to conditions agreed upon as to dates of installment payments, interest charges, and other factors, which were determined in each case according to local circumstances and customs.[2] Prior to the allocation of any grant, a thorough inquiry was conducted by the Committee as to the reliability of the applicant and the feasibility of the proposed project.

Detailed rules governing allocation of funds and rigid arrangements for disbursement of money to applicants were established. Funds were released through the local Jewish community or through an out-of-city Committee member residing in a given locality. These agencies were also entrusted with the task of following-up on the utilization of the grants.[3]

The "Charity" Principle

Notwithstanding the businesslike arrangements for dealing with grants (the principal members of the Committee were financiers and bankers), some of the leading members, almost from its inception, considered the Committee's work as falling within the framework of charitable activities funded by publicly collected money to be granted to persons in need of the Fund's assistance, albeit for specified economic purposes.

Eventually, there was to be considerable debate and difference of opinion as to the character and goals of the Society in which the ideas of the founders would be pitted against those of a younger generation. The "young Turks" would clamor for a change in methods which, they claimed, smacked of traditional charity rather than of new and more socially-motivated programs which they considered more appropriate to the times. But this complex and often confused dispute did not arise until much later. For a number of reasons and, in a way, independently of the will of the founders, the organization was for the moment slowly and carefully embarking on a program of "small but useful deeds."

On December 10, 1880, from its offices at 4, Angliiskaia Naberezhnaia Street, St. Petersburg (which remained for many years the central offices of the organization), the *Remeslennyii Fond* began distributing subventions to qualified individual and institutional applicants.

An account in the name of the Provisional Committee was opened at the St. Petersburg State Bank (*Gosudarstvennyi Bank*). Initially, checks drawn against the account were to be signed by any two of the following officers: Poliakov, Baron Gunzburg, Zak, and Bakst. (This procedure was later changed.)

At the Committee meeting of March 7, 1881, rigid fiscal arrangements were established. All funds received in St. Petersburg were to be invested in interest bearing bonds and dividend producing stocks. No more than 5,000 rubles in cash to meet current needs were to be held in the bank at any time. In this highly systematized organization of the Society we can see not only the hand of the banker-leaders of the Committee but also the influence of Bakst, who was known to be a man of formal and methodical ways.

In 1881, Nikolaii Vesoler[4] was appointed secretary and

accountant to the Provisional Committee. His function was to provide technical assistance to Bakst in the day-to-day work of the office which, with hundreds of applications coming in from many towns and townlets, was becoming voluminous.[5] The volume may be gauged by the fact that the Committee decided to hold regular meetings twice monthly (on Tuesdays, after at least a 14 day interval).[6]

In the meantime, the *Remeslennyii Fond* was becoming a subject of continuous debate in the press. Long before the establishment of the Fund, the subject of Jewish labor and agricultural settlements had been discussed in the Jewish press as part of a great debate about how to bring about changes in the social and economic conditions of the Pale. The Russian-Jewish periodicals *Rassvet*, *Ruskii Evreii*, and *Voskhod*, perhaps with more emphasis than in the Hebrew and Yiddish publications, reported on the situation in Jewish agricultural settlements and the status and prospects of existing handicraft schools.[7]

The need for change had been recognized by all groups of the Jewish community, and the creation of the Provisional Committee was greeted with enthusiasm by the Jewish press.[8] *Rassvet* (No. 27, August 3, 1880) called on Russian Jews to assist in the appeal launched by the Provisional Committee: "This [program] is of a general and radical character and will have centuries-long impact and historical significance."

In the same vein, *Russkii Evreii* (No. 36, Sept. 2, 1880) emphasized the need of broad communal support for the newly organized project of productivization of the masses, which had met with "remarkable sympathetic unanimity . . . since everyone understands that this is a cause for all the people." The Hebrew language *Hamelitz* (No. 35, Oct. 2, 1880) reported on the establishment of the Committee and the first steps undertaken.

The Committee thus began its activities under a bright star, at least so far as Jewish public opinion was concerned. It was soon, however, to face a grim reality.

At its fourth meeting, held on December 23, 1880, the

matters dealt with by the Committee concerned organizational questions and distribution of funds.

On March 1, 1881, Tsar Aleksandr II was assassinated at the hands of the underground People's Will. The event brought a drastic change in the situation of the Jews of Russia.[9]

Under a New Tsar

The Committee's next meeting took place on March 7, 1881, six days after the assassination. There is nothing in the minutes of this meeting to indicate the reactions of the members to the event, but there can be no doubt as to what these reactions were. Patriotic, wealthy, not in sympathy with the revolutionaries, the founders of a project created in celebration of the 25th anniversary of Aleksandr II's reign were undoubtedly horrified by the senseless act of terror.

Aleksandr III (1881-1894), who succeeded his father, was a man of limited vision. Educated and influenced by the notorious Procurator General of the Holy Synod, Konstantin Pobedonostsev, he believed that Russia must be protected from alien Western "ideas of progress and freedom." Under his rule, every effort was made to turn back the flow of Russian history and, particularly, to abolish the liberal reforms instituted by Aleksandr II.

Soon after the assassination, a secret Russian society, the so-called *Sviataia Druzhina* (Sacred League) was formed with the aim of defending the Tsar against his enemies and promoting "truthful Russian ideas" as opposed to those of foreign and local "detractors" of the fatherland. Bent on fighting sedition, the government program included systematic anti-Jewish pogroms (even under the most favorable interpretation, the pogroms were at least tolerated by the authorities).

Immediately after the assassination, *Novoe Vremia*, *Russ* and many other publications in the pay of the government offered their readers a simple explanation of the malaise being felt throughout Russian society: the presence in Russia of alien, scheming Jews who were not only perverting the established Russian Christian order but were somehow also guilty of the murder of the Tsar. A wave of pogroms occurred in 1881 and 1882. One after another, Jewish communities in cities such as Elisavetgrad, small towns in Khersonia, Kiev, and small towns in the Kiev region, Odessa, Warsaw, and, later, Balta among many, many others—fell victim to a barbaric lawless fury.

Within a year, the government had introduced the so-called *Vremennye Pravila* (Temporary Rules) which brought havoc to Jewish social and economic pursuits.

The new rules, also called *Maiiskie Pravila* (May Rules), promulgated on May 3, 1882, further reduced the areas of the Pale by forbidding Jews to settle in the countryside. Property outside the towns could not be purchased in the name of a Jewish purchaser. Jews were forbidden to conduct business on Sundays and certain other Christian holidays. Jewish artisans living outside the Pale were permitted to deal only in goods produced by their own hands. Infractions against the rules were followed by immediate confiscation of merchandise and expulsion of the offenders. These administrative restrictions, the expulsions and harassment, limited the economic opportunities of the Jews. It became difficult, if not impossible, for a Jew to earn a living.

In the face of pogroms, aggravated by "legal" assaults by the authorities, the Jewish masses began to see their salvation in emigration. The great emigration of Jewish refugees from Eastern Europe to the United States began at this time.

Under the prevailing conditions, the economic programs envisioned by the recently established Provisional Committee had to be drastically curtailed. That they nevertheless continued must be attributed in large part to the devotion and perseverance of the small group of founders, and especially to the exertions of Bakst.

During the 19th century, the Russian Jewish population had increased substantially. The census of 1897 put the total Jewish population of the Empire at 5,189,401. With the exception of some 207,700 living in towns now closed to Jews, the bulk of the Jewish population still lived in the Pale.[10] By the end of the century, a Jewish factory and workshop proletariat had gradually grown in the Pale, producing for both local needs and the larger market outside the restricted area.[11] Along with industrial plants there had also sprung up specialized shops employing from three to five workers and producing linens, wearing apparel, shoes, candy, and other commodities.[12]

Until the emergence of the modern Jewish labor movement and a crystallized socialist ideology, internal differences within the Jewish community were only in an early stage of development. Impoverished masses and prosperous Jews alike suffered at the hands of an inimical Gentile society.

Given the poverty prevailing in the Pale, the Provisional Committee, notwithstanding old and new restrictions, directed its first moves precisely toward enlarging the economic base of the Jewish community by facilitating productivization and extending its activities wherever possible to areas outside the Pale by developing marketable crafts.

The Committee at Work

It might be said that, in the beginning ORT activity was relief-oriented, providing assistance to specialized categories of individuals in need of what we might today call "constructive relief work." Subsidies, however, were given only to individuals engaged directly in labor (handicrafts and agriculture). No grants were made to persons training for management of labor.[13]

This policy provoked debates among the members of the Committee. In 1885, for example, according to the minutes of a meeting of the Committee, an interesting discussion arose in connection with an application for a grant made by 11 Jewish students of *Lesnoi Institut* (Institute of Forestry).[14] Bakst objected to extending support to these students on the ground that this would be contrary to the established principle of supporting laborers rather than persons preparing for management of other people's labor. In this particular case Bakst was overruled, but it is clear that the decision with respect to the students of *Lesnoi Institut* did not in fact change the basic policy of the Committee.

Over the years, ORT concepts of labor management, particularly in certain technical areas, have undergone considerable change, so that it is especially necessary to bear in mind this original attitude of the founders which was to color the outlook of ORT for decades to come.

At its meeting of April 6, 1881, approximately one month after the assassination of Aleksandr II, the Provisional Committee dealt with only routine matters. It enlarged its membership with the inclusion of Arkadii Kaufman, Grigorii Rabinovitch, and Iakov Rosenfeld, who accepted the Committee's invitation to join it. Co-optation of new members was a procedure that was to be resorted to many times in the future. Ippolit Wavelberg joined the Committee in this manner about a year after the inclusion of Kaufman, Rabinovitch, and Rosenfeld. The new members did not change the social composition of the Committee. All were of the Jewish upper class and successful in business or the professions.

There was no lack of funds. In addition to the 204,000 rubles initially contributed to the fund, there was a steady influx of contributions from members of the Committee and individuals from the Pale.

From the archival documents that were preserved, it appears that the Committee proceeded in accordance with its original plans, which were based essentially on economic opportunities opened up by the liberal legislation of Aleksandr II. Its program included assistance to artisans, agricultural settlements, and vocational training for Jewish youths. To the extent that this can be judged from the records, no significant changes occurred in this program during the period ending in 1906.

In the course of the first two years ORT operated with a small budget. Of the 13,820 rubles allocated, 12,045 were actually disbursed to enable 86 artisans and their families to resettle in cities in the interior of Russia. Of the 1,537 rubles allocated for local assistance, 937 rubles enabled 12 artisans to purchase necessary equipment and 600 rubles was for assistance to artisans in Kovno who had been victimized by a fire; 3,626 rubles were allocated, and 2,276 actually disbursed, to 13 Jewish vocational schools or vocational departments in Jewish elementary schools in Dombrova, Dubno, Elisavetgrad, Zhitomir, Kishinev, Minsk, Mir, Odessa, Orsha, Ostrog, Starodub, Taganrog, and Kherson.

Eight students in technical schools (*technicums*) in Elets, Kremenchug, Uman, Vileika, and St. Petersburg were granted stipends in the total amount of 440 rubles to enable them to continue their studies, of which sum 397 rubles were in fact disbursed. In addition, an unspecified number of Jewish colonists in the areas of Ekaterinoslav, Kiev, Kherson, Volynia, Kovno, and other localities received 1,965 rubles to assist them in agricultural pursuits for which 6,865 rubles had been allocated. The total amount allocated during this initial period was 26,289 rubles, and the total amount actually disbursed was 18,221.[15]

The records show that allocations and disbursements for the approximately nine year period 1880-1889 (Table 1) were at substantially the same level, with some fluctuation in amounts of subsidies allocated to various fields.

TABLE 1

Allocations and disbursements by the Provisional Committee
November 4, 1880 – September 1, 1889

	Allocated	Disbursed
	(in rubles)	
1. Transfer of artisans	29,464.02	25,166.02
2. Local subsidies to artisans	36,117.70	35,636.84
3. Subsidies to vocational schools, including vocational training in folk-schools, Talmud Torahs, etc.	43,084.46	26,057.18
4. Grants to students in specialized vocational schools (railroad, agricultural, gardening, etc.)	5,513.96	5,309.90
5. Subsidies to farmers	32,619.85	29,255.10
	146,799.99	121,425.04

During these first nine years, 29,464 rubles were allocated, and 25,166 actually disbursed, to help 233 artisans and their families relocate in appropriate places of work; 185 artisans received 35,636 rubles out of a total allocation of 36,117 for purchase of equipment, special assistance to victims of fires, and other purposes.

43,084 rubles were allocated, and 26,057 actually disbursed to 42 vocational schools or departments in Jewish elementary schools or special training workshops among others in the following cities: Balta, Bobruisk, Borisov, Brest-Litovsk, Velizh, Vinnitsa, Grodno, Dinaburg, Korsun, Kremenets, Krynki, Mogilev, Molodechna, Pinsk, Pereiaslov, Piriatin, Riga, Kovno, Rosieny, Sventsiany, Simferopol, Sokolka, Surazh, Fastov, Tukum, Shaki, and Shklov.[16]

The sum of 5,513 rubles was allocated, and 5,309 actually disbursed, for students in technical schools, among others, in Warsaw, Vilna, Volkovisk, Volozhin, Gorodishche, Dinaburg, Dubno, Kiev, Kovno, Korets, Medzhibozh, Mstislavl, Pinsk, Novogrudok, Samara, Surazh, and Tolochin.[17] The sum of 32,619 rubles was allocated, and 29,255 disbursed, to farmers in areas of Bessarabia, Kiev, Vitebsk, Novgorod, Orel, Samara, Tula, and Tavrida.[18]

Thus, during the approximately first nine years of its operations the Committee allocated 146,799 rubles, and actually disbursed 121,425, for various activities in behalf of Jewish artisans, farmers, vocational trainees, and students in technical schools.

Requests for grants to educational institutions as well as for outright assistance to individuals in need began to be received immediately after the establishment of the Committee.

While the data given above apply to the regular activities of the Committee, it should be noted that because some Committee members were relief-oriented, subsidies were occasionally granted for purposes other than those prescribed by Committee rules. In most cases such requests were rejected.

One example of an exception to the rules involved two

persons who have since become part of Russian Jewish history: in 1881, the sculptor Mark Antokolskii urged the granting of a subsidy of 200 rubles to a talented young painter, Kadushin, who wished to study graphic arts. The request was clearly outside the Committee's concern, but in view of Antokolskii's recommendation, a monthly subsidy of 100 rubles for a one-year period was granted. Later that year, when Kadushin's work had achieved an extraordinary success, Committee members personally contributed a supplementary sum of 40 rubles.[19] There were other instances of Committee members meeting requests out of personal funds.

During its first nine years the Committee was distributing funds at the rate of about 13,000 rubles annually. In terms of cost of living (at the time, two rubles were equivalent to one American dollar), this was a considerable sum. Its activities were, of course, limited by the May Rules of 1882, which were particularly restrictive with respect to relocation of Jewish artisans in the Russian interior and with respect to agricultural settlements. Committee minutes of those years mention many instances of grants denied because of government harassment and chicanery. Funds were available, but the Committee could not use them to alleviate the ever-increasing needs of the Jewish masses. This situation did not change with the accession of Nikolai II (1894-1917).

Quarter-Century Balance Sheet

The new ruler of Russia, like his predecessor, was a man of limited gifts and deeply anti-Semitic outlook. He had retained, as his most influential counselor, Pobedonostsev who, along with Durnovo, the minister of internal affairs, had always been an advocate of anti-Jewish policies.[20] When, in the 1890's, the ICA[21] tried to convince the government in St. Petersburg of the desirability of settling Jews as farmers in Russia, Pobedonostsev replied that "the Jews are displacing us, and this does not suit us."[22] Later, questioned as to the future of the Jews in Russia, he stated:

"one third will die, one-third will leave the country, and one third will be completely dissolved in the surrounding population."[23] Any improvement in the Jewish situation was against the wishes of the rulers in St. Petersburg, and the application of Pobedonostsev's philosophy did not encourage extension of the Committee's programs.

While Committee expenditures rose from 20,000 to 25,000 rubles annually, during the first decade of the reign of Nikolai II, this amount was far from adequate given the vast needs.

As will be seen from Table 2, from November, 1880 to December, 1906, a period of some 25 years, the Provisional Committee, out of a total fund of 1,132,214 disbursed only 703,287 rubles.

By 1906, the Provisional Committee, limited though it was by the anti-Jewish policy of the government and harassment by local authorities, nevertheless had on its rolls 285 dues paying members and was extending assistance in varying degrees to Jewish endeavors in some 350 towns and townlets of the Russian Empire, involving some 20,000 to 25,000 individuals. A fraction of the more than 5,000,000 Jews; nevertheless, a vital service.

The Russo-Japanese War, which broke out in January

TABLE 2

Disbursements by Provisional Committee[24]
November 4, 1880 – December 3, 1906

	Amount (in rubles)
1. Transfer of artisans	32,489.02
2. Local subsidies to artisans	174,184.23
3. Subsidies to vocational schools, including vocational training in folk-schools, Talmud Torahs, agricultural schools, etc., and to students in training.	251,180.95
4. Building and maintenance of vocational schools in Dvinsk and Tsekhanovka	74,294.58
5. Farmers	121,708.76
6. Administrative expenses	49,625.17
	703,482.71

1904, and the obvious inability of the Tsarist bureaucracy to conduct extensive war operations in the Far East successfully, created a revolutionary mood in the country. Russians clamored for a change. Strikes and demonstrations were followed by bloody repression. In October, 1905, in the face of increasing unrest, the Tsar issued a manifesto promising freedoms and a legislative parliament (Duma).[25]

Coming of Age

The 1905 Revolution, which was followed by a wave of pogroms, was nevertheless a mixed blessing for the Russian Jewish community. The achievements of the revolution were short-lived—the reaction came in 1906—but they provided a breathing spell for many social initiatives.

Having begun its activities in 1880, not long before the crisis brought on by the assassination of Aleksandr II, ORT came of age, reaching its 25th anniversary during the revolutionary events of 1905.

The Provisional Committee, which had not succeeded during the early years in having its bylaws approved by the authorities, now initiated moves to correct this undesirable situation. The draft Bylaws submitted in the mid 1880's had traveled from one government bureau to another, with no decision being reached on "this grave question." The Tsarist authorities did not favor a society working for the betterment of Jewish conditions. It refused to approve the bylaws and refused also, in 1882, to grant the Provisional Committee the right to acquire small parcels of land to be used for settlement of Jews wishing to go into farming.

Taking advantage of the Political "spring" that began in 1905, the Committee held a series of special meetings to discuss the new conditions obtaining in Russia, the possibilities for enlarging its activities, and the preparation of new bylaws to replace those written more than 20 years before.

In June, 1906, a revised version of the bylaws was submitted for registration in accordance with the new and more liberal law of March 4, 1906. They were duly registered on September 5, 1906, and published in *Senatskie Vedomosti* (Official Gazette) on November 11, 1906.[26]

Among those invited to participate in these meetings was Leon Bramson, at that time only peripherally concerned with the work of ORT. He was destined to become a leading man in the Duma and later in the 1917 Revolution. Until his death he led ORT and personified it throughout the world.

In accordance with Article 33 of the Bylaws, the first meeting of the new Society for Handicraft and Agricultural Work among Jews in Russia, ORT (see Footnote 16, Chapter II), which replaced the Provisional Committee and continued its activities, took place on December 3, 1906.

Baron Horace Gunzburg was elected President of the Society, and Ippolit Wavelberg was elected treasurer. Isaak Berger became the executive head.

The new ORT received from the Provisional Committee the unexpended balance of the Committee's funds, amounting to 428,731 rubles.[27]

Chapter IV

The Great Debate

Twenty-five years is not a long time in the life of a developing organization but it is sufficiently long for the organization to have undergone many changes in program and personnel. In the case of ORT, by the time it had reached its twenty-fifth year, it had lost many of its founders by death, among them Poliakov, Fridland, Rosenthal, and Zak.

The death, in 1904, of Bakst was a great loss. Bakst had devoted all his time and thought to ORT. As one ORT leader, eulogizing him, put it, "Bakst was ORT, and ORT became Bakst." However respected by most of his colleagues, his work was not viewed with complete approval by the upcoming younger generation. It is true that, as often happens with organizational endeavors, some ORT activities, with the passage of time, had indeed become routinized and lost their excitement under Bakst's stubborn direction.

Differences in personality and temperament doubtless contributed to the tensions that pervaded the organization but issues of greater consequence lay behind the discontent with Bakst's rigid direction. A profound conflict had emerged in *Weltanschauung*, in irreconcilable attitudes toward the fundamental question of Jewish needs. These differences were further exacerbated by the coming into their own of the Russian Jewish intelligentsia who had not only been educated in Russian schools but were under the influence of the growing revolutionary mood of the country.

As early as the 1890's, the ORT organization, then still the Provisional Committee, was attracting young professionals who saw the need for a broader framework of ORT activities and closer contact with the Jewish masses. They demanded the adoption of what they considered a more generous social outlook. They wanted to replace what they viewed as a philanthropic approach of a Committee sitting in far-off St. Petersburg, and directed by a group of respectable *shtadlonim*, with a more responsive approach, working from local bases for the Jewish community as a whole. Under the conditions then existing in Tsarist Russia there was little that could be done to radically reform the structure of ORT, but in the post-revolutionary climate the dispute erupted into the open and a great debate began between the opposing factions.

The St. Petersburg Committee, while it did not encourage opposition, did not try to stifle it. In the long run, this open-mindedness contributed to the establishment of a democratic structure. A principle was affirmed: the ORT leadership was willing to listen. This democratic spirit remained with ORT and was to be effective in the future in resolving internal differences, personality clashes, and even the threat of wholesale splits as a growing ORT spread its activities throughout the Jewish world.

The Old and the New

The St. Petersburg leaders naturally did not wish to share their monopoly of decision making and control of funds with people more closely connected with the beneficiaries of ORT than with its benefactors, individuals whom they viewed as belonging to a different, perhaps lower, social class. From the beginning they had legally endowed the Provisional Committee, sitting in the capital city, with executive powers of initiative and decision. They did not share and did not favor what they considered the radical suggestions of "young Turks."

For Bakst personally there was an additional reason to resist change. He loathed the Russian revolutionary movement, did not appreciate the writings of the celebrated Russian progressive thinkers, and was careful not to admit into the ORT organization men or ideas connected with the "radical milieu."

Perhaps, in a subtle sense, Bakst was more European than many of the "young Turks." He had been schooled abroad and had a healthy respect for the evolutionary processes of Western society moving gradually in bringing about social change. In terms of the Russian political picture of his time Bakst was a moderate, if not a moderate leaning toward center-right. As has already been indicated, he participated in the work of commissions created by the Tsarist government; among others, a commission to study the Jewish situation. He openly rejected all-embracing social schemes aimed at immediate radical solutions of the "Jewish question."

Within ORT, he advocated the maintenance of the status quo in the structure and financial base of the Provisional Committee until, under better political conditions, it would be possible to enlarge ORT activities and create a powerful Jewish agency working in the economic field.

The younger generation of ORT members, like their peers among the Russian intelligentsia, believed in far-reaching social initiatives. They disliked Bakst and what he stood for, and they did not trust him. They never forgave him for his anti-revolutionary stand and his collaboration with the representatives of the right.

There were efforts to blot out Bakst's role in the development of ORT. After his death, which preceded by a year the changes brought about by the revolutionary events of 1905, his name gradually disappeared from ORT materials. This attitude continued for decades—probably, unconsciously.[12]

While focused on Bakst, the opposition of the younger

ORT activists survived his death and was directed against the entire ORT leadership, the monopoly of the *shtadlonim*, and the general direction of ORT policy. They charged the St. Petersburg leadership with a lack of initiative and a lack of perspective that resulted in few achievements.

Persistence of Original Idea

Meanwhile, in the course of the first twenty-five years of ORT (1880-1905), and under the impact of the rapid industrialization taking place in Russia, the number of Jews gainfully employed in industrial and, to some extent, agricultural pursuits had increased considerably. These increases reduced somewhat the number of Jews in the so-called non-productive occupations, but obviously not enough to radically change the structure, so that much needed to be done to alleviate the poverty and the economic imbalance.

Moreover, it was becoming obvious that even those Jewish wage earners engaged in productive occupations (workers, artisans, peasants) were, more often than not, in need since they were for the most part concentrated in occupations that were not solidly based economically and were always the first victims of any economic downtrend.[3] Jews were over-represented among tailors, cobblers, barbers, and watchmakers; even in normal times they had to compete sharply for clients. In the prevailing anti-Jewish climate they were constantly harassed, and suffered under local anti-Jewish administrative restrictions.

The guiding idea of the ORT founders in the 1880's had been to promote productivization. They wanted to separate Jews from uncertain business deals and marginal commercial activities where they served as intermediaries, rather than engaging in occupations that required them to work with their hands. The goal was to bring about a gradual change in the work configuration of the Jewish Pale. As did the men of the Enlightenment, the founders believed that once the Jew was educated in a productive occupation, his disabilities would begin to disappear.

The *maskilim* were over-optimistic in their evaluation of the social developments and spirit of the times. Much more was required to integrate Jews into the surrounding Christian society on a basis of equality than had been foreseen by the enlightened Jews.

With the growing industrialization of Russia it was becoming clear that productivization and resettlement of individual Jewish artisans, while important, were not enough. Russian areas beyond the Pale often did not provide sufficient markets for Jewish artisans, forcing newly established artisans to seek new locations. It became necessary to think, with perhaps the same sense of urgency, about measures to promote more profound transformations in the Jewish social milieu within which the acquired *metier* (and the equipment supplied for the *metier*) would be attractive to the individual artisan and keep him from seeking a way out of his misery by emigration.[4]

As the Russian artisan class continued to grow, it was necessary to think about how to put the Jewish artisan, whether master or hired man, in a situation in which he could compete and possibly even provide superior services. The dilemma was a critical one. It was to demand ORT attention under different conditions and in other countries in the future.

A Social Direction

Such an approach required a great change in both the program and direction of ORT activities. It called for the abandonment of case-by-case assistance in favor of broader policies. It also called for the initiation of a system of cooperative actions directed to the Jewish collectivity as a whole.

While some of the criticism directed at the St. Petersburg leadership undoubtedly reflected a recognition of the new social and economic circumstances, and thus represented a constructive overview, there were political overtones in this criticism which the founders unhesitatingly rejected and the younger members consciously promoted.

As was the custom among the Russian and Russian Jewish intelligentsia, practical moves, if considered at all, were always seen in ideological terms. Moreover, some of the criticism reflected the expectations engendered in the community and in the press in the still "liberal" years of the reign of Aleksandr II. In some Jewish circles the creation of ORT was greeted as a kind of revolution which, if permitted to develop, would radically change the social and economic structure of the Jewish Pale. Measured against this far-reaching goal, and illusory as it may have been, the accomplishments of ORT, in the eyes of the radicals, were small indeed.

Balance Sheet of That Time

Looking back on this first great conflict in ORT from a present perspective it would appear natural to ask: Was a radical change in program and leadership possible under the conditions prevailing in Tsarist Russia? And, concomitantly, what was the situation in ORT and what were ORT's achievements, if any?

To devise a critical framework within which it would be possible to pinpoint positive and/or negative aspects we must return to the distant past and see things as they were then.

The creation of the Provisional Committee and its functioning required sponsorship of individuals of the stature of Baron Gunzburg, a Poliakov, a Rosenthal, men of wealth and, to the Tsarist authorities, politically trustworthy. They were men who did not hesitate, in their petitions, to express to the "beloved Monarch" their feelings as "faithful servants." Without the sponsorship of such men, who had high social standing and connections, permission to establish the Provisional Committee would not have been forthcoming.

Even with this exceptional sponsorship it took twenty-six years to obtain registration of the organization, and the effort ultimately succeeded mainly because of changes in the laws resulting from the events of 1905. It would have been surprising if a group of liberal activists had at that time been able to change the framework of ORT and, in addition, maintain the necessary connections with rich Jewish families, the authorities, and local affiliates.

The answer to the first question must be in the negative. As for the second, one is inclined to conclude that, shortcomings notwithstanding, the ORT founders had succeeded, despite the general decline that characterized social and political efforts in Russia in the 1880's, in building a solid foundation for future development and future social achievement.

This would appear to be borne out if one takes into account the social impact of ORT's initial ventures: their geographical spread, which was without precedent in Jewish life in Tsarist Russia, the number of people involved centrally and locally; and, most important, the significance of ORT as the locus of a new approach and training ground for Jewish social work in Russia.

As often happens in the course of the development of seminal ideas, some aspects of an initial endeavor become obsolete with the passage of time. The doctrines of the founders undergo adjustment due to the pressure of events. Called-for additions are grafted onto original propositions. The essence of the ORT idea—development of productive labor in its various forms, as determined by the times and by geographic and social conditions—has for decades been the guiding principle of ORT endeavors. It has proved a sufficiently attractive and realistic objective to permit the maintenance of the framework of ORT in many countries and continents, and accounts for its unprecedented growth.

The great debate was a conflict of generations in which the younger urged restructure in their image and the elders tried to build on the old.

New Initiatives

In the social climate of the first decade of the 20th century significant changes took place in Jewish life in Russia. Social demands were becoming more vocal and political activities more visible. To the Jews, the Kishinev pogrom (1903) brought home the fact that Pobedonostsev's pessimistic dictum about the future of the Russian Jews had not been a passing fancy of a reactionary bureaucrat. This realization brought responsible Jewish bodies face to face with the need for concrete remedial efforts.[5]

No time was wasted in soul-searching, although soul-searching there was, both in the provinces and in St. Petersburg. With the help of the "young Turks," and perhaps under pressure from local affiliates, some internal reforms had been introduced. It was suggested that the possibility of introducing Jewish artisans to non-Jewish professions be investigated in order to diffuse excessive concentration in a few marginal occupations.

Gradual changes appeared in the operations of the St. Petersburg center. Five thousand copies of a new set of bylaws were sent to interested persons and agencies inviting them to join ORT. "Selective membership" of the earlier days gave way to an opening of the doors to broader Jewish circles. An outline of an elaborate program of far-ranging activities was submitted for comment and suggestion to some three hundred Jewish schools, Jewish societies, selected Jewish individuals, and Jewish publications, the first time such an action had been taken.[6]

The document embodying the plan was entitled "Project of a Plan of ORT Activities Among the Jews in Russia." The proposal included much that was new in ideas and practical approach. It proposed to direct ORT programs toward ameliorating the economic and social conditions of Jewish artisans and peasants through the establishment of cooperative societies and loan funds that would help Jewish producers attain more stability in their workshops and agricultural pursuits. It emphasized the necessity of planning for the geographic distribution of Jewish productive workers in order to avoid excessive competition or projects in areas where it might be impossible to practice a given trade.

As early as 1907, ORT had appointed J. Rosenfeld as a traveling agent to inform local communities of ORT plans, survey local needs, and report the results, together with local suggestions, to the attention of the St. Petersburg center.

A number of commissions had been created in 1908. One was to survey the economic conditions of Jewish artisans and workers; another was to prepare a program for a forthcoming conference of heads of Jewish vocational schools devoted to vocational training in schools and in outside facilities.[7] There was also a commission for the establishment of new local ORT divisions, and a commission for fund raising.

Among the individuals associated with the new tasks were J. Gurevitch, Ruben Blank, M. Bolotin, and Leon Bramson, the latter having become more and more active in ORT work.[8]

To strengthen liaison with local affiliates, the St. Petersburg center took advantage of the frequent private travels of such leading members of ORT as Moiseii Krol, G. Levinson, and Jacob Frumkin.

The efforts of the ORT leadership to enlarge the organization's activities and make them more responsive to the wishes and needs of the Jewish masses apparently did not satisfy the demands of the younger ORT generation, who believed that, as constituted and perceived in the Jewish Pale, ORT was failing to promote an understanding of its purpose and, so, failing to arouse the sympathies of the Jewish masses.

The Conflict Is Joined

The conflict within ORT came into the open in 1909, the year Baron Horace Gunzburg died, but was probably not connected with the passing of this outstanding Russian Jewish leader.

At the April 16th General Assembly (general membership meeting), J. Gurevitch, a very able "young Turk," moved for a vote on the question of the exclusion from ORT programs of all forms of charity. "The General Assembly," read the motion, "considers it necessary that the Society reject assistance to individuals . . . and concentrate all its forces on measures of a general character . . . aimed at the development of economic self-help."

Without going into the details of the conflict, it should be emphasized that ORT's so-called charitable work was in fact much more than simple philanthropy. It was a natural outgrowth of the initial moves by the *Remeslennyii Fond* to fulfill its aims. While both sides knew this, the point was a moot one, for what was involved was a clash between two radically different approaches.

As is often the case in such debates, "code words" and key formulations are often more revealing than complex expositions of points of view. "Charity" and "philanthropy" signified, for the participants on one side of the argument as well as for their contemporaries, much more than what we would today consider their meaning to be. In this debate the "code words" were "*shtadlonim,*" "rich Jews of St. Petersburg," "arrogant self-appointed protectors of the Jewish masses," and such expressions as "general approach to the community" and "self-help" reflected the ideas of the developing Jewish radical groups.

The "young Turks" wanted to apply radical social measures, which the old founders and their followers feared would bring the organization into conflict with the Tsarist authorities. This was the crux of the split within the leading circles of ORT.

After some unsuccessful efforts at compromise, Gurevitch's motion was adopted, 47 in favor and 29 against. The "young Turks" had won the battle.

Immediately after the vote was taken, Galpern (at that time Acting President of ORT), G. Sliosberg, S. Meerson, D. Feinberg, I. Wavelberg, and M. Shafir resigned from the directing committee. Efforts at reconciliation were made. At the next General Assembly, held on May 3, 1909, the deliberations of the previous Assembly were re-examined, resulting in the withdrawal of the resignations.

Return of the six leading members did not essentially alter the decision with respect to "philanthropy." But the Assembly agreed that in "exceptional cases the Committee has the right to extend help to individual artisans, with the proviso that such cases will be reported to the next Assembly of members."[9] Perhaps this was considered a compromise, but in fact it was face-saving to permit the return of the offended leaders.

The Second Birth

A new and different ORT emerged from these memorable meetings in 1909. It was an ORT reflecting a profound shift in the social structure of the leading circles of Russian Jewry. New men, some with, for that time, radical political leanings, had come into the top ORT councils. While they did not take over, their influence was to be substantial.

In 1909, Leon Bramson was delegated to attend the Jewish Conference in Kovno, where he presented an ORT proposal of a comprehensive program of vocational training and general productivization. In 1911, Bramson, now the executive head of ORT, participating in the All-Russian Congress of Artisans, again presented a broad plan, elaborated by ORT, for increasing the productivization of the Jews. He spoke with great force about the necessity of liquidating the Pale and extending civil equality to the Jews of Russia.[10]

He made a direct appeal: "We expect from you, from the representatives of Russian labor . . . that upon leaving this conference . . . you will conclude that the time has come to abolish . . . every type of barrier and repression of laboring people independently of their origin and their nationality." This was a substantial departure from the traditional attitude of the ORT founders, who had shunned pronouncements with political connotations.

There were some in ORT ruling councils who did not appreciate the new ways or, perhaps, the new voices heard in ORT circles. There was even a formal appeal for a return to the old ways, including the system of individual assistance.[11] But there was no way back. The majority of ORT activists were now men of "the left."

Nevertheless, the revolution in ORT directing councils, with its mixed leadership of partisans of the old and representatives of the new, at least in the period of the last years before World War I, did not result in the development of the broad programs that were the goal of the younger members, although the emphasis had shifted perceptibly away from assistance to individual artisans to concentration on vocational training and the establishments of schools, cooperatives, and similar projects. There was more openness to the ideas of the "progressive" intelligentsia and greater realization of the need to become more vocal at conferences and meetings of professional, social, and cultural agencies working toward general change in Russia.

New Directions

Most significant in the coming to leadership of the "young Turks" (approximately 1908-1909) was the emergence of a process of modernization of the ORT framework, however limited by prevailing political conditions.

Under Stolypin,[12] it was difficult to develop large social undertakings focused on the needs of the Jewish people. Moreover, such projects demanded substantial funding, and reports of the time indicate that large contributions were not forthcoming. Nevertheless, modernization of ORT went forward slowly, taking, as it developed, several forms. One by one, a number of specialists were added to the ORT staff, most of whom had been trained in Russian universities and whose outlook was very much that of the "young Turks."

A special conference of delegates of interested groups was convened in 1910 to consider small loan activities, the establishment of cooperative ventures for artisans, and other matters. As a result of a study of social conditions outside the Pale and a survey conducted in 89 localities, ORT opened local information offices to offer advice to Jewish artisans who wished to settle in the interior, where there were few, if any, Jews, particularly in the Volga and Ural regions.

Much attention was given to cooperative enterprises, and continuing subsidies were extended to, among others, carpentry groups in Bobruisk, Ekaterinoslav, and Zhitomir; a textile cooperative in Zhdunskaia Volia; mutual help loan societies in Gomel (shoemaking), Vilna (tailoring), Bialostok (mechanical woodworking), and Dubossary, where a loan society assisted artisans in many trades.

The so-called producer-cooperatives were particularly favored. It was this type of Jewish economic self-help that became important later under different circumstances and in different countries, in some cases with ORT participating in these important endeavors.

Cooperatives, very much favored by the "progressive" elements, were not always appropriate to the situations existing in Jewish areas where there was a severe lack of resources and where acquisition and maintenance of raw materials often presented insurmountable difficulties. The functioning of cooperative societies was much discussed in St. Petersburg. It is easy to imagine the intensity of these debates, which involved, in addition to technical considerations, the political commitments of ORT leaders. In working out arrangements for support of cooperatives, ORT was in close contact with many local institutions devoted to their development, including the Jewish relief society Pomoshch in Kiev and similar societies elsewhere in Russia.

After much study and debate, ORT began a campaign for the introduction of Jewish workers in many areas where such labor had been almost totally absent. In 1909, it was instrumental in organizing and then subsidizing courses for electricians in Vilna and, in 1910, courses for automobile drivers and automobile mechanics in St. Petersburg.[13] ORT activities were thus closely connected with the modernization of Russia.

The Vilna courses, for example, were started in advance of the city-projected introduction of an electrical street car system. The field of automobile mechanics was in its beginnings in Russia, and it was felt that Jewish young men could profitably enter into the new vocation. (The drivers' project was privately funded by M. Ginzburg.)

An interesting pilot idea of ORT was the establishing of commercial agricultural garden plots in small towns and townlets of Lithuania. It was believed that these could produce vegetables that could be marketed in nearby areas at little expense for transportation and other services. After a thorough inquiry conducted by Samuel Sistrin of the ORT staff, the project was dropped. It deserves mention, however, because some ten years later it was resurrected in Evsektsiia circles and functioned for a short time under the Bolsheviks.

ORT representatives and lay members made frequent visits to the Jewish Pale to study the operation of new projects and to suggest methods of attracting local workers to them and, if necessary, help local artisans with technical advice. In its surveys, ORT staff made use of the services of the Jewish Statistical Society of Vilna and other local agencies.

Program of Publications

A detailed discussion of ORT programs during this period will not be given here, but one important activity should be mentioned: endeavors in the field of technical publication, an initiative destined to become a significant future activity. An ORT textbook, *Forms of Economic Self-Help among Artisans*, by L. Zak, was published in the Russian language in 1911. It covered cooperative enterprises, loan *kassas*, purchase of raw materials, producer-cooperatives, and other matters. It included a discussion of assistance to the unemployed, old age pensions, and trade unions.

An essay by N. Aronovitch on vocational education of

artisans appeared as a supplement. The publication was viewed as a general introduction to ORT programs and plans. The 3,000 copies issued were sold at 75 kopeks each. A year later, the textbook was published in a Yiddish translation by Kh. Gurevitch. On the strength of the great interest among residents of the Pale in all types of cooperative undertakings, the Yiddish version was issued in 5,000 copies and sold at 25 kopeks each. It was greeted with enthusiasm by individuals and organizations alike. An interesting discussion arose in St. Petersburg concerning the advisability of using Yiddish—considered jargon in some Jewish circles—in ORT publications.

ORT established, in 1912, two prizes for books in Yiddish, one of 300 to 600 rubles for a book on tinsmithing, and one of 250 to 500 rubles for a book on mathematics adapted to the needs of artisans. Unfortunately, the manuscripts submitted were not favorably received by the judges. Before the beginning of the war, ORT had published a manual on furniture making by A. Kostelianskii and a manual on tailoring by S. Margolin. Both authors were on the staff of ORT.

Diversified Approaches

ORT continued its program of subsidies to selected artisans, selected agricultural projects, and Jewish vocational schools and vocational classes in other schools, and facilities for preparation and improvement in artisan trades.

In the period immediately before World War I, it was extending subsidies to vocational schools for both boys and girls, and for training in outside workshops in, among other places, Dvinsk, Tsekhanovets, Orsha, Kremenchug, Mogilev-Podolsk, Minsk, Novogrudok, and St. Petersburg.

Some grants given for vocational education were pared and some were discontinued when it became apparent that, in cases where ORT subventions represented only a small part of the school's budget, these subventions were not needed. In the case of certain schools, particularly those under semi-private sponsorship, it was felt that they had established themselves sufficiently not to require ORT assistance. With a treasury limited by less than successful fund-raising, the savings thus realized permitted experimentation in other fields.

ORT also continued to subsidize resettlement of artisans in the interior, but on a small scale since, as we have seen, this program was adversely affected by the May, 1882 rules.

Organizational Spread

In the climate of the short-lived political spring ushered in by the events of 1905, ORT was able to establish local divisions in various parts of the Empire. There were ORT affiliates in Kovno, Moscow, Ekaterinoslav, Odessa, Samara, Kherson, Kiev, Ekaterinburg, Riga, Minsk, Bialostok, Lida, Dvinsk, Berdichev, Krivoi Rog, Sventsiany, Uman, and other cities.

Judging from available reports, there was only loose contact between the center in St. Petersburg and some of the local affiliates, while in some cities the center maintained mandated representatives.

ORT membership rose from 285 in 1906 to 866 in 1908; 1,037 in 1909; 1,556 in 1911; 1,951 in 1913; and reached 2,098 in 1914.[14] Appropriations reflected the limited ORT activities: 44,574 rubles in 1909; 61,951 in 1911; 64,778 in 1912; and 75,778 in 1914, the first year of the war.

For a long time, and particularly in the period after the 1905 revolution, the ORT leadership had given much thought to the "question of organization." Organization was a recurring problem representing another aspect of the struggle for control, again pitting the older against the younger generation. Later during the war years some of the work was organized by means of special committees and special departments under separate direction and to a large degree with independent financial control. In this area, too, with Bramson assuming the executive management of ORT, the "young Turks" had won the battle.

Leon Bramson

Bramson was elected executive head of ORT in 1911, the year of the Beilis Affair.[15] He remained in the post until 1914, when he resigned to devote himself to political and social activities, but returned to active ORT work in 1915 and was elected vice-president.[16]

The name of Leon Bramson will appear increasingly in these pages until, as was the case with Bakst in an earlier era, it will become synonymous with ORT. A picture of Bramson and his place in Russia and among Russian Jews will perhaps facilitate an understanding of the future development of ORT.[17]

Bramson was born in Kovno, Lithuania, in 1869, the son of a pioneer in pro-Palestine circles. In 1887 he went to Moscow to study law. During his years at the university he was an anti-Zionist; he declined to join a student Zionist group, B'nai Zion. He remained anti-Zionist throughout his life, but in 1934, after visiting Palestine, he softened his anti-Zionist position.

In Moscow he formed a student group devoted to the study of Jewish history. Boris Bogen, who was later associated with Jewish social work in the United States, was among the members of this group. Until old age, sensitive and stubborn in devotion to his work, Bramson retained his capacity for concentration on chosen goals. He knew not only how to make people work but how to make them do so with enthusiasm.

He was a good writer and researcher. He was the author or co-author of, among other works, a bibliography of sources of Russian Jewish history that grew out of his participation in Moscow history circles. The bibliography was later published and became a significant tool for scholars in the field.[18]

In his early years Bramson was associated with the educational work of the Society for Enlightenment and also wrote and for a short time edited the Russian Jewish periodical *Voskhod*. In 1899 he joined the ICA (Jewish Colonization Association) and was instrumental in conducting the economic statistical inquiry on Russian Jewry.

Like many other Russian Jewish intellectuals, Bramson participated actively in Russian politics. He was elected from the Kovno district to the first Duma, where he joined and became one of the leaders of the Trudoviks (labor group), which represented essentially the interests of Russian peasants and was ideologically associated with the Russian populist movement.[19] He was one of signers of the Vyborg protest against the dissolution of the first Duma and was among those arrested for this act. Later, he was influential in conferences of Jewish Duma deputies.

During the March, 1917 revolution, Kerensky offered him a ministerial post, which he declined, although he remained active in political affairs. He contributed to the preparation of the text of the Emancipation Law and was intimately connected with its adoption by the Lvov-Kerensky government. As a representative of the Trudoviks he was a member of the executive committee of the Soviet of Workers and Soldiers Deputies and chairman of its finance committee. Later, he was a member of the committee for the preparation of the Constitutional Assembly. He was tried as an enemy of the October revolution and the Bolshevik dictatorship in December, 1917, and sentenced to "social condemnation." Soon after the trial he left St. Petersburg, went to Kiev, then to Odessa, and from there emigrated abroad.[20]

Bramson was part of a Jewish generation that identified completely with Russia, Russian culture, and Russian aspirations. Unlike many of his contemporaries, however, he at the same time devoted much of his thought, time, and uncommon talents to his Jewish brethren.

Chapter V

Years of Turmoil
World War I and Revolutions

The blood libel case against Mendel Beilis ended in Beilis' acquittal in 1913. Russian Jewry emerged from the bleak episode with some hope of a better future. But matters soon took a turn for the worse.

On July 18, 1914, Germany declared war on Russia. For centuries, large Jewish masses had lived along Russia's western borders, and it was precisely there that the confrontation between Russia and her enemies, Germany and Austria, began. Tens of thousands of Jews were displaced. They found refuge for a short time in Warsaw, where they added to the already substantial number of poor and unemployed Jews. Immediate relief was needed. Many Jewish organizations began to develop programs of financial assistance and legal protection, the latter much needed to counteract measures promoted by the anti-Semitic elements of the army.[1]

For ORT, the year 1914 began without great upheaval. The leadership continued to strive for enlargement and improvement of its operations. In February, 1914, some five months before the outbreak of the war, an ORT conference was held in St. Petersburg at which the main topic of discussion was expansion of activities.

71

Invitations to the conference were sent to 53 organizations, including 14 ORT affiliates, 9 loan funds, 7 societies for the promotion of vocational training for children, 10 vocational schools, 3 mutual aid societies, 2 artisans' clubs, societies providing social services to Jewish workers in Vilna, Vitebsk, and Warsaw, the Society of Artisan Labor in Warsaw, the Pomoshch Society in Kiev, the Jewish Statistical Society in Vilna, the Carpenters' Loan Society, and EKO.[2] Also invited were four individuals representing ORT in various cities, and five individuals serving on various ORT commissions. The conference was a deliberate move on the part of the leadership to democratize the organization by bringing local people, including ORT beneficiaries, into the elaboration of ORT plans.

In all, 56 persons participated in the conference: 43 representatives of various agencies, 11 individuals connected with ORT bodies, and two deputies of the Duma, N. Fridman and E. Gurvitch. The presence of the Duma deputies enhanced the prestige of the proceedings and perhaps gave them a political dimension. Proposals were made to bring to the attention of the Duma the legal restrictions hampering the development of productive forces within the Jewish economy. Among participating ORT leaders were Sliosberg, Bramson, Gurevich, and Blank.

For three days the delegates debated ORT programs. It was decided to maintain and even reinforce the standing ORT policy of promoting local community initiatives and supporting self-help projects aimed at the development of artisan labor and small individual enterprises. The policy calling for avoidance of individual assistance except in cases where such assistance would be useful for the general community was reconfirmed.

For the first time, it was decided to revise the original goals of the organization by de-emphasizing assistance to Jewish agricultural projects. This decision was motivated by the persistence of severe legal restrictions but also, in large degree, by the continuing colonization work of ICA (Jewish Colonization Association) which was also active in the field of vocational education in Russia.

It should be noted here that the ORT-ICA relationship was not always well-delineated. In fact, there was growing between them a vexing jurisdictional conflict in the area of vocational education. While there were historical reasons for both organizations to maintain programs of vocational training, as time went on it became obvious that it was both educationally unsound and financially onerous to support two separate efforts having the same goal.

As in the earlier conflict within ORT, the controversy with ICA took on an ideological dimension. To some ORT "radicals," ICA represented a charitable *shtadlonim* organization which, through an established bureaucracy, was able to develop its programs without a shred of communal control. ORT activists appreciated ICA's achievements in some areas, and in particular the bringing together of the "rich West and the poor East." But they felt strongly that "the business of Jewish vocational education . . . had to be concentrated in one communal democratic organization, ORT."[3] It was an extended debate, with both sides presenting an array of arguments for their own point of view, but without much effect. The conflict was taken up by the Jewish press, and the ORT people, who were experiencing financial difficulties, insisted particularly on the need for Jewish organizations to practice austerity.

In terms of the quality of the participants and the level of debate, this ORT conference, held in the early part of 1914, was an important one. The rapid evolution of events in Western Europe and Russia could not have been foreseen, and ORT planned its work, as did many other organizations, without realizing that it was already too late to think in terms of normal operations. The war made many programs irrelevant. The new conditions called for quite different actions.

Response to War Conditions

ORT Committee minutes of 1914 do not cast light on the Committee's immediate reaction to the beginning of hostilities.[4] The Committee's first meeting under war conditions took place in the fall of 1914 when the situation in the Jewish communities in the war zone and surrounding areas was becoming extremely grave. Vast territories near the front were under military control. The anti-Semitic High Command, in the hands of two notorious Jew-baiters, Grand Duke Nikolai Nikolaevich and General Nikolai Ianush-kevich, was conducting mass campaigns of persecution of Jews, promoting among the population and in the press fantastic stories of Jews serving the German enemy. The Jews provided a convenient scapegoat to explain the military defeats.[5]

In October, 1914, the ORT Committee in St. Petersburg, in another departure from formulated policy, embarked on a new field of activity: it established a Relief-Through-Work Department aimed at finding gainful occupations for Jewish artisans and workers, victims of the war. This new activity placed ORT in a quite different position. It was now in war relief. It was in the labor market looking for work opportunities for its "clients," and was thus in much closer contact with people.

It is difficult to determine precisely how this innovation came about. With masses of Jewish refugees unable to find ways to earn a living, the idea was probably around. We do know that sometime in 1914 a group of ORT volunteers, with the permission of the Committee, established a special commission to study the possibilities of providing jobs for unemployed Jewish artisans and workers. This group, which eventually came to include more than a hundred members, was especially interested in ORT's new and as yet untried experiment.[6]

In any event, the Relief-Through-Work Department was quickly established. To avoid duplication of effort among the many organizations engaged in war relief, it was decided to include in the direction of the Department members of ORT active in various Jewish agencies, among which were EKOPO and OSE.[7]

Eventually, the volunteer group transferred to the Relief-Through-Work Department practically all of its functions and agreed to provide the funds necessary to cover the Department's administrative expenses. EKOPO and, later (1915), ICA also contributed to the Department's budget.

From the beginning, the Relief-Through-Work Department had a degree of autonomy not given to other ORT functional services. Jacob Tsegelnitski, who was later to head ORT activities in the Soviet Union, was the first *deloproizvoditel* (executive) of the Department. Toward the end of 1915 he was replaced by J. Khurgin, but he remained active as a member of the directing group of ORT.

Meanwhile, Boris Brutskus (brother of the Julius Brutskus mentioned earlier), an economist and leading member of the ORT Committee in St. Petersburg, had elaborated a plan under which local ORT affiliates would be charged with organizing work programs for the Jewish unemployed.

Local ORTs, particularly those in the northwest areas of the Pale, were to be provided with orders obtained from the government for production of war items. It was felt that the authorities would favor such an initiative since it would provide the war effort with a mass of specialized labor. The general mobilization having depleted the reserves of manpower, ORT leaders counted on this support of the authorities and on the help of Russian volunteer organizations working for the war. Some ORT leaders believed this important project should be administered from the Center in St. Petersburg but, after some discussion, Brutskus' proposal to delegate responsibility to local affiliates was adopted.

The new department began to function promptly. Two experts, Wolf Latski-Bertoldi, a future Minister of Jewish Affairs in the Ukrainian Rada, and Jacob Lestschinsky, a noted economist, were engaged to survey the situation and make plans for the actual work. They began by visiting the cities of the Pale: Vilna, Minsk, Zhitomir, Uman, Kovno, Fastov, Dvinsk. They collected material on the status of Jewish refugees who, without planning, had been moved by the military out of the war zones and who, as had been the case earlier in Warsaw, increased the numbers of local Jewish poor supported by the communities and various organizations in many towns.

The War Years

Human tragedy cannot be measured. The contemporary reader who has lived through the fateful years of the Nazi Holocaust will probably find it difficult to imagine the degree of misery endured by the World War I generation of Jews. We can give here only some details of the horrors caused by the military and, sometimes, civilian authorities in the course of deporting Jewish populations from areas close to the front.

Entire populations were hastily evacuated, lodged in barracks, often under military guard and without provision for kosher food. Some victims of this extraordinary action were then brought to the interior of Russia, in contradiction to the laws pertaining to the Pale. The advancing German army overran some 800 small towns and villages, destroying centuries-old Jewish life in the border areas.

The authorities, both in the interior and in the Pale, did not know, and probably did not wish to know, how to deal with the problems facing the expelled Jews. In Ekaterinoslav the local administration and regional authorities deported Jewish refugees who had been sent there on orders from Petrograd. In August, 1915, one thousand Jews were expelled from that city, where they had already acquired gainful occupations.[7] The same situation occurred in Pskov.[8] Some 7,000 Jews passing through Kursk, including some who were seriously ill, lived for a month in a freight train because local authorities refused them permission to enter the city.[9]

Many Jewish organizations conducted relief programs on behalf of the displaced Jewish populations, but the efforts of ORT deserve special mention for their originality and for the social dignity inherent in the determination to help people by providing them with work.

The Relief-Through-Work Department extended substantial credits and organizational assistance to various artisan cooperatives capable of executing government orders for
military goods. The program included shoemaking shops in
Vilna, a home-tailoring project manufacturing uniforms for
the army in Dvinsk, and a number of loan funds in the
southwest region. A cooperative purchasing project for
shoemakers in Bobruisk and a similar enterprise in Minsk
also received aid. It was estimated that some 4,000 individuals benefited from these efforts.

It soon became apparent that supplying the army with
goods produced by Jewish workers was beset with insurmountable obstacles, some caused by lack of governmental
coordination and the legal restrictions still in effect. Chaotic
transportation conditions made it impossible to deliver manufactured goods within the stipulated time. Already in February, 1915, some seven months after the outbreak of hostilities, it had become obvious that local efforts by Jewish
artisan cooperatives to obtain government orders had best be
discontinued.

The attention of ORT was now transferred to coordinating its efforts on behalf of displaced and unemployed Jews in
rear areas where there was an increasing demand for
specialized labor. Some moves in this direction had been
made by the Work Division of the Warsaw Jewish Relief
Society, but they were not successful, since the work required the employment of persons familiar with the labor
market and a central office to coordinate information and
activities.

Labor Bureaus

The Relief-Through-Work Department lost no time in responding to the new conditions. In fact, relief-through-work
activities were repeatedly discussed by responsible ORT
bodies, and ORT soon embarked on one of its most important efforts of the war period. It established labor bureaus in

various cities to survey the labor market and find jobs for Jewish refugees. ORT provided the bureaus with funds and assured them of the support of interested local groups.

In time, local groups of volunteers and additional labor bureaus were established. The bureau in Vilna began functioning in April, 1915. Minsk, Ekaterinoslav, Kiev, Vitebsk, Odessa, Smorgoni, Elisavetgrad, and Orel followed suit. By the end of July, 1915, 25 labor bureaus had been set up. With the number of Jewish refugees from the frontier areas increasing, bureaus were opened also in the interior—in Samara, Saratov, Perm, Moscow, Tambov, and Tula.[10]

As of January 1, 1916, there were 72 ORT labor bureaus functioning in Russia, some in such far-off (for Russian Jews) places as Vologda, Kaluga, Novgorod, and Orel. In fact, 81 offices were opened, but nine had to be closed because they were in military areas. Among those closed were the bureaus in Vilna, Smorgoni, and Warsaw. There were to be additional closings necessitated by the war.

While the development of these activities was extraordinary in terms of numbers and geographic spread, the actual finding of jobs proceeded slowly. The Relief-Through-Work Department initiated measures to assure orderly search for employment and to maintain contact with industrial enterprises. It issued instructions in late 1915 describing the aims and methods of the program. It prepared reports and control forms which it placed at the disposal of local officials.

In the course of 1915, 41,209 unemployed Jews had registered with some 30 labor bureaus that submitted reports. Of this number 17,423 were referred to enterprises in need of workers. During the two years 1915 and 1916 over 60,000 unemployed were registered with the ORT Labor Bureau and 25,000 out of this total were referred to jobs.

Through the labor bureaus, ORT was not only doing an important task for the unemployed Jews, but was also performing a patriotic duty of the first order for the state. Under the conditions of general mobilization it was providing high-quality labor to do the work required by the depleted economy. The variety of labor put at the disposal of the Russian economy is illustrated by table 3, below.

In addition to assistance to those seeking work, the Department provided financial aid to some 28 artisans' shops in, among other cities, Vilna, Minsk, Lublin, Dvinsk, Fastov, and Warsaw, serving 435 master artisans and 154 trainees. Some of these shops had to be closed due to their proximity to the war areas. Some 30 machines for shoemaking and tailoring and looms for knitting stockings were put at the disposal of local offices for distribution among Jewish artisans. The Department was also active in organizing "patronates" which provided vocational education for Jewish children. During 1915, the total expenditures of the Depart-

TABLE 3[a]

Occupational distribution of persons registered and persons referred to jobs by ORT labor bureaus
(as of January 1, 1916)

Occupational category	Registered	Referred to jobs
Tailoring	7,444	4,459
Leather work	2,610	1,354
Textile weaving	330	135
Woodworking	667	401
Food handling	939	335
Printing	644	414
Metalworking	1,136	854
Construction	838	397
Agriculture	51	14
Office work	5,927	1,606
Professions	2,317	623
Mercantile	1,417	—
Unskilled labor	2,780	3,863[b]
Miscellaneous	3,782	1,075
	30,882[c]	15,530[c]

[a] *Otchet Za 1915 god., op. cit.*

[b] Apparently, among the unskilled laborers referred to jobs were some belonging in the miscellaneous category.

[c] The difference between these figures and those given in the text above is accounted for by the fact that due to the war situation the figures from Warsaw and Lublin are not included.

ment rose to 120,369.58 rubles, of which 95,547.29 were provided by EKOPO, 12,822.29 by the Commission of Volunteers, and 12,000 from the regular budget of ORT.

Broader Impact

The scope and importance of the Relief-Through-Work Department activities went far beyond efforts to provide jobs for needy Jewish artisans and workers. In fact, the Department had a considerable impact on the development of communal Jewish self-help programs and an even greater impact on the development of general Jewish social initiatives in many cities throughout Russia.

Following the example of the labor bureaus, refugee Jewish artisans and workers organized their own mutual-help societies to overcome the shortage of food supplies created by the war by supporting cooperative restaurants, cooperative lodging in hotels, and small loan *kassas* providing cheap credit.

During the war, Russian and Jewish dissenting groups were growing and looking for ways to expand their efforts; local labor bureaus were soon joined by local Jewish workers' organizations, and even representatives of Jewish labor parties, looking for safe ground for their own activities. The radically minded younger generation viewed these self-help efforts as their great achievement, indeed as a "new democracy" that they had brought to Jewish communal life. They were continuing the debate with the representatives of the "old guard."

Vestnik Trudovoi Pomoshchi Sredi Evreev (Messenger of Labor Help Among the Jews), a "thick" monthly magazine, begun with the assistance of ORT in 1915 under the editorship of Boris Brutskus, devoted many articles to this question, with some of the followers of the "old guard" objecting to the appropriation of the concept of "democracy" by the younger "radicals." In response, *Vestnik* pointed out that the younger members of ORT included not only men younger in age, but, more important, younger in spirit and initiative. It emphasized the importance of the labor bureaus as instruments of "popularization of the ideology of labor among the unorganized and partially employed periphery of our people . . . introducing for the first time elements of clearly spelled out social policy in the framework of our open communal efforts."[11]

A large majority of those associated with the relief-through-work programs among staff, lay members, and supporters of ORT as well as local activists belonged to the political "left." (The reader should not confuse the modern American and Western European political terminology with the classifications used in pre-Bolshevik Russia when "left" included socialists of many colors and general progressive organizations active in social endeavors.)

Among the "leftists" were Tsegelnitski, Latski-Bertoldi, Lestschinsky, M. Litvakov (future ideologist of the *Evsektsiia*), Z. Litvakova, L. Epstein, G. Aronson, and Anin, all of whom were associated with Jewish socialist groups. Among Jewish communal workers during this period the labor bureaus were sometimes referred to as "centers of sedition" *(kramola)*. All of the "leftist" groups were staunchly democratic.

The relief-through-work programs began as an effort to meet the needs of artisans and workers deported from the war zones. It soon became apparent, however, that it was both unfair and communally impractical to give priority to the newcomers in an area, leaving the local Jewish unemployed without aid. After much debate, ORT decided to extend its work assistance to all needy artisans and workers without distinguishing between old settlers and refugees.

Under conditions of war and the necessity to help victims of the war, ORT activities had to be focused largely on relief-through-work programs directed by the special department.[12] In 1915, 58 cities and towns were visited and surveyed by ORT representatives. Even a partial listing of the locales surveyed demonstrates the vast geographic spread of these efforts: Balashov, Bobruisk, Vilna, Vitebsk, Vologda,

Minsk, Moscow, Odessa, Penza, Perm, Romny, Samara, Saratov, Simbirsk, Simferopol, Tula, Kherson, Tsaritsyn.

Some of these places were in the Russian interior where, following a considerable softening of Pale restrictions, Jewish refugees from the war areas were brought by the authorities. As of January 12, 1916, 172,317 refugee Jews had been assisted by EKOPO in 384 towns of 52 *gubernias* (regions),[13] and ORT offices operated in some of these.

Expanded Activities

It was not clear whether, after the outbreak of the war, ORT would be able to continue its activities. There was a period in 1914 when some leading ORT people, as well as leading members of other social organizations, believed that systematic ORT work could not be maintained under the existing conditions and that programs would have to be radically changed. Fortunately, this did not become necessary. While many ORT programs had to be adjusted to war conditions, ORT work as a whole made considerable progress during this period.

During the war years ORT supported 34 vocational training workshops serving some 2,000 individuals, 23 artisans' shops, 56 labor bureaus serving more than 60,000 clients, and 31 vocational "patronates" for 2,300 children. Thirty-seven ORT affiliates were in operation during that time. Expenditures in 1915 rose to 273,721.36 rubles and in 1916 to some 541,000.[14]

It is interesting to note that the 1915 budget included a 44,305 ruble one-time grant from abroad (36,600 from Jewish workers in the United States and 7,705 from Jewish artisans in London). The ORT Center apparently was not informed about the precise purpose of these funds so that we find this amount recorded as a transitory item in the 1916 budget estimate. We know from material that became available later that these funds included the United States contribution of the Arbeiter Ring[15] and was appropriated for the relief-through-work program.

The considerable rise in cost of operations created a grave problem for the ORT leadership. Writing in the October, 1915 *Vestnik*, Bramson noted that ORT's financial situation, reflecting the growth of activities during the war years, was unsatisfactory. He noted also that changes in the scope of its work had transformed ORT into a "large enterprise." Apparently ORT operations were growing so complex that direction and, to some extent, policy-making had become managerial responsibilities. Experts and technicians with specialized knowledge had acquired a larger role in the execution of programs, diluting the control exercised by the lay leaders.

At the beginning of the war some 85 percent of the ORT budget was covered by EKOPO. It was not certain how long this subvention would continue, since part of EKOPO's funds came from the authorities, and the Ministry of the Interior had made it known that its grants would be cut, particularly those for relief-through-work programs. At the beginning of the war the state had extended financial assistance to Jewish organizations dealing with relief but, as the war progressed, some of these grants were discontinued.

Many proposals were made for intensifying fund-raising. One was to appeal to Russian-Jewish emigres in New York and London who had maintained their personal and cultural connections with the Old World. Bramson suggested the dispatch of a delegation to New York, London, and other Jewish centers in the West that might establish direct contact with Jewish organizations, and especially with Jewish labor, to obtain additional funds.

The Bramson proposal was not new. Already in 1913, in the course of a similar discussion of financial problems, the Fund-Raising Commission had suggested an appeal to Russian Jews in the United States and the sending of a delegation to New York with the specific mission of informing them about ORT activities and obtaining their financial support.[16]

No action was taken on the "delegation" idea in either 1913 or 1916, but the idea did not die. In the end it proved to be probably one of the most significant proposals made to ORT councils during the trying war years.

On November 10, 1916, ORT held its General Assembly, at which, after a lengthy presentation by Bramson, it was decided to establish a special financial department to take steps to find new sources of financial support. Bramson's presentation at the 1916 General Assembly was his last act during this period in ORT history. At the same Assembly, he tendered his resignation from the ORT Committee. ORT sources do not reveal what motivated Bramson's resignation. Miron Kreinin, who presided at the Assembly, did not refer to the reasons for it.[17] It may be assumed, however, that Bramson left active ORT work to return to the Russian political arena, where his talents as an organizer were badly needed.[18] In fact, he took over the day-to-day responsibilities in connection with the projected 5th Duma electoral campaign. His apartment on Rozhdestvenskaia Street was transformed into a Trudovik party office, and it was there that much of the negotiations took place.[19]

The elections to the 5th Duma never took place. Russia was losing the war and the general situation in the country was rapidly deteriorating. The mobilization of masses of Russian peasants, heavy casualties, and lack of supplies both at the front and in the rear, disrupted the normal functioning of the state. The lack of central direction and continuous changes at the top made it impossible to achieve the sacrifices necessary to continue the war. On February 26 (March 10), 1917 without serious resistance on the part of its supporters, the Tsarist regime collapsed, and on March 2 (15), Tsar Nikolai II abdicated.[20]

For the Jews of Russia the fall of the monarchy represented a promise of freedom. Aleksander Kerensky, at that time Minister of Justice in the Provisional Government, was entrusted with the task of preparing a report on national and religious restrictions in Russia. On March 20, the Lvov-Kerensky Provisional Government issued an emancipation decree abolishing the special restrictions that for centuries had afflicted Russian Jews.[21]

Under the new conditions of equality it appeared, at least at first, that new horizons were opening for ORT activities in the cities and towns of Russia. We shall not detail this crucial period of Russian history. The continuing war soon brought chaos, with masses of disaffected deserting soldiers, dissatisfied workers and peasants clamoring for peace and radical change. On October 25 (November 6), 1917 came the debacle. Lenin's small Bolshevik party seized power. The Bolshevik hurricane covered the cities and villages of the great country and rapidly produced a merciless civil war and, in its wake, pogroms perpetrated by the Ukrainian *haidamaks,* the White Army and Green and Red Army partisans. According to available data, there were some two thousand pogroms in the Ukraine during the civil war years 1917-1920. There were pogroms also in areas under the White Army and under the so-called Belorussian battalions. One after the other, Poland, Latvia, Lithuania, Estonia, Georgia, Armenia, Azerbaidzhan, and the Ukraine declared their independence.

In the summer of 1919 the Bolsheviks abolished all Jewish communal organization, including all social agencies, applying, as it were, the old recommendation made by Derzhavin to Tsar Paul I. Under the difficult conditions produced by a malfunctioning economy, Soviet authorities permitted "technical" organizations, including such organizations as ORT, OSE, ICA, and EKOPO, to operate, although under strict government control.[22]

While here and there ORT programs were maintained, systematic, long-range work became impossible. We shall later discuss in detail ORT work during this period under the Soviets and in areas under the control of various governments, but it should be noted here that whatever the usefulness of ORT may have been at the time, it was now a Soviet ORT, with radically changed structure, leadership, and range of activities. In fact, during this period much of ORT activity was carried on beyond the Russian frontiers, some in newly formed states. Some activities were cut off from Petrograd by the civil war, and those within reach were going through a difficult period of adjustment.

Bramson, an avowed anti-Bolshevik and, after October a member of the Union for Renaissance (of Russia), left Petrograd and, with many other political opponents of the new regime, went to the Ukrainian capital of Kiev, where he resumed to some extent work in local ORT activities.

In the meantime the central ORT Committee in Petrograd decided to send a delegation abroad to establish liaison with and to inform the Jews of the world of the staggering economic problems facing the Russian Jews after years of war and pogroms and, at the same time, to organize a fundraising campaign for the benefit of Russian ORT as the instrument of Jewish rehabilitation acceptable to the new regime.

Little is known about this decision taken in Petrograd, but we may surmise that there was no objection on the part of the Soviet authorities, since foreign currency was badly needed in Russia, and any foreign help at the time was welcome. In ORT, too, there was a dire need of funds. The rich had fled the Bolsheviks, and private donations were not forthcoming. In 1919 the Soviet bureaucracy had not as yet developed the rigidity and intolerance which, at a later period, made contacts with agencies outside Russia extremely difficult, if not altogether impossible.

The Delegation

The Petrograd Committee appointed two delegates to undertake this mission, Bramson and David Lvovich. While the selection of Bramson was a natural one, that of Lvovich was somewhat surprising. Whatever Bramson's politics, he was an old and highly esteemed leader of ORT, while Lvovich was clearly an outsider. In fact, Lvovich, passing through Kiev, was himself surprised when L. Joffe, the ORT representative there, informed him of his appointment.

Born in 1882 to a well-to-do family, Lvovich had graduated in law and economics from St. Petersburg University and had also studied engineering in Munich. As a student he had been active in the Zionist movement and, later, in the Zionist-Socialist (Territorialist) party, whose ideological bent was not favored in ORT circles. He was also connected with the Russian Socialist-Revolutionary party.[23] He participated in the so-called Angola project, Angola having been suggested as a Jewish territory-to-be. In 1907 he advocated the inclusion of emigration and colonization in the program of the Socialist International, and in 1908 he had visited the United States in connection with Jacob H. Schiff's "Galveston Plan," which contemplated sending Jewish emigrants from Eastern Europe arriving in New York to Southern areas in the United States. Lvovich resided in the United States during the war, but returned to Russia where he was elected on the slate of the Socialist-Revolutionary party to the Constituent Assembly (January, 1918) which was to establish the future regime in Russia. He was one of the few speakers at the first (and last) session of the Constituent Assembly which was soon dispersed by the Soviet military. In between his various political activities he was an industrialist who maintained international business activities, later in Germany and the United States. He became interested in ORT activities, particularly its agricultural and cooperative projects.

Given some of his past activities, Lvovich was not, perhaps, the most suitable propagandist of ORT ideas. He was apparently selected for the delegation because of his familiarity with the West and his long-time interest in the economic situation of Russian Jewry. Whatever might have been the objections to the choice of Lvovich, he went into ORT work with his characteristic enthusiasm and was soon to play a large role in building ORT work outside Russia.

The idea of sending a delegation to the West had, as we have indicated, first been suggested in 1913. In 1916, Bramson, elaborating his plan for enlarging ORT resources, returned to the idea, but the war and revolution had made the project impractical. Such facts as we have do not make clear whether the aims of the delegation were limited to informing foreign sources on the Russian situation and raising funds for Russian ORT. We must assume that, given Russian conditions, they were. Looking back we do know that something very different in both quality and scope of ORT work came out of this project, which opened up a new and significant era in ORT history. We may, therefore, ask ourselves: Was the extension of ORT activities to the countries of the West an idea born to Bramson, or to Bramson and Lvovich, in Europe after they had familiarized themselves with general conditions in the West and with the situation of Jewish refugees in many of the countries of the West? Or did it evolve naturally out of contact with already-functioning ORT organizations in Poland, Latvia, Lithuania, and countries formerly part of Russia? We shall come back to this very important question, but at this point we will merely record that in January, 1920, together with other refugees from Bolshevism, Bramson left Odessa, where he had gone from Kiev, and went to Paris. Lvovich, then in Minsk, went to Vilna after the Poles took over the area, and in 1920, after a short period in Poland, joined Bramson in Paris.

Bramson and Lvovich immediately began to develop the activities of the ORT delegation, establishing contact with international Jewish organizations and making plans for future work. Thus, in 1920, ORT inaugurated its activity in countries outside Russia and the former Russian Empire.[24]

Chapter VI

New Beginnings
After World War I

The war changed the geopolitical map of Europe. After Versailles, newly independent states appeared in the areas formerly belonging to Russia, Austria-Hungary, and Germany. In all of them, Jewish populations, representing larger or smaller minorities, each with its own social, cultural, and economic problems, faced neighbors not always sympathetic.

The Versailles treaty, it is true, provided for autonomy for minorities, but this provision was adhered to for only a short time in some of the new states, in others it was never applied. The aggressive nationalism prevailing everywhere made formal equality before the law a de facto fiction. The political and legal status of the Jewish minorities in Poland, Latvia, Lithuania, and Bessarabia (now Rumania) was a subject of continuous conflict between the minorities, governing authorities, and dominant national groups.

The "Cold Pogrom"

The Jewish economic situation was grave, since in addition to war and, in some places, pogroms, Jews were victims of all kinds of discriminatory laws and practical restrictions. In addition, Russia, the great consumer of Polish goods, was now off limits, and local markets were in many respects closed to Jewish producers.

The functions performed by many Jews as intermediaries in business transactions were not needed in the new, geographically small areas, and outsiders were not favored. Some of the new states soon adopted systematic policies of anti-Jewish boycott. Poland was one of several states that instituted a policy of excluding Jewish workers, Jewish artisans, and Jews in the liberal professions from gainful occupation, intensifying an already critical situation.

Anti-Jewish discrimination was manifested much more in the economic area than in attitudes toward Jewish religion and Jewish cultural endeavors. The number of Jews employed in productive occupations was constantly decreasing. Unstable border conditions created unhealthy outlets for not-quite-lawful economic activities, and some Jewish inhabitants of these areas used the opportunities thus offered to make a living.

Figures on Jewish populations affected by the new geopolitical conditions will indicate the scope of the problem: In 1921, in Poland, there were 2,845,000 Jews, 10.5 per cent of the total population; in Latvia, some 100,000, about 5 per cent of the total population; in Lithuania, 155,000, about 6 per cent of the total population; with the new borders of Rumania (including what was formerly Russian Bessarabia), there were some 800,000 Jews, about 5 per cent of the total population.

The Jews in these areas not only had to change their passports (national allegiance) but underwent a substantial change in their social-economic status. Emergency aid and rehabilitation were urgently needed. Present and future breadwinners had to be directed toward the limited occupational opportunities open to Jews.

Renewals in the New Geography

It was under these conditions that local ORT committees, prepared to begin the work of Jewish rehabilitation, sprang up in many of the cities formerly part of the Russian empire. Many of these efforts were initiated with the assistance of local Jewish political groups which, notwithstanding differences in outlook, displayed rare unanimity in supporting ORT work and mobilizing local resources.

It would appear that the ORT delegation in Paris soon realized that its relationship with the ORT center in Petrograd was becoming tenuous. ORT in Russia was now a Soviet institution not only subject to strict control by the authorities but also, of necessity, representing a Sovietized outlook on Jewish life and Jewish economic problems. Dealing with a Soviet institution from Paris, the center of "capitalist reaction," was a difficult matter.[1]

The delegation in Paris was very much concerned with its obligations to the Jews of Russia and it continued energetically to promote all kinds of assistance to ORT projects there. At the same time, it was drawn to the task of undertaking assistance to Jews in the newly established states where, in addition to the indigenous communities still connected by family, personal, and sometimes language ties to Russia, there were also large numbers of Russian refugees, including victims of Ukrainian pogroms.

Examining the beginnings of ORT activity outside Russia, it becomes clear that the development of ORT in the former Russian areas of Vilna, Kovno, Kishinev, Revel, Helsingfors, and Vyborg, where Bramson and Lvovich were completely at home, was a most natural undertaking for the ORT delegation in Paris. Such activities were in fact a continuation of ORT's Russian endeavors. At the time (the early 1920's), Lithuania, Latvia, and Bessarabia were, to large numbers of Russians, still Russian areas, and many Russian Jews shared this feeling.

New Structure

Once embarked on actual functional work outside Russia, in addition to assistance being extended to ORT projects in Soviet Russia (discussed in a later chapter), Bramson, aided by Lvovich, and perhaps in consultation with other friends now abroad, initiated a new structure for ORT activities outside Russia, a step that was to result in spreading ORT ideas and ORT work to Jewish communities the world over.

Bramson readily attracted to ORT many individuals among the Russian-Jewish emigrants in Paris, Berlin, London, and later, to a degree, in New York. The first ORT chairman in Paris was A. Alperin. The first chairman in Berlin was Jacob Frumkin, who for years had been concerned with ORT in Petrograd. In London, the first chairman was A. Halpern, the son of a former ORT chairman in Russia.

Thus, ORT penetration into the countries of Western Europe was spearheaded by Russian-Jewish emigre circles who were indeed the pioneers of ORT outside the borders of Russia. Under Bramson, ORT maintained its Russian character for many years; in spirit and style it was Russian, not Soviet.[2] In its first operations abroad, Russian remained the language of ORT. Meetings were conducted in Russian and minutes of meetings were recorded in that language. It was some time before ORT succeeded in integrating itself into Western Europe and, later, in other areas, and become, as it were, a "native" component of Jewish communal life.

Paris Interval

Bramson, immediately after arriving in Paris, renewed his contacts with representatives of Western Jewish organizations. Having served as an ICA (Jewish Colonization Association) executive in Russia, he was in a position to inform the ICA organization of the worsening situation of the Russian Jewish community. A special report, containing extensive statistical data, was prepared by the Paris delegation and submitted to both ICA and the American Jewish Joint Distribution Committee (JDC). Similar reports on the conditions of Russian Jewry were sent to Jewish organizations in the Scandinavian countries and to the Workmen's Circle (Arbeiter Ring) in New York.[3]

Both Bramson and Lvovich participated in the World Relief Conference (*Welthilfskonferenz*) held in Karlsbad in 1920, which sought to unite relief activities for needy Jews in the war areas. The Conference was under the chairmanship of the Zionist leader Leo Motzkin, who was of Russian origin, as was the secretary of the Conference, Israel Jefroykin, a well-known Jewish writer and activist of pre-World War I days.

It is interesting that the Conference, which visualized its activities in global terms, included the kind of constructive work that was the domain of ORT. Notwithstanding its stipulated objectives, and apparently persuaded by Bramson, it soon voted to grant ORT a subsidy.

ICA was most helpful to ORT. It was the first agency to make a substantial financial contribution to it. The second was JDC. During the period 1920-1922 the ORT delegation in Paris received from various Jewish organizations, including ICA, JDC, the Federation of Ukrainian Jews in London, and other Western European Jewish agencies, contributions amounting to $179,471.

Materials relating to this period indicate that Bramson was not satisfied with the limited activities initiated by the Paris delegation. Already at the Karlsbad Conference in 1920, he and Lvovich had had occasion to meet individuals from Latin America, South Africa, the USA, and England, and in these encounters discussed Jewish economic needs in various countries, especially those of war refugees.

By that time Bramson had accumulated considerable information on Jewish needs almost everywhere in the newly created states in Europe and had come to the conclusion that the work of the Paris delegation must be expanded and its framework adjusted to the new and larger tasks. Looking ahead he saw the Paris delegation as a stepping stone to putting ORT on the European map.

Birth of World ORT Union

After some preparatory work in the Paris office, accomplished with the help of Michel Kivelevich, secretary of the delegation, a conference of European ORT organizations, the first of its kind, took place in Berlin in August, 1921. It was a small affair in which were represented 12 local committees and ORT initiative groups in Vilna, Grodno, Brest-Litovsk, Pinsk, Piotrokow, Warsaw, Kovno, Kishinev, Kiev, Paris, London, and Berlin. It was, in fact, a conference of ORT people from Poland, Lithuania, and Bessarabia, representatives of three Western capitals, and one from Soviet Russia (Tsegelnitski, formerly head of the pre-war ORT Relief-Through-Work Department in Petrograd and later head of ORT in Soviet Russia, who had recently arrived in Berlin).

Among the participants were Dr. Z. Szabad, I. Okun, and B. Kagan from Vilna; M. Zylberfarb and Dr. J. Krouk from Warsaw; J. Jaszunski from Grodno; A. Roitman from Kishinev; Prof. S. Frankfurt, Dr. J. Frumkin, Dr. D. Lvovich, and Dr. A. Syngalowski from Berlin; D. Mowshovitch from London; Bramson, I. Jefroykin, M. Schein, and V. Tiomkin from Paris.

The delegates represented both functional ORT organizations in Eastern Europe and supporting groups in Paris, Berlin, and London, the role of the latter three being mainly to facilitate contacts with local Jewish organizations making financial grants for the work of ORT.

The conference heard reports from experts dealing with Jewish agriculture, vocational training, and related subjects. Bramson presented an elaborate plan for developing ORT work outside of Russia which was a blueprint of things to come. He was already seeking appropriate forms for a larger structure, the contours of which he only dimly perceived, while maintaining a continuation of ORT objectives elaborated in Old Russia.

Bramson's plan was approved by the conference. Under it, local ORT societies and committees were to constitute the new ORT Union of local and regional (national) affiliates.

The principal task of the ORT Union was to "create new ORT committees . . . undertake a vast propaganda campaign in order to find the financial means necessary to achieve ORT aims . . ." and, most important, "extend ORT activities to new fields." Emphasis was placed on the necessity of local self-help and local participation in ORT budgets, not only as a means of financing local projects, but as a social principle distinguishing ORT from traditional patterns of charitable work.

Zalman Szabad was elected chairman of the 18-member Central Council of the new ORT Union. Bramson was vice-chairman, and Lvovich was a member of the Council. A Central Board, the executive body of the new organization, included Bramson, Lvovich, and Tsegelnitski. Jaszunski and Zylberfarb, of Poland, were elected alternate members of the Central Board, and Dr. Aron Syngalowski was elected secretary-general.[4] Berlin became the seat of the Union and remained so until the advent of the Nazis in the early 1930s.

The first secretary-general of the Union, Aron Syngalowski, had only recently been attracted to ORT. He was to become one of its foremost builders and its most eloquent spokesman.

Born in 1889 in Baranovich, in the Minsk region, Syngalowski in his early youth had been active in Zionist Socialist party work in Russia. Zionist-Socialists were exponents of the territorialist ideology that had also attracted Lvovich. Abroad, Syngalowski pursued his studies in law and philosophy in Berlin and other cities.

During his university years and after graduation he was interested mainly in literature, social thought, and literary criticism. A gifted man, his talents were highly regarded in the German-Jewish community, where he earned a well deserved reputation as a scholarly, capable exponent of the national Jewish outlook. A born orator, his brilliant presentations in Yiddish hypnotized his audiences.

In Search of a Financial Base

With the ORT Union established and its organizational structure more or less defined, financing became a matter of prime importance. The ORT organization abroad required a stable financial base for its development, and it was incumbent upon Bramson to secure such a base.

Leon Bramson (1869-1941)
Prominent leader in Russian and Jewish political movements, member of the first Duma (Parliament), outstanding leader of Russian ORT, and initiator of World ORT.

David Lvovitch (1882-1950)
Prominent activist in Russian political movements, was elected to the
Constituent Assembly in 1918, then joined the ORT delegation abroad
and became a founder of World ORT.

Aron Syngalowski (1889-1956)
One of the great Yiddish orators of his time, an activist in Jewish
political movements, leader of World ORT, participant in its founding,
and a leading exponent of the ORT idea.

FOUNDATION of the ORT-UNION   BERLIN   JULY 1921

Founding conference of the ORT Union, Berlin, 1921,
attended by delegates from 12 local committees of Eastern Europe,
Paris, and Berlin.

Soon after the conclusion of the first ORT Union Congress, Bramson and Syngalowski went to the United States to solicit funds.

For Bramson, an administrator with broad management experience in both Jewish and Russian affairs, it was a natural role.[5] Syngalowski, with his fervid oratory, was able to evoke an enthusiastic response from the Jewish masses in the United States. His oratorical skill was in contrast to Bramson's dry "Misnagid" style.[6]

The pair remained in the United States from April to October, 1922, and suceeded in obtaining substantial financial support from and through various Jewish organizations.

This was the first of a series of financial campaigns conducted by Bramson, Syngalowski, and Lvovich in many countries which later involved other ORT representatives, and they became a regular feature of ORT activity. This method of financing necessitated traveling to distant countries, where differences in exchange sometimes made it difficult to transfer funds, and this entailed technical preparation involving local communities, local politics, and substantial expense.

As the volume of ORT work grew, so did the amounts collected and disbursed. The new form of financing had a marked impact on ORT, gradually making it an even "bigger enterprise" than that foreseen by Bramson in 1916 in Russia. This, of course, was to come later. In the early 1920's ORT needed all the selfless devotion of its leaders and workers to survive.

The Bramson-Syngalowski visit signified the formal beginnings of ORT in the United States, although American Jews had extended financial support to ORT in Russia during the war years (see Chapter V). We shall return to this important part of ORT history, but it should be said here that Bramson and Syngalowski succeeded in attracting to the ORT idea many influential Jewish leaders.

One of them was Herbert H. Lehman, later a Governor and Senator of New York State. Scion of a well-known Jewish mercantile and banking family, Lehman was throughout his life intimately associated with Jewish communal work and participated actively in the work of ORT.

Shortly after their arrival in the United States, Bramson and Syngalowski helped to establish the American ORT, of which Jacob Panken was the first president and Louis B. Boudin was the first vice president. Both were associated with various parts of Jewish labor circles in the United States.

Program Takes Form

The functional activities initiated by the Central Board of ORT developed slowly. In the beginning, the Paris delegation and, later, the ORT Union responded mainly to local initiatives in places where the ORT idea was an organic part of Jewish communal life. Lvovich, who had been in the Russian-Polish border area and then in Poland, noted that already in 1919, before going to Paris to meet Bramson, he had participated in the creation of ORT groups in Minsk (temporarily under Polish rule), Vilna, and Grodno.

During this period the political situation in the border regions was constantly shifting, with power changing hands between Russia and Poland.[7] Bramson himself, immediately after arriving in Paris, made contact with leading Jews in Kovno, Riga, and other cities.

The revival of ORT activity in the newly created states at first concentrated mainly on rehabilitating Jewish agriculture in small towns where it was an important part of the Jewish economy. Similar agricultural projects had been envisaged by the ORT center in Petrograd early in 1919 and, interestingly, had been strongly supported by local Zionists who were interested in organizing agricultural *Hachshara* (preparation for agricultural work in Palestine). These projects, also involving gardening, were developed in Bobruisk, Borisov, and Slutsk, as well as in Vilna and Minsk.

During the year 1920 the Vilna ORT committee surveyed some 2,000 Jewish farms in the Vilna, Grodno, and Minsk regions. Credits were arranged for 1,131 agricultural units for acquisition of seed and horses and for the repair of housing facilities. In addition, ORT supported an agricultural school in Velichany and rehabilitation work in many Jewish colonies victimized by the war.[8]

The Vilna Technikum

In 1921, ORT opened a technical school in Vilna, the Technikum, which played an important part in promoting vocational education among Jews in Poland. It will be remembered as one of the significant Jewish institutions in pre-World War II Poland, as will Israel Okun, its director during the first three years of its existence. Later he was replaced by Matvei Schreiber.

The school provided opportunities for specialization of many young Jews who, due to prevailing unfriendly conditions, had had to interrupt their high school studies, or who had graduated from folk schools and found it necessary to continue their education outside of the state schools, where they faced a *numerus clausus* (quota) against Jews.

The Technikum's three-year program was on the level of higher technical schools in Europe in both theoretical courses and practical work. It provided two courses of training, an electrical course and a mechanical course. The Technikum made a significant contribution to Jewish education in preparing technical textbooks in Yiddish. This work required a great deal of innovation in finding, indeed creating, appropriate Yiddish terminology. Fifteen technical Yiddish textbooks were published by the school. In 1923 the Technikum had 104 students; in 1930, 230. By 1935 the number had dropped to 144. The Vilna Technikum was recognized by the Ministry of Education and had the status of a state school. It is interesting that after taking Vilna in 1940 the Soviets gave the Technikum the status of a college.

In the New States

ORT began its work in independent Lithuania in 1920. The vocational school in Kovno was opened in that year, and the one in Vilkomir in 1922. The Kovno school had three departments—machine shop, women's garments, and tailoring. It was under the direction of G. Karnash. Late in 1924 it became a state recognized technical high school.

The local ORT also conducted an apprenticeship program under which, after the initial year or 18 months, apprentices were paid for their work. It encouraged the establishment of artisan cooperatives, helping Jewish workers to obtain needed raw materials.

In 1921, 1,240 Jewish trainees in Lithuania participated in 17 ORT-conducted gardening projects in 11 cities. In many cases gardening was an important source of additional income for Jewish families.

In 1922, in Bessarabia, a substantial number (8,000-9,000) of Jewish families, with the assistance of ORT, derived their living from agricultural pursuits. In this area, Jewish farming was facilitated by agrarian reforms introduced after World War I, when Bessarabia became part of Rumania.[9]

ORT Purchase Bureau

In order to facilitate the acquisition and distribution of locally needed supplies, the Paris delegation established the ORT Purchase Bureau. One of the first practical tasks of the Bureau was the acquisition of tools and materials needed by Jewish artisans in the war-devastated areas of Eastern Europe.

Quantities of tools and equipment brought to France by the American army were available for purchase, and the Purchase Bureau bought 243 crates of instruments for distribution in Poland, Lithuania, Bessarabia and Russia. Unfortunately, Jewish artisans in these countries were accustomed to Russian and German tool measurements and experienced difficulty in learning the American system.

This situation led to tightening of overall procedures so that when an ORT Purchase Bureau was established in Berlin (1921), it had charge of both purchasing and distributing tools, thus avoiding annoying misunderstanding. Industrial products were at that time available in Berlin at lower prices, and transportation from Berlin was more expeditious.[10]

Much of the work in Eastern Europe was at the trial-and-error stage and required constant review and change, as well as close inspection of vocational education and the system of extending credits to artisans.

A set of minutes of the Central Board (*Pravlenie*) in Berlin gives an interesting picture of ORT activities of that period. The variety of plans and projects, the range of initiatives, and the voluminous details involved are truly astonishing.

On July 13, 1921, the Berlin Center granted 60,000 Deutschmark to an agricultural cooperative in Keidany to enable it to buy 12 cows (20 had been planned initially). Pending discussion of the locally-prepared budget, it approved the opening of a shoe repair shop in Kovno. In August, 1921, it arranged the shipment of parts for the electrical laboratory at the Vilna Technikum. It also invited Maier Mendelson, a chemical engineer from Warsaw, then in Berlin, to organize a chemical department at the Vilna Technikum. It prepared textbooks needed in various schools and issued publications describing the role of ORT in the productivization of the Jewish masses.

All these activities were handled by a very small staff. However, inspectors and instructors were being sent to Lithuania, Poland, and Rumania (Bessarabia). This required some *savoir faire*, more than a little energy, and, perhaps, "connections" in order to obtain visas needed for entry into the independent states, as well as funds to meet the cost of these missions.

The minutes indicate that funds were slow in coming in, and that in some cases it was necessary to observe caution in accepting certain subventions since, despite the good will that prevailed, ORT work and that of JDC and ICA were, at the time, not clearly delineated.[11]

All told, during the period 1920-1923, ORT expenditures for all activities (vocational education, assistance to artisans, and agricultural projects) amounted to $396,965.

Reconstruction Begins

The year 1922 saw the end of civil war in Russia and the beginning of a solidified regime. About the same time, the newly established post-Versailles independent countries had stabilized their borders and begun to function in a steady and predictable way. The new situation, of course, had repercussions on the social and economic status of the Jewish communities. The time of emergency, of "first aid," was past and it was necessary to turn to problems of long-range reconstruction.

The challenge was a great one for ORT, which, unlike many other Jewish organizations providing assistance to war victims, had for decades emphasized long-term goals and spearheaded the introduction of Jewish labor into industry and agriculture, insisting on the necessity of changing the occupational structure of the Jewish community.

Against this background, the ORT Union prepared an overall plan and several area plans for future activity. The new tasks required increased financial resources and an improved and strengthened organizational base. The available ORT leadership, comprised mainly of Eastern European Jews, had little experience of work in countries outside the old Russian Empire or with Jewish communities in the West. Adjustment took some time, but through hard work and changes in its ruling councils, the ORT Union succeeded in insuring not only the maintenance of its work, but its expansion.

It would not be amiss to state here that the existence of contemporary ORT organizations the world over was due primarily to the organizing talents of Leon Bramson, who, assisted by Lvovich and, later, Syngalowski, established in Berlin, in the early 1920's, a firm foundation for future ORT activity. Other individuals were later to participate in the building and expansion of ORT, but in the early 1920's, during the critical formative years, Bramson's role, which entailed not only important policy decisions but the devotion of much time to office routine and the establishment of successful administrative procedures, was outstanding. [12]

Chapter **VII**

Consolidation and Expansion

The 1921 ORT conference, or, as it is now known in official ORT documents, the Founding Congress of the World ORT Union, signified the end of the ORT Delegation as an important instrumentality of ORT activities abroad. The Delegation was no longer needed, at least not for work outside of Russia. A new structure was now created, outside Russia, which had as its organizational base and expression the ORT Union.

Delegates to the First ORT Congress came mainly from the former Russian provinces. Bramson and his colleagues were aware that in order to maintain activities beyond the critical period of the war's aftermath it would be necessary to "naturalize" ORT concepts abroad, particularly among Jews of the West who represented the only important source of much-needed funds. No time was lost. Within two years following the First Congress, the ORT Union had launched a significant program combining propaganda and organization.

An "ORT Week" was organized in Poland in June, 1923, dedicated to ORT work in Jewish economic reconstruction. A special publication, *ORT Woch*, to which Jewish writers and artists contributed, was issued. Propaganda meetings were held in Warsaw, Lodz, Piotrokow, and other places. A similar "ORT Week" campaign was conducted in Rumania in 1924 and in Berlin in 1925. Efforts to spread the ORT idea were undertaken in other communities, but it was in Poland and Rumania, and perhaps also in Lithuania, that these efforts took on substantial proportions.

The Danzig Congress

In June, 1923, the ORT Union convened its Second Congress, this time in Danzig, a free city existing under a special regime. The Second Congress was a far cry from the first small conclave held in Berlin in 1921. Twenty-six local ORT organizations were represented with, this time, delegates of functioning ORT organizations in Paris, Danzig, and Berlin participating.

ORT had already established, in Paris, a Labor Bureau for immigrants looking for work. In Danzig, it organized training shops for Jewish emigrant youths passing through that port city. In Berlin, in 1921, together with the Jewish community and the *Arbeiter Fursorgeamt* (Labor Exchange), it opened two tailoring shops.

Later, in 1925, with the help of Dr. Wilhelm Graetz and Rabbi Leo Baeck, it succeeded in attracting the support of broad sections of the German Jewish community under the sponsorship of the local ORT society. This was an important first step, since the ORT Union offices were located in Berlin and needed a local base with access to the authorities.

While the Soviet ORT was not a part of the ORT Union, Soviet delegates and a report on work in Soviet Russia were expected at the Danzig Congress, and an appropriate item was included in the agenda. No representative from Moscow attended, however, for "reasons independent of his will."[1]

The Danzig Congress gave much thought to organizational problems, including the difficult financial situation. Worsening economic conditions in the West naturally affected ORT. This notwithstanding, the leadership not only continued its ongoing work but decided to enlarge its programs in terms of both geographical distribution and content.

A session of the Congress was devoted to discussion of a report on vocational training and technical education presented by L. Frenkiel and Dr. E. Kohn. ORT leaders had always been aware of the philosophical and methodological aspects of ORT's education system. These matters had previously been discussed in Russia; but it was only in the West, where ORT was expanding its programs to cover many countries and different cultures, that its pedagogical rationale was subjected to thorough examination. This question will be discussed in more detail later.

The Danzig Congress made a number of major decisions. It enlarged the governing body, electing Bramson, Lvovich, Syngalowski, Frankfurt, Zylberfarb, Tsegelnitski, and Tiomkin, all Russians, to the Central Board, the executive body of the ORT Union, which represented the inner circle directing the day-to-day work. Later, Dr. L. Haas and Dr. A. Hantke, of Germany, became members of the Board through cooptation, bringing for the first time a Western element into the ORT governing body.

The new Central Council, originally composed of 21 members and later expanded to 41 (20 through cooptation), also reflected the general Westernization of the organization. The Council included many outstanding Jewish personalities, among them the historian Simon Dubnow, the future French Socialist Premier Leon Blum, Dr. J. Brodnitz of Berlin, D. Mowshovitch of London, Dr. Henry Moskowitz of New York, and Senator M. Kerner of Warsaw. Dr. Chaim Zhitlowsky of New York was elected chairman of the Central Council, replacing Szabad of Vilna. In 1925, Zhitlowsky was replaced by Dubnow.

The ORT leadership recognized that it could not always rely on unpredictable fund-raising campaigns. A permanent financial instrumentality that would serve as a regular channel of funds of support and loans to Jewish farmers and artisans in need of machinery and equipment would have to be created.

A start in the direction of establishing a permanent financial structure was made at the Danzig Congress, with a decision to establish a Jewish Reconstruction Fund and a Cooperative Tool Supply Corporation. An elaborate plan of a Reconstruction Fund was presented to the Congress by Bramson and Lvovich, who brightened the detailed proposals with his infectious optimism and self-assurance. After much preparatory work, involving complicated legal details, the Jewish Reconstruction Fund was registered in London in 1924 as an independent stockholders' corporation with a capitalization of $1,000,000. The value of a share of stock was fixed at $10, or 2£, at the prevailing exchange rate, with stock to be issued in blocks of 10,000 shares.

It was anticipated that the major Jewish relief organizations would subscribe for substantial blocks of stock with the majority holdings to be retained by ORT. Among the Fund's founders in London were Elkan Adler, S. Beloff, M. Shalit, J. Visotsky, and D. Mowshovitch.

ORT Reconstruction Funds were established simultaneously in the United States, France, and Germany for the purpose of raising capital. Among sponsors of the Fund in the United States were H. Moskowitz, Louis Boudin, Morris H. Waldman, B. Charney Vladek, Dr. Zhitlowsky, Howard S. Cullman, and Paul Warburg; in France, Leonard Rosental, Louis Ascher, and Dr. Zadock-Kahn.

Among the signers of a special ORT appeal in France were Prof. Silvain Levi, Leon Blum, Paul Painleve, and Edmond Fleg; in Germany, Rabbi Leo Baeck, Paul Nathan, Prof. Warburg, and Wilhelm Graetz supported the drive for the Fund.[2] N. Soloweitschik was elected chairman. Campaigns were conducted in the United States, Germany, France, England, and other countries. By 1929 the resources of the Fund amounted to $602,000.

The personalities involved in the undertaking were men of great influence. They included bankers of international reputation, among others. That they lent their names, prestige, and, in many cases, their time and money to the support of this innovative ORT project is testimony not only to their generous instincts but to the will and energy of the ORT leadership whose powers of persuasion were indeed extraordinary.

Supplying Tools

The second initiative emanating from the Danzig Congress, the Cooperative Tool Supply Corporation, was organized in London in 1924. Its objective was to facilitate acquisition, on credit, of machinery, equipment, and raw materials needed by Jewish artisans and farmers. In fact, it was intended to continue, but on a larger scale, and perhaps by more sophisticated methods, the work of the Purchase Bureau that had functioned between 1920 and 1923. In establishing the Tool Supply Corporation, some ORT old-timers no doubt drew on their experience in ORT work in Russia, particularly during the war, when the St. Petersburg ORT had supplied machinery to needy artisans.

Lvovich was particularly active in the organization of the new corporation, the founders of which included, in addition to the ORT Union, the Central Union of Jewish Cooperatives in Eastern Europe, and a number of individual ORT supporters from ORT groups as well as financial circles in London.

Capitalization was set at £10,000, with 51 per cent of the stock to be held by ORT. Later, a corporation of the same name was created in Berlin which took over the day-to-day tasks, with London remaining financial and administrative center.

In time, the Tool Supply Corporation developed a "commercial" approach to its operations. Instead of distributing machinery to artisans in need, as had the Purchase Bureau, it sold machinery and raw materials to beneficiaries, on credit, at below-market prices. Artisans and farmers receiving machinery through the Corporation executed notes which were held by various local Jewish cooperative banks for collection.

The Corporation was able to procure the necessary articles on nine to twelve months' credit; artisan and farmer beneficiaries were given up to eighteen months for repayment at an annual rate of 12 per cent, or about half the 2 to 2.5 per cent monthly interest rate prevailing at Jewish cooperative banks.

In 1926 the Corporation's capital fund stood at $75,000, in 1927 at $150,000, and in 1928 at $356,000. In 1929, Agro-Joint became a partner.[3] By the end of 1929 the Corporation had agencies in all the countries of Eastern Europe. It maintained close contact with some two hundred German business firms able to supply needed items.

The Tool Supply Corporation, which in a way supplemented the Reconstruction Fund, provided a means of productive existence for thousands of Jewish artisans and farmers. In the 1930's, mobilizing private resources, it enlarged its activities and was serving as a channel through which American Jews, individuals and *Landsmanschaft* circles, sent machinery and tools to their families and to Jewish producer-cooperatives in the old countries of Eastern Europe.[4] (See discussion of ORT in the United States and Soviet Russia.)

Foundations of the Post-World War I ORT

The 1923 Danzig Congress was a watershed in ORT development. After some three years abroad, in close contact with Western Jewry, including the Jewish community of the United States, the ORT leadership had brought about a deliberate change in the general orientation of the organization.

Still working mostly in the East, ORT was now firmly established in the West and not merely in terms of geographical location. True to ORT tradition, the leadership took into consideration both immediate Jewish relief needs and long-term Jewish social and economic trends as these became apparent following years of war and revolution. There was, of course, much debate in ORT circles about the significance of unfolding events, some of which had underlying political overtones.

For the Jews, as well as other minority groups, the new European reality did not correspond to the Wilsonian dream of justice and national equality. Lvovich on numerous occasions pointed out that the ORT directing group represented better than any other comparable Jewish assembly the entire spectrum of Russian political life—it included Bundists, Zionists, Trudoviks, Zionist-Socialists, and even Mensheviks. This multiplicity of political ideologies notwithstanding, all of the active leaders agreed that ORT was faced with a Jewish life fundamentally different from what it had been a decade before. The world had changed, and not for the better.

Amid the ruins of the old order and the new emerging structures the choices were difficult. Imaginative programs were projected to ensure long-term help. In retrospect, we know that ORT plans and forecasts were not always borne out by later developments.

Among the planned ORT programs were agricultural and vocational training projects in Soviet Russia where, it seemed, opportunities were opening up not only through the "back-to-the-land" movement among the Jewish masses, but by the readiness of the Soviet government to participate in efforts at productivization of large numbers of Soviet Jews. Alas, the grim reality of things to come belied these hopes, but in the early and mid-1920s it was difficult to foresee the events that were to come.

What happened in the Soviet Union was an extreme instance. It was also not easy to establish long-range working schedules in the newly formed states of Poland, Lithuania, and Latvia, and in Bessarabia, now part of Rumania, where conditions were in a state of flux.

The Tsarist Pale of Settlement had disappeared, but harsh restrictive policies continued to hamper Jewish integration into the new societies.[5] A wave of pogroms swept over many Jewish communities in Poland and did not sub-side until about 1922. One of the dominant Polish political parties, the En-Deks (National Democrats), led by Roman Dmowski, proclaimed a fight against the Jews as its prime political goal.

Whatever may have been his personal feelings, Marshal Joseph Pilsudski, the head of the Polish state, who had begun his career as a socialist and had come to power as the result of a coup in 1926, did little to stop anti-Jewish excesses. He did stop open encouragement of anti-Jewish actions, but local administrations, consisting of large numbers of Dmowski's followers, continued the anti-Jewish policies of old.

Rumania, which also had a significant Jewish population, had a history of strong anti-Jewish bias. Under Prime Minister Ionel Bratianu, many legal measures were enacted limiting Jewish citizenship rights and occupational opportunities which went counter to the international obligations assumed during the peace talks. Later there were pogroms in all parts of the kingdom, including newly acquired Bessarabia.

In Lithuania, where anti-Jewish bias existed but did not manifest itself in such extreme forms as in Poland, the Jewish community from the beginning enjoyed full national autonomy, with a Minister for Jewish Affairs and a representative Jewish National Council. With the coming of the Fascists and the assumption of power by Waldemaras in 1926, practically all forms of Jewish autonomy were abolished.

To a degree, autonomous Jewish life in Latvia and Estonia was maintained for a longer time than in some of the other states. Jewish creative efforts were hindered less in terms of legal status and economic opportunities, but by the 1930s the squeezing of the Jews out of the economy took on, under the Fascist regime, an acute and systematic character.

During the 1920s substantial numbers of Jewish emigrants, including many looking for educational and professional opportunities closed to them in some of the new states, left Eastern Europe for countries of Western Europe, Palestine, and the United States. But the hard challenges of the anti-Jewish environment provoked tough responses. Jewish communities took measures to ensure continuous Jewish existence in the lands of their fathers and forefathers.

The struggle of the Jewish population to establish a *modus vivendi* alongside their Christian neighbors required patience and continuous effort, in which the Jews drew on their long experience of living in unfriendly surroundings. In time, as the result of agrarian reform, a native peasant class in many of these states opened limited market opportunities to Jewish artisans, who were always ready to bring their skills, and in some cases ready-made goods, to the villages.

Broader Vision in Action

In the mid-1920's, ORT, adjusting to the new economic patterns emerging in Eastern Europe, saw new opportunities.[6] By supplying needed machinery, it was able to considerably improve the competitive capability of Jewish artisans. With old channels of assistance not always available, ORT organizations often had to change work plans to suit local conditions.

ORT was frequently called upon to respond to emergency situations by means not always in consonance with its immediate goals. In the mid-1920's, for example, the Polish authorities, without prior notice, required that Jewish artisans affiliate themselves with the Polish Craft Guild. To do so, Jewish artisans would have to take a special qualification examination, conducted in Polish, a language in which most of them were not proficient.

This was a blatant anti-Jewish measure camouflaged as a means to upgrade the standards of the crafts. The Jewish artisans asked for help. ORT, with its decades of technical experience, responded to the emergency by quickly setting up courses in Polish and refresher courses in various crafts in many cities.[7]

The ORT education system continued to expand and included both vocational training in schools and shops and the

די טישלער־אפטיילונג

A workshop in cabinet-making in the Jewish vocational school in Dvinsk established prior to World War I.

Another shop in the Dvinsk vocational school, with belt-driven machines.

Outside view, indicating large size of the Dvinsk school.

Jewish peasants in Pruzshan, in the region of Grodno, Poland, after World War I.

Blacksmith shop supported by ORT in Eastern Europe in post-World War I, specializing in metal work.

ORT school in handweaving, Lodz, 1920.

ORT tailoring workshop in Kovno, 1922.

בשת למודים אין אַ קלפון דיר האַנטװ.סיוף ,אָרט, בריסק.

Classroom in the ORT school in Brest-Litovsk, 1925.

Mechaniczny Kurs
Poiiozoch „Cotton"
Tow. „Ort" w Łodzi
1928

ORT cotton stocking mechanical training course in Lodz,
Poland, 1928.

Agricultural cooperative "Spring," Ukraine, 1927.

Class in furniture design in the ORT school in Kishinev, 1929.

so-called patronates or apprenticeships for children. It provided training at various levels, preparing students for jobs as well as giving them special technical education such as that provided at the Vilna Technikum and similar schools. However, unlike many programs of vocational training conducted by other organizations which focused essentially on economic aspects, ORT programs endeavored to take into account the future societal status of trainees, thus emphasizing the educational importance of training in vocational schools as against apprenticeship training in shops.

In some cases this concept may have resulted in limiting the number of beneficiaries, but it was basic to ORT work from the very beginning in Russia, and was consonant with the social vision and democratic orientation of the ORT leadership. Table 4 will illustrate the application of this concept.

Table 5 gives the social background of ORT trainees. It underscores the fact that the largest number came from families engaged in small business, that is, from the social groups that were feeling the most severe effects of change in their countries. It is significant that children of parents with professional background frequently turned to vocational training, a decision born in necessity.

ORT-supported vocational schools, training courses, shops, and patronates functioned in the Polish cities of Kobrin, Kowel, Sarny, Piotrokow, Brest-Litovsk, Warsaw, Grodno, Bialostok, and Vilna; in the Rumanian cities of Bendery, Kalarash, Orgeiev, Resika, Beltsy, Iassy, and Kishinev; in the Luthuanian cities of Kovno, Vilkomir, and Ponevezh; in the Latvian cities of Dvinsk, Riga, Lubny; in the free city of Danzig; and in Berlin and Paris.

Participation of ICA and JDC

A close collaboration developed between JDC, ICA, and ORT in all practical areas of vocational training despite the fact that ICA and JDC were extending direct support to a

TABLE 4

Students at ORT Vocational Schools
(outside Soviet Russia)
1922–1925

Country	Number of Students			
	1922	1923	1924	1925
Poland				
Vocational schools	1,341	1,261	1,034	1,061
Courses for adults	211	426	651	1,348
Patronates	150	263	718	263
Technikum	133	104	130	137
Total	1,835	2,054	2,533	2,809
Rumania				
Vocational schools	67	284	277	420
Courses for adults	45	629	682	707
Total	112	913	959	1,127
Latvia				
Vocational schools	143	152	163	148
Courses for adults	15	—	—	—
Total	158	152	163	148
Lithuania				
Vocational schools	203	172	91	111
Courses for adults	52	68	55	—
Patronates	60	74	67	26
Total	315	314	213	137
Danzig				
Courses for adults	—	—	32	—
Paris				
Courses for adults	—	—	—	148
Berlin				
Training shop	—	15	15	17
GRAND TOTAL	2,420	3,448	3,915	4,386

number of vocational schools and that, from time to time, there were serious differences of opinion as to educational approach and methodology.

As early as 1922, a JDC commission, under the chairmanship of Dr. Bernhard Kahn, had argued that apprenticeship training with master artisans would yield better results than training in vocational schools, the system favored by ORT.

TABLE 5*

Social Background of ORT Vocational Trainees 1922–1925[9]

Parental Occupation	Per cent
Small business	44.3
Artisan	16.6
Worker	15.4
Professional	5.9
Other or not recorded	17.8
	100.0

*Based on a sample survey conducted in Warsaw; figures are believed to be representative of the general situation.

During this period, ORT programs received substantial support from JDC, although reduced JDC subsidies in 1924 forced ORT to curtail for a time its own grants to local schools and training centers. These grants represented an important part of local budgets.[10]

TABLE 6

ORT Grants for Vocational Training (outside Soviet Russia) 1923–1925

Country	1923	Amount 1924	1925
Poland	$53,200	$42,500	$60,630
Lithuania	25,300	18,500	10,500
Latvia	9,900	5,650	3,890
Rumania	4,100	5,050	11,430
Berlin	140	400	1,180
Paris	—	—	2,670
Danzig	420	1,000	—
Total	$93,060	$73,100	$90,300

The reduction in JDC subventions came at a time when the vocational programs were undergoing continuous development. New initiatives were taken everywhere, and in some cases old vocational schools and other vocational projects joined the ORT system.

In Poland, there were a women's tailoring shop in Vladimir-Volynsk, a school in Warsaw, courses for dressmakers in Rovno and Bialostok, courses for tailors in Lodz, a mechanical hosiery-knitting shop in Lodz, and courses for locksmiths in Vilna; in Rumania, the old vocational school, *Trud* (Labor), in Kishinev; in Lithuania, courses for tailors and auto drivers in Kovno; in Latvia, courses for seamstresses in Riga; and in Germany, courses for auto drivers in Berlin.

As a result, the number of students and trainees in ORT institutions increased from 2,420 in 1922 to 4,326 in 1925 and to 7,242 in 1928 (1,503 in the USSR and 5,739 outside the USSR).

TABLE 7

ORT Vocational Trainees, by Countries
1928

Country	Number of Trainees
Poland	3,735
Rumania	1,449
Latvia	376
Lithuania	137
Germany	42
USSR	1,503
Total	7,242

According to type of training, ORT trainees were distributed as follows:

TABLE 8

Vocational Trainees in ORT Institutions, 1928

Type of Training	Number of Institutions	Number of Trainees
Vocational school	33	3,128
Courses and training shops for adults	31	2,499
Patronates (children)	9	1,314
Vilna Technikum	1	301
Total	74	7,242

Growth Problems

The increase in the number of ORT-supported institutions created educational and financial problems. Some school buildings were in urgent need of repair, others needed additional space for laboratories, clean rooms, and more equipment. In some cities, ORT succeeded in realizing economies by consolidating various activities in the same location.

In the long run, however, resources were insufficient to cover the enlarged programs. In addition, the expanded education system necessitated continuous retraining of instructors who had been teaching their crafts for many years. To meet this need, ORT arranged for instructors to be sent periodically to Berlin, Vienna, or Bucharest for refresher courses. Retraining courses in woodworking and locksmithing for ORT instructors, financed by ORT, ICA, and JDC, were organized in Warsaw.

In 1927 the ORT Union and ICA convened a conference in Warsaw of directors of vocational schools. Specialists in vocational education from outside Poland who participated in the meetings could utilize the information acquired at the conference in their own countries.

In 1928 the ORT Union organized an exhibit related to its work which was seen in Warsaw (October 30—November 3), Cologne (December 2-6), Berlin (December 18-27), Frankfurt (January, 1929), and in New York in 1929.

For Jewish Farming

As has been noted, ORT's early efforts in agriculture were directed toward assisting the small Jewish farm undertakings that had survived years of war and unrest after having achieved a degree of success. This was particularly the case in Poland under the German occupation, where a number of Jewish families took to farming lands left unused by Poles evacuated during the Russian retreat. This move to the land had been encouraged by the German authorities.

After the war, when refugee landlords and peasants returned home and claimed their lands, Jewish agriculture in Poland was reduced. The agrarian reform introduced by the government for the most part ignored Jewish needs, even in cases where returning landlords were willing to give over to Jewish families the lands they had worked on during the German occupation.

On pragmatic grounds, and for local economic reasons, the ORT leadership felt strongly that Jewish agriculture should be supported and, where possible, expanded. To some extent ORT was able to pursue its endeavors through a special subsidy provided by ICA for loans to farmers, although in many cases strict legal conditions stipulated by ICA made ORT loans to beneficiaries difficult.[11]

Nevertheless, a limited amount of constructive work was done, particularly in the districts of Vilna and Grodno, where assistance to Jewish agriculture had been initiated immediately after the end of the war. Later, ORT encouraged the development of Jewish agriculture in the districts of Warsaw, Pinsk, and Brest-Litovsk, and helped to establish agricultural cooperatives in the Volin region which played a helpful role in 1925, when the region suffered a poor harvest.

From 1923 to 1925, ORT made 1,053 loans for repair of buildings, acquisition of livestock, and purchase of equipment and seed. Among ORT beneficiaries were many *Hechalutz* groups preparing their members for emigration to Palestine.

There were fewer agricultural undertakings in Lithuania and Latvia, although in the Suvalki region in Lithuania there was a considerable number of Jewish families engaged in gardening and farming. ORT work in Lithuania was essentially limited to providing seed on credit. Similar work was done in Latvia, particularly around the Dvinsk region.

In Bessarabia the situation was totally different. Here, there was an old Jewish agricultural settlement where some thousand Jewish vintners were still at work in nine colonies organized during the reign of Nikolai I. Before World War I some three thousand Jewish families were engaged in growing tobacco there, and the area was still attracting Jewish farmers. Jewish colonists had acquired about an additional thirty thousand acres of land, and it was there that ORT tried to give them various kinds of assistance. A supply center was established in Kishinev where Jewish farmers and vintners could acquire, on credit, much of the machinery they needed.

In many districts ORT provided machinery and small tools "on hire." It also extended credit to local *Hechalutz* groups. Some of these activities had to be curtailed in 1925 due to lack of funds; work was limited mainly to advisory services and, in some places, hiring out of needed machinery.[12] ORT agronomists and instructors regularly visited Jewish farms, giving advice and teaching new methods of agriculture, animal care, and related subjects.

In 1925 ORT participated in the agricultural exposition held in Kishinev, where it was awarded a gold medal for its achievements in the field of Jewish agriculture.

ORT agricultural work was conducted in, among other places, Alexandreny, Rishkanovka, Manzir, Faleshty, Gertop, and Rishkava.

Organizational Growth

During the 1920's there was an important development among local ORT affiliates as they intensified their efforts to promote increased local support for ORT initiatives. These efforts at self-help were important, and not only symbolically. Complete data are not available, but there is no question that there was a significant growth in membership.

Figures for the mid- and late 1920's for Poland indicate that membership there rose from 2,490 in 1926 to 3,539 in 1928, and in Rumania from 1,667 in 1926 to 2,348 in 1928. Local membership in Eastern Europe rose from 5,518 in 1926 to 7,381 in 1928. The situation was less satisfactory in the United States and the countries of Western Europe, where it was more difficult to establish clear organizational identification for supporters of ORT.[13]

Fund-raising campaigns, combined with frequent communal presentation of ORT ideas and the organization of ORT groups, was one of the major tasks of ORT, involving considerable effort, including the issuance of various publications in Yiddish, Russian, French, and other languages.

In the 1920's the principal source of ORT income was and came from JDC and ORT fund-raising drives in the United States. ICA and Jewish relief organizations in Europe were also generous supporters of ORT. As the ORT Union succeeded in integrating its activities in the countries of Western Europe, financial support came from Germany, England, France, Italy, and Austria. Gradually, also, local sources in Eastern Europe became contributors to ORT income.[14] In certain areas and under prearranged conditions, ORT conducted united campaigns with OSE and Emigdirect.[15]

In its fund-raising campaigns ORT succeeded in attracting a number of outstanding Jewish writers, journalists, and political activists who, despite ideological differences, volunteered to bring the ORT idea to the Jewish masses of the various countries of Europe, Africa, and Latin America, including small Jewish communities not heretofore active. Interestingly, ORT was in contact with Jewish communities in the Far East, where it used the services of the well-known Jewish leader in Harbin, Joseph Blum. At various times ORT representatives around the world included the well-known writer S. Poliakov, the Menshevik S. Shchupak, the Revisionist leader Joseph Schechtman, N. Kaminski, M. Feinleib, N. Halperin, Dr. Gran, and Dr. Gergel, and they all participated in fund-raising.

For 1923-1925 ORT income stood at $761,000, half of which came from independent campaigns. For 1926-1928 income from all sources amounted to over $815,000, including approximately $540,000 from the United States, about $130,000 from Western Europe, and some $145,000 from Poland, Rumania, Latvia, and Lithuania. Disbursements amounted to $763,000 in 1923-1925; $933,000 was budgeted for 1926-1927 through 1928-1929 (July 1 to June 30).[16]

In 1929 the ORT Union included 62 affiliated organizations, functional and supportive, in 14 countries, including

China, where at that time there resided a substantial number of Jewish refugees from Russia.

The Third Congress

In summer 1926 there took place, in Berlin, the Third ORT Union Congress, with 64 delegates representing Poland, Rumania, Lithuania, Latvia, England, France, Germany, and the United States. ORT in the Soviet Union was represented by members of the ORT Union Central Board.

This was an important but routinized assembly dealing with current organizational and financial matters. A new Central Board was elected which in turn appointed an Executive Committee, with Bramson as chairman. In accordance with the By-laws of the ORT Union registered in Berlin on April 25, 1927, which provided that a Congress should be convened every three years, the Fourth Congress was to be held in 1929. But in July, 1928, the Central Board, using its prerogative, decided to postpone the event until 1930 to coincide with the planned celebration of ORT's fiftieth anniversary.

A large number of working papers (some of great interest) were prepared for the forthcoming celebration. Unfortunately, the economic crisis in the United States and the strained finances of the ORT Union made it necessary to postpone the planned celebration. In fact, it was never held; the Fourth Congress was not to be convened until some eight years later. The ORT leaders could not know, nor did the world around them, that Nazism was at the door of the Weimar Republic.

VIII

ORT in the Soviet Union

Technically, ORT continued its activities on Soviet Russian soil through 1918-1922, but it was only after this period, when the USSR was created, that we can speak about ORT work in the Soviet Union.

After the liquidation of the *kehila* in 1919, the Jewish community in Russia was in disarray. Some Jewish functional organizations were permitted to continue their activities, albeit under strict government control: ORT, OSE, EKOPO, and ICA became part of the peculiar system of Jewish social services acceptable to the new regime. Most of the old Jewish communal leaders, including the old-timers of ORT, had either gone abroad or were in opposition to the new regime. Most of their places were taken by individuals acceptable to the Bolsheviks.

Having fought against Jewish autonomy in all its forms, the Soviet government under Lenin—with Stalin as Commissar of Nationalities—had to do something to provide for Jewish needs since there was no longer a *kehila* to perform these functions. Against its own doctrines and contrary to its propaganda, the government created within the Stalin Commissariat a Commissariat for Jewish Affairs. This was a

131

departure from the original Bolshevik conception of the status and future of the "skeleton" Jewish nation on the way to "extinction."[1]

In Petrograd, now part of the RSFSR (Russian Soviet Federated Socialist Republics), efforts to aid Jewish victims of the pogroms of the civil war period were centered around EVKOM (*Evreiiskii Komisariat*—Commissariat for Jewish Affairs), and later around *Evreiiskaia Sektsiia* (Jewish Section of the Communist Party).[2] EVKOM was to provide for the rehabilitation of the substantial number of Jews who did not fit socially and economically into the new Soviet society.

In addition, there were large numbers of Jews concentrated at the Rumanian and western borders who were hoping to emigrate to Bessarabia (now Rumania) or to the new independent states created in the formerly Russian western areas and who were in urgent need of help. The Council of People's Commissars allocated 500,000 rubles for this work in 1919. The advance of Denikin's White Army from the south into Bolshevik centers put an end to this prospect.

The Soviet Jewish Service Apparatus

In 1920, with the approval of the government, a Jewish Social Committee (*Yidgezkom*) was created to coordinate work on behalf of the Jewish population. This was a sort of umbrella organization uniting the authorities (*Evsektsiia*), the functional Jewish organizations (ORT, OSE, and others), and various Jewish political groups.

As to the latter, like the Russian political parties, they did not have sufficient freedom to operate within the framework of their ideologies and programs; the non-governmental political parties represented in *Yidgezkom* consisted mostly of individuals from leftist splinter groups that had in one form or another already accepted the October coup d'etat or were on their way to capitulation. Only a small minority of these parties, which hoped to do good work for the Jewish people and at the same time conserve their political image, participated in *Yidgezkom*. *Yidgezkom* was controlled by the Soviets, a logical arrangement since from October, 1917, on, Soviet Russia was under a rigid ideological regime organically hostile to all competing political groups.

While the Communists did not cherish the idea of a united front with Jewish political groups and organizations—"united fronts" were to come later—the decision to permit the maintenance of activities such as those of ORT, OSE, ICA, and, later, JDC, was dictated by several important considerations. The critical situation of Jews called for emergency measures, and the old Jewish organizations had had decades of experience in responding to Jewish needs.

Liaison with outside Jewish groups was useful at a time when Russia was isolated from the West. In dire need of foreign currency, Russia welcomed the opportunity of attracting funds from abroad. In 1921, the non-Communist groups, ready to compromise but objecting to dictation by *Evsektsiia* and other Soviet agencies, resigned from *Yidgezkom*.

By 1922, according to reports of *Yidgezkom*, it was supporting, among others, some 100 vocational schools for children and youth. This and other work was accomplished partly through the help of JDC, which subsidized various relief and reconstruction projects in the USSR. *Yidgezkom* was dissolved in 1924, the Bolsheviks apparently feeling that there was no longer a need to maintain a fictitious non-party agency.

After the Revolution

After the revolution the Jewish Pale of Settlement began to crumble, and the economic foundations of Jewish life were destroyed. Traditional Jewish occupations were becoming obsolete in an economy geared to centralized planning. In 1919-1920, Soviet ORT conducted a survey of Jewish artisans and peasants in the west and south of Russia. Incomplete as it was, the survey revealed the extreme gravity of the situation created by revolution, civil war, and pogroms: More than half of the previously existing artisans' shops had been destroyed and the number of apprentices employed in them had been reduced by 60 to 70 per cent. Many of the shops had been closed because their equipment had been destroyed and replacements were difficult to obtain.

According to an analysis of the census figures for 1897, about 40 per cent of the Jewish population were employed in industry as owners, workers, or artisans; some 35 per cent were in commerce (merchandising, small shopkeeping, and transportation); and about 25 per cent were without definite occupation. Under Soviet conditions the majority of the Jewish population became *lishentsy*, that is, persons who, because of their non-proletarian origin, had no civil rights, were unable to obtain employment, and could not claim housing facilities.

The situation of the children of *lishentsy* was tragic. They could not gain admission to schools or universities. In order to obtain employment they had to conceal their origin.

Jews in small towns faced starvation. Their plight was worse than it had ever been under the Tsars. Under the impact of these dire conditions there arose a back-to-the-land movement.[3]

Back-to-the-Land Among Jews

Agrarianization and productivization of the Jews, goals long promoted by ORT, became practical choices for many Jewish families. Thousands of applications for settlement on the land poured into ORT offices in various cities, and Jewish families in large numbers joined the agricultural cooperatives.

In some Ukrainian districts, and to some extent in Belorussia, farming became an important means of livelihood. ORT continued to furnish technical advice and economic aid to the old Jewish colonists in the southern Ukraine, who had suffered greatly during the pogroms and civil disorders. It also promoted new Jewish agricultural settlements in suitable areas.

This work was carried out under difficult conditions. Russia was breaking up. The Ukraine was fighting for independence, and parts of the western areas were under assorted regimes and social systems. Nevertheless, between 1918 and 1921 new ORT settlements were organized in Berdichev, Kamenets-Podolsk, Vinnitsa, Cherkassy, and Novgorod-Volynsk.

Agricultural training courses and an agricultural cooperative in the port city of Odessa were enlarged, and a club was created to promote farming pursuits among Jewish youth and adults. To popularize its programs and attract Jewish schoolchildren, ORT created small vegetable gardens at some 50 Jewish primary schools.[4] A technical volume on Jewish farming was issued by the local ORT in Kiev.

As the back-to-the-land movement in Russia grew, Jewish families interested in farming converted from small-scale agricultural working groups (artels) on the outskirts of the cities to larger settlements wherever land was available. Brutskus, in Berlin, estimated that during this period (1918-1925) additional 45,000 desiatin (approximately 120,000 acres) of land were allotted to Jews in the neighborhood of their former homes.

All told, in 1921-1922 some 50,000 Jews were engaged in farming. This number rose to 75,000 in 1923, 100,000 in 1925, and about 120,000 in 1926.

The New Economic Policy (NEP) instituted by Lenin somewhat improved the Jewish situation, permitting a degree of small-scale entrepreneurial initiative, but this easing of conditions was of limited significance and duration.[5] Jewish needs continued to grow, and the movement to the land, particularly in the Ukraine, was expanding.

In 1924 the Soviet government created KOMZET, a special committee for agricultural settlement of Jewish toilers. Later, a voluntary society for agricultural settlement of Jewish toilers, OZET, was organized to propagandize settlement on the land, social services for settlers, and solicitation of funds abroad. The creation of KOMZET and OZET and the farreaching initial plan to colonize 100,000 Jewish families, created a stir within *Evsektsiia*.

KOMZET, under the chairmanship of Peter Smidovich, was assigned to administer substantial areas of land in the Ukraine, Belorussia, the Crimea, and Russia proper. A special committee to promote Jewish agricultural settlement was also created in Minsk, capital city of Belorussia. Later (1928), there was the Birobidzhan project, which was thoroughly debated by Jewish Communists, some of whom expressed fears that such a move was a step in the direction of Jewish nationalism and a Jewish middle-class hostile to the proletarian USSR.[6]

For the moment, Soviet support of the back-to-the-land slogan, and particularly the statements made by Kalinin, then Chairman of the Presidium of the Supreme Soviet and formal head of state, were greeted with enthusiasm in Russia and in Jewish circles abroad, especially in the United States. Several Jewish international organizations expressed willingness to participate in relief work in Russia.

Negotiations with the Soviets

Work in Russia was a natural and organic part of the ORT Union program. While Soviet ORT was not affiliated with the ORT Union in Berlin, the latter was prepared to undertake systematic efforts to support ORT work in Soviet Russia.

In the face of rigid Soviet administrative practices and the limited funds at the disposal of the Berlin Center, this was not always easy. Soon after the first ORT Union Congress (1921) the Central Board of the ORT Union in Berlin met with I. Rashkes, representing *Yidgezkom*, who had come to Berlin to discuss Jewish needs with Jewish organizations abroad. Lvovich and Tsegelnitski informed the *Yidgezkom* representative that the ORT Union was ready to include Soviet ORT projects in its overall programs provided that the Soviet authorities agreed to follow, in Soviet Russia, certain general principles governing ORT activities elsewhere, one of which was the organization of local ORT committees.

In the early 1920's such committees were generally based on tripartite representation, one-third elected by the general membership, one-third consisting of representatives of local Jewish economic organizations and cooperatives, and one-third comprising technical experts with special competence in the areas of ORT concern. (Later, this organizational arrangement was abandoned and election of ORT committees was left to the membership.)

While local work was under the jurisdiction of local committees and professional staff, in many places, particularly in the important cities, the ORT Union also had a representative to supervise projects and serve as a liaison with the Center in Berlin. It insisted on application of these arrangements in Soviet Russia although aware that, according to Soviet law, only members of trade unions could be considered for ORT committee membership, which permitted the Soviet authorities to exercise control of their activities.

ORT Union leaders believed, however, that despite rigid Soviet regulations such an arrangement would help to diffuse, to some extent, Soviet control of ORT work in Russia. After lengthy discussion, Rashkes accepted the ORT Union conditions and indicated that he did not anticipate objection on the part of Avram Merezhin, the head of the Jewish Department of Narkomnats (Commissariat for Nationalities) and a leader of *Evsektsiia*,[7] particularly if ORT Union representatives were to be chosen from among the old Russian ORT activists.

He pointed out that when the Narkomnats (Commissariat for Nationalities) "communized" ORT in Petrograd, it did so in order to safeguard the organization and conserve its professional staff, whose special competence was much appreciated by Soviet officials.[8] This was an interesting statement even if partly motivated by Rashkes' desire to please and impress his negotiating partners. Perhaps he meant to convey that "communization" or nationalization of social institutions which could be useful to Soviet society was Bolshevik policy.

Archival materials on the episode are scant, but it is worthy of note, particularly if it is borne in mind that Rashkes was a thorough *Evsekovets* and well aware of the danger of contradicting the party line.

The ORT Union communicated to ORT in Russia and to the Commissariat for Nationalities the gist of the discussions with Rashkes. Soviet ORT was asked to begin the reorganization of the local ORT committees and was informed that the ORT Union would appoint representatives to serve with local Soviet ORT committees, selecting individuals acceptable to the regime.

In expectation of a prompt reply, the ORT Union contacted the Soviet Consulate in Berlin to request permanent entry visas for the members of the Central Board who might have to visit ORT projects in Soviet Russia. At the same time, the ORT Union began to look for people willing to serve in Soviet Russia.

It was a difficult and delicate task. Candidates had to be both acceptable to the Soviet authorities and conversant with ORT programs and ORT views as to the future of Jewish social and economic life. After some canvassing, the candidates were selected, among them L. Joffe (for Kiev), A. Weinstein (for Odessa), R. Logunova (for one of the cities), and A. Joffe (for Moscow). After deliberation and changes necessitated by circumstances not always in accord with what ORT wanted, the old ORT activist Tsegelnitski of Petrograd sometime later went to Moscow as head of ORT there and as representative of the ORT Union in Moscow. (The lay chairman of Soviet ORT in the early 1920's was U. Golde.)

Tsegelnitski, an agronomist, had come to Berlin from Russia and had remained there for several years while retaining his Soviet citizenship and connections with the country of his origin. During his stay, he was one of the leading men of the ORT Union.

A Different Reality

As time went on it became apparent that establishing rapport with Soviet ORT was not as simple as it might have appeared after the meeting with Rashkes. *Yidgezkom* was interested in Jewish money from abroad and not in cooperation with the ORT Union, and it was not ready to accept foreign interference in Jewish social work in Soviet Russia; this was, after all, the province of *Evsektsiia* or its people in *Yidgezkom*.

Opinion was deeply divided in the ORT Union with respect to strategy in confronting the Soviet attitude. Everyone realized that *Yidgezkom* was dragging out completion of formal arrangements and leaving the ORT Union in the dark as to its real intentions.

Speaking at a meeting of the Board in July, 1922, Lvovich intimated that if large funds were available to ORT these might be used to smooth the way to reorganization of local committees and remove obstacles in the way of communication with Soviet ORT. We do not know if delivery of substantial amounts of foreign currency would have alleviated the difficulties, but we do know that during his stay in the United States, soon after his visit to Berlin, Rashkes voiced objection to sending funds collected by the Ukrainian Jewish Federation through the ORT Union in Berlin, and requested that the money be sent directly to ORT in Russia, this despite the promises made in Berlin. It has since become clear that Rashkes was playing a double game, trying to fulfill his mission by any means at his disposal. Negotiations were protracted and communications voluminous. The leaders of the ORT Union in Berlin were facing the complex problem of establishing relations with Soviet officials, who proceeded, as they have to this day in other areas, on the theory that "anything goes in dealing with the capitalist enemy."

The Soviet Contract

Tsegelnitski went to Moscow in 1923. He succeeded in making a short-term contract with Soviet ORT, which was approved by the ORT Union in December of that year. Under its terms, the ORT Union assumed the obligation to send to the Soviet Union, over a period of several months, the sum of $5,000 monthly. Simultaneously, a conference of ORT leaders, taking into account the difficulties involved in pursuing ORT work in Soviet Russia, took a softer line with respect to the reorganization of local ORT committees there. They decided to inform Tsegelnitski of doubts in the Berlin office concerning the acceptability of the many candidates that Soviet ORT had suggested for inclusion in the reorganized local committees.[9]

Inception of Programs

Some work was undertaken even before the formal status of the ORT Union was clarified. Already in the fall of 1921, a shipment of seed was dispatched to the old Jewish colonists in the southern Ukraine for the next year's sowing. This was a godsend since Russia was experiencing a poor harvest and resultant famine.

In addition, there was a shipment of needed machinery and equipment. The seed included 80 tons of barley, 650 tons of maize, 120 tons of millet, and 32 tons of various garden seeds. This seed was not available in the area of the old Jewish colonies. Part of the shipment was intended to provide food for the families of the Jewish settlers.

In 1922 the ORT Union sent 11 carloads of machinery and tools to the agricultural settlements. It was the first Jewish organization to bring help to Jewish colonists seeking to reestablish themselves in the areas of the old Jewish settlements in the south. Later there were ICA and JDC and, in 1924, the newly founded Agro-Joint (see Chapter VII), which devoted its efforts and substantial funds to Jewish agricultural programs.

In 1923 ORT decided to confine its work to special projects, including assistance in the restoration of buildings ruined during the pogroms. The ORT Union in that year again dispatched seed and machinery to Jewish settlers who had experienced a poor harvest. The cost of this operation, about $100,000, was covered by JDC and ORT in equal amounts. There was also an attempt to create a fund in Berlin to assist Jewish farmers who had poor harvests in southern Russia.

The ORT Union provided assistance to various Jewish vocational programs in Russia, where trade schools, while included in the state system, still depended on outside help. Among them were some old ORT institutions, but a large number had by then been established by Soviet ORT with the help of the state. Arrangements between the ORT Union and Soviet ORT made it possible to subsidize these schools partly out of funds underwritten by JDC, Welthilfskon-ferenz, and other Jewish relief organizations.

It was a modest program: in 1923, 29 schools with 2,920 pupils, which dropped to 11 schools with 1,209 pupils in 1924 and 11 schools with 1,224 pupils in 1925. The decrease was due primarily to the difficult financial situation in Berlin. ORT Union subsidies for vocational training in Russia fell from $58,000 in 1923 to $13,650 in 1924 and to $6,950 in 1925. Nevertheless, ORT Union financial support was much appreciated during the transition period following the civil war.

Difference, Debates, Abrasions

It was not only because of its natural connections that ORT work in Russia, after the revolution, was at the center of ORT Union concerns. It should be borne in mind that the Jewish population under the Soviets had reached some 2,700,000 and that its economic and social plight had deeply worried fellow Jews the world over. Writing in the 1950's, Syngalowski noted that "from 1921 to 1938 ORT activity in Russia was the most important item in our program."

During those 17 years life was not always easy for ORT, not only because Jewish circles were divided in their opinions about helping Jews in Russia, but also because of difficulties connected with work in the Soviet Union.[10] After the October revolution some Jewish leaders objected to any relief work in Russia, feeling that this would benefit the Soviet regime, which, understandably, they did not favor. It came to a point that, at a meeting of the Welthilfskonferenz held in Prague in 1923, ORT was severely criticized for supporting Communist initiatives.

In any event, the "Russian question" ("*Russkii Vopros*," in the apt formulation of Aronson, then Secretary General of ORT), was always present on the agendas of ORT councils. It arose not only in connection with programs of assistance per se, but as a subject of continuous and passionate debate as to the advisability of conducting relief work under Soviet conditions. On occasion, the ORT Central Board called special meetings to discuss problems connected with ORT work in Russia.

ORT Union leaders disagreed on many of the issues involved. There were skeptics and adversaries of Russian programs, enthusiastic partisans, and individuals who, out of practical considerations, accepted the opportunities as they presented themselves in the mid-20's. Overriding this divergence, there was the official ORT position, approved in Danzig in 1923, which acknowledged the importance of the Jewish back-to-the-land movement for the thousands of Jewish *lishentsy*. This position embraced an obligation to help the suffering Jewish masses without subscribing to Soviet political propaganda which saw Jewish agricultural settlements and vocational productivization as serving farreaching socialist goals. At the same time the ORT Union was naturally interested in supporting all efforts to maintain and expand crafts and vocational training, the traditional purpose of ORT.

The "Russian Question"

The debate on the "Russian question" within ORT circles had strong political connotations, particularly in the 1920s, when a subtle political, and perhaps psychological change came over many European intellectuals, who, under the impact of the war and disappointed by the aftermath of Versailles, began to reevaluate their political views and look to the East for the solution of social and economic ills.

It was a time when the Bolsheviks intensified the campaign against the West, appealing particularly to emigres who were having a hard time, inviting them to return home to take part in the construction of the new socialist society. This propaganda was especially felt circa 1922-1923 in Berlin. *Ex Oriente lux*—writers, actors, and artists looked to Moscow for the new wisdom that would replace the disappearing virtues of the West. Many Yiddish writers and artists who had left Russia after October were affected, among them David Bergelson, Aleksandr Khashin, Der Nister, and Nahum Shtif. Observing the vitality of Yiddish publications, schools, and theaters in the Soviet Union they felt that they were missing a great opportunity by remaining in the bourgeois West.[11]

This pro-Soviet mood also penetrated ORT Union circles. There were indications that some ORT people both at the top and on the staff, sympathized with and, in differing degrees, shared the "great Soviet perspectives."

Among other ORT Union intellectuals, Syngalowski was also shifting to the left. A devoted Yiddishist and lover of Yiddish literature, he was close to Bergelson, the great Yiddish writer, who was then undergoing a deep psychological crisis. We do not know, but we may surmise that Syngalowski was influenced by the views of the group around Bergelson.

Bergelson, while in Berlin, had been close to the ORT Union. In 1924 he went on a mission on behalf of the ORT Union, visiting Bukovina and Bessarabia. In the course of a few years he openly changed his orientation, resigned from the social-democratic Yiddish daily in New York, the *Forward*, and began his collaboration with the pro-Soviet press abroad and with Communist *Emes* in Moscow. In 1925-1926 he launched a pro-Soviet magazine in Berlin, *In Shpan* (In Harness). The magazine, of which only two issues appeared

(1926), was under the editorship of Bergelson and Khashin, both of whom had accepted the Communist line. In 1934, Bergelson went to Birobidzhan and Moscow where, despite his formal Communist credentials, he was arrested and, together with other Jewish writers, murdered on August 12, 1952. Aronson has reported that Syngalowski was connected with the publication and was part of the editorial group. Because of his official connection with the ORT Union, his name did not appear on the masthead of *In Shpan*.

Whatever the degree of his shift to the left, Syngalowski was an old territorialist, and the idea of a large Jewish settlement, with Yiddish as the language and perhaps with separate Jewish institutions, had a special attraction for him.

Describing the political debate in Berlin Jewish circles, Aronson rightly suggests that the pro-Soviet mood was generated primarily by the promise of Jewish colonization, which was astutely propagandized by Moscow. For the first time in history, a national government was establishing, as it were, out of the poor and unhappy former inhabitants of the Pale, a healthy Jewish nation. It is easy today to smile at the naivete of many who believed in the Soviet promises, except that we now know the result, which was not the case in the 1920's.

The pro-Soviet mood was present outside Western Europe, too. Many Jewish writers, journalists, and labor leaders in the United States, who had occasion to visit the Soviet Union or follow the developments there, also shared for a time the pro-Soviet illusions, generously minimizing the harsh Soviet reality. Among them were such labor leaders as David Dubinsky, the scholar Horace Kallen, and the poet H. Leivick. Later, all of them were in the forefront of anti-Communist battles.

Syngalowski soon realized the dangers inherent in intellectual fellow-traveling and shed his illusions about the "great Soviet experiment," bringing to an end the interval during which he had put at risk the democratic outlook of the ORT Union and perhaps its future.

Bramson, a firm anti-Bolshevik and intimately connected

with the Russian democratic emigration, soon took a strong hand in liquidating left fellow-traveling among ORT personnel. He obviously feared that the ORT Union would be viewed as a pro-Soviet institution, which was not only not the case, but which might have disastrous consequences for its practical programs. In a characteristic move, Bramson, the ever-wise administrator, invited Avraam Ben-Adir, a staunch anti-Bolshevik Yiddish writer and a former leader of the Jewish socialist-territorialist group in Russia, to take over the ORT publication, *Wirtschaft Un Lebn*, thus signaling to all sympathizers of the Soviet experiment that the ORT Union was not with them.[12]

A New Framework

Finally, on October 9, 1925, the ORT Union concluded an agreement with the Soviet Commissar for Foreign Trade concerning its support for Jewish agricultural settlement in the Soviet Union. Approval of the Soviet government was given on March 25, 1926. In the negotiations for the agreement the Soviets were represented by Avram Merezhin and the ORT Union by Tsegelnitski. Under its terms the ORT Union was permitted to proceed with its program of "promoting agricultural occupations among the Jews" with an investment, during the one-year period covered by the agreement, of not less than $75,000.

On May 24, 1928, the ORT Union concluded a supplementary agreement with KOMZET covering ORT activities in the area of industrialization of the Jewish masses, which by that time had been included among the tasks of KOMZET. The signatories to the agreement were Smidovich for KOMZET and Tsegelnitski for the ORT Union. The ORT Union was empowered to import and distribute within the USSR machinery and tools needed by Jewish *kustars* (home workers), artisans, artisan-cooperatives, and agricultural settlers.

By this agreement there was created an organizational framework for the distribution of needed tools to thousands of Jewish artisans and *kustars* working at home and outside of recognized cooperative institutions. It was expected that this arrangement would provide opportunities for work to thousands of Jews who were unable to find places in the Soviet economy. [13]

The agreement, which covered a five-year period, stipulated that within that period the ORT Union was obligated to import, without imposition of customs duties, materials of the value of not less than three million rubles, distribution of the items to be approved by KOMZET. The ORT Union was given the right to bring into the Soviet Union technicians and other personnel needed for the performance of ORT services, provided the number did not exceed 10 per cent of total ORT personnel.

The agreement was to be automatically renewed at the end of each five-year period unless either party, on three months' notice, indicated a desire to terminate. At the expiration of the contract the ORT Union was to have the right to transfer abroad not more than 50 per cent of funds received from beneficiaries for imported items. Thus, after years of démarches and negotiations, the ORT Union had established a comprehensive base for its programs in the Soviet Union.

Impact of Soviet Power Structure

These ORT agreements were concluded during times that were hardly propitious, or under the best auspices. Lenin had died in 1924, and a ferocious battle for the succession had followed. Trotsky was considered the natural successor, but he was not to attain that position. At the Fifteenth Congress of the All-Union Communist Party, held in December, 1927, there appeared a deep division in the ruling circle. (Trotsky had already been expelled from the party.) Stalin, at first in alliance with other leaders, and then by himself, succeeded in taking over party and power.

Trotsky had stood for rapid industrialization and, concomitantly, strict measures against the "village *kulaks*," who, according to him, were in the process of starving the cities by means of a systematic grain blockade. Trotsky represented the "left opposition." Stalin, with Rykov (for a time Chairman of the Council of Commissars) and Bukharin, the respected theoretician of the party, fought Trotsky from "the right," trying to win over the peasants who rightly felt that they were being unfairly treated by the regime. Stalin defended the individual peasant and preached gradual industrialization in order not to destroy the important union (*smychka*) between city workers and village peasants, advocated in his time by Lenin. Trotsky lost the battle and early in 1928 was exiled to Alma-Ata in Turkestan. Early in 1929 he was forced to leave Russia and went to Turkey.

With Trotsky out of the way and "the right" (Rykov, Bukharin, Tomsky) weakened by inner dissension, Stalin, in a complete turnabout, in 1929 proclaimed total collectivization of the villages and rapid industrialization as "the order of the day." He had taken over the Trotskyist ideas.

The first Five-Year Plan had to be amended to fit the new political line borrowed from the defeated "left opposition."[14] The new policy signified the end of NEP and the total reshaping of the Soviet economy.

It was, in fact, a second Bolshevik revolution, launching the country, exhausted by the "war Communism" of the earlier years, on a new and costly experiment of overall planning, a violent reversion to revolutionary action that brought untold suffering to all classes.

During the NEP period Soviet authorities had begun to recognize the importance of artisans to the economy. In 1925 artisans were even benefiting from certain tax advantages, and the government promised to prevent actions that would impair the status of the private artisan. The return to rigid planning, however, could not but adversely affect the Jewish *kustar* and Jewish artisan and, in fact, the great majority of the Jewish population which was not prepared for the rapid change.

Nor was it clear what effect the collectivization would have on Jewish farmers. Throughout the country peasant properties were taken over and collectivized, and produce was being requisitioned without regard to the needs of the peasants. Millions of peasants were uprooted, and entire villages, without advance notice, were exiled to Siberia. Hundreds of thousands of children—the *bezprizornye*—of the destroyed families, left behind, roamed the roads of Russia. Communist agricultural functionaries and police decimated the villages.

A Mission to Russia

Throughout this time the world Jewish organizations had maintained their efforts in support of Soviet Jewry. The Central Board of the ORT Union decided to send a delegation to the November 15, 1926 OZET conference in Moscow. Some of the ORT Union delegates—Tsegelnitski (Moscow), Lvovich and Syngalowski (Berlin), Zylberfarb and Kagan (Warsaw)—familiarized themselves with the general mood and the problems facing the Russian Jews, and visited many colonies in the regions of Odessa, Kherson, and the Crimea.

This mission marked the consolidation of ORT Union activities in the USSR and to a large degree established the limits of its efforts there. With first-hand information now available, ORT intensified its work on behalf of Jewish colonists in the districts of Odessa and Pervomaisk (formerly Balta), near the Bessarabian border. In Belorussia, ORT was active in the areas of Minsk, Bobruisk, and Mogilev, where it extended loans for the development of poultry farms.

In 1929-1930, assistance in these regions was extended to 4,143 households in 108 localities. During this period agricultural work was predominant in ORT programs in the Soviet Union.

Toward the end of the 1920's the Jewish settlements in the Ukraine were combined by the government into three large

Jewish national districts: Kalinindorf (1927), Novozlatopolie (1929), and Stalindorf (1930). Later, in 1931, there were created two national Jewish districts in the Crimea: Freidorf and Larindorf, and some settlements in Belorussia. The largest and most prominent Jewish agricultural settlement project was Birobidzhan, established in 1928 and in 1934 officially designated a Jewish autonomous region.[15] Around 1930, along with the expansion of Jewish settlements in the Crimea and Ukraine, collectivization came to the Jewish colonies. 94 per cent of Jewish farmers were collectivized in Freidorf (Crimea) and 99 per cent in Novozlatopolie (Ukraine).

Collectivization did not affect the Jewish settlements as disastrously as it did the peasantry-at-large. Of necessity, and on the advice of experts, some Jewish settlements had adopted cooperative practices long before collectivization, since the cooperative system had helped them to overcome much of the hardship that came with revolutionary changes.

Nevertheless, collectivization radically changed the agricultural economy, practically closing opportunities which had been open to private social initiatives.

The wide-spread Soviet practice of unearthing *kulaks*, including some who were Jews, created upheaval in some of the Jewish colonies. In Kalinindorf and other places many settlers left the villages and returned to the city. A report of May 24, 1929 by Boris Smolar, the Jewish Telegraphic Agency writer on Russian affairs, that four Jewish colonists in the Crimea had been sentenced to three years' imprisonment on trumped-up charges which Smolar felt was intended to set an example to neighboring non-Jewish peasants, aroused concern in Jewish circles in the West.

The new agricultural regime also brought some technical changes. Up to about 1930, ORT loans to Jewish settlers were distributed through Jewish cooperative banks and loan *kassas*, but later, in the 1930's, these credit institutions were liquidated, compelling ORT to conduct its operations through the newly established Agrarbanks.

Urban Programs

ORT interests included assistance to city dwellers, artisans who were finding it difficult to adjust to Soviet conditions. In this area it focused on cooperative undertakings— producer-cooperatives, mutual-aid societies, loan funds— which not only made it easier to obtain needed commodities and raw materials but to a large degree legitimized the status of artisans in Soviet society.

In cooperation with Soviet economic agencies, ORT was instrumental in establishing new industrial undertakings, among them a brick factory in Lipovtsy, artels in Mogilev-Podolsk and Chernigov, artels in Kiev and Kharkov, and cooperatives in the Crimea. Individuals accepted in the ORT programs, former *lishentsy*, were rehabilitated and had their civil rights restored. In time, as industrialization attained high priority in the USSR, this program acquired particular importance.

With help from the ORT Union, Soviet ORT supplied artisans with machinery and tools, helped modernize their shops, and expanded opportunities for additional manpower. Homeworkers also received loans for machinery. In the five years 1926-1930, with ORT Union assistance, some 400 machines were supplied to 60 old and new cooperatives. The imported machines considerably increased the productive capacity of the cooperatives, bringing into the labor force an additional 6,000 Jewish workers. Some 2,000 foreign machines were given directly to various beneficiaries, including individual artisans and members of the declassed *lishentsy*, affording them an opportunity to form artels or join existing cooperatives.

All told, during the five-year period 1926-1930 the ORT Union imported from abroad and distributed 2,946 machines, some of which had been sent as gifts by relatives in the United States.

In connection with this type of assistance, the ORT Union initiated a campaign in Western Europe and the United States urging contributions of machinery and tools, rather than food and money, for relatives in the USSR. (This will be related in detail in a later discussion of ORT in the United States.) ORT Union-supplied machines were distributed in 152 towns, 163 townlets, and 16 villages to, among others, tailors, shoemakers, barbers, hatters, and wood-workers. ORT Union also maintained supplies of machine parts, enabling technicians to repair some 5,500 discarded machines in 132 towns which for years had remained unused for lack of parts.

ORT Union imports included six million knitting machine needles and 160 tons of yarn, which were not available in the domestic market and were distributed in 269 towns.

ORT instructors played a notable role, traveling about the areas of Jewish concentration and providing technical help and advice to Jewish artisans. The work of these instructors was especially important during the period of intensive industrialization when new technical skills were introduced and Jewish artisans had to acquire the new specializations. In all, 700 cooperative societies, including producer-cooperatives, societies for mutual aid, and loan funds, benefited from ORT Union support.

Vocational Programs

Even after the end of the civil war, when these schools were integrated into the state educational system, the ORT Union maintained its traditional interest in vocational schools. Unable now to deal directly with the schools, it organized and supported a vocational training program providing evening courses, workshops, and courses for Yiddish-speaking vocational teachers.

In these programs, which were conducted in many cities, 25 per cent of the trainees were women, whose earnings helped their families. In cooperation with KOMZET, ORT extended grants for such projects as school buildings, specialized libraries, and technical equipment. Again in cooperation with KOMZET it helped, in an advisory capacity, in selecting and directing Jewish youths into the mixed educational and vocational schools established by the state.

Rise of Soviet Economic Structure

The intensive industrialization and collectivization in progress in the Soviet Union had a great impact on the social and economic activities of the Jews. *Evsektsiia* translated the government policies into Jewish terms. Under socialist conditions, it said, the Jewish proletariat to be created out of the masses of poor Jews would be in the vanguard of a consolidated Jewish nation, an organic part of the socialist society being established in the Soviet Union.

Beginning in the 1930's (the decision to inaugurate collectivization came on January 5, 1930), the ORT Union, collaborating with Soviet ORT, had to take into account that things were no longer the same in Russia. In the early and mid-20's ORT traditions were still alive. Now the organization was being integrated more and more into Soviet economic institutions, its personnel were being sovietized, and its work was being adjusted to the Five-Year Plans. These changes were reflected in the language of ORT reports, which adopted the party formulation of "building socialism in one country."[16]

In 1930, ORT in the USSR underwent a further metamorphosis when to a large degree it was amalgamated with OZET, theoretically a voluntary Soviet agency for agricultural settlement. This signified even more rigid control by the authorities and was a portent of things to come.

ORT Union leaders debated whether they should continue their programs under the new conditions. They questioned whether an international Jewish organization could conduct a program under those conditions, and whether, as the long-time adversaries of work in Soviet Russia believed, the time had come to break the contract and liquidate the program. The Jewish press on both sides of the controversy joined the debate. The Zionists came out strongly against continuing the activities; they preferred to see the funds used in Palestine. By then Stalin had alienated a large part of the Jewish "left," the socialist circles in the West, and doubts appeared also in this sector.

The problem, a serious one, is, under different conditions and with other elements, still with us. The question was: Who would be the losers if the relief work was discontinued? Looking back, and knowing what was to follow, it would appear that the ORT leaders came to the right decision. They maintained the programs, feeling that it was incumbent upon them to continue to bring to Soviet Jews whatever assistance and technical knowledge they needed to help them to adjust to the conditions prevailing in their country. It was a difficult decision, but it was based on their understanding of Jewish efforts at self-help in Russia, and their reading of developing Soviet policy.

At the beginning of the Five-Year Plans the Soviet government badly needed foreign capital. This was perhaps one of the reasons why it accepted outside help in promoting productivization among Soviet Jews.

In fact, Soviet authorities continued to assign large areas of land for Jewish colonization. Between 1925 and 1927 it allocated some 260,000 *desiatin* (about 700,000 acres) for Jewish settlement. Later there was the Crimean project, with initial projections of an additional acreage of 300,000. In terms of direct financing, however, as of 1929 the total amount expended for Jewish agricultural projects was 22,500,000 rubles, of which only 5,800,000, or a little over 25 per cent, was furnished by the state.[17]

The total amount expended by the ORT Union in the USSR during the period 1926-1930 came to about 4,700,000 rubles: 3,225,000 for machinery and raw materials for cooperative groups and individuals; 902,000 for agriculture; 248,000 for vocational training; 57,000 for technical assistance, and 288,000 for various other purposes. These funds came from the United States (JDC, *Landsmanshaften*, handtool collections) and ORT campaigns conducted in many countries.[18]

The Thirties

In its ongoing work the ORT Union dealt primarily with the ORT Center in Moscow, but Soviet ORT also had offices in Leningrad, Kiev, Kharkov, Odessa, and Minsk. Its work involved a large number of local contracts covering business arrangements in various cities and with various industrial enterprises. ORT was financing wholly or partially the establishment of factories in the Ukraine, Belorussia, the Crimea, and, later, Birobidzhan, all of them entailing complex local arrangements with Soviet institutions and government authorities.

ORT activities from 1931 on underwent significant changes. Farming had become a less important factor in the productivization of Soviet Jews although there was still a reservoir of Jewish families seeking an opportunity to settle on the land.

The country needed manpower for its developing industry and Jews were mobilized into the labor force along with other groups in the multi-national state. In 1924 the number of Jewish wage and salary earners was 394,000; by 1931 the number had risen to 787,000; official sources cite 1,100,000 for 1935.[19] Thus, after a long and difficult period of transition, some 35 to 40 per cent of the Jewish population of the Soviet Union had been integrated into the Soviet economy. While many of the economic problems faced by Soviet Jews a decade before had been eliminated, the social cost was great in terms of splitting families, geographical displacement, and a severing of Jewish roots.

No great changes occurred in the status of the Jewish agricultural settlements except that the younger generation was attracted to industry by higher pay and less work. Even some older persons left the Jewish settlements to return to the city.

There were still Jews who, because of age or for other reasons, such as Sabbath observance, needed help in adjusting to the new Soviet society. ORT assisted these individuals in many ways, particularly through supplying machines, tools, and raw materials.

ORT continued to subsidize short-term vocational courses for youths needing speeded-up vocational instruction, but it did not extend grants for training programs requiring longer periods of schooling.

The ORT program in the USSR was becoming stabilized at a reduced level. As of 1932 ORT supported 60 cooperative loan societies, 60 producer-cooperatives, 246 *artels*, and 24 social organizations—a total of 390 organizations with 30,000 to 35,000 gainfully employed Jewish workers.

In addition it promoted significant research on Jewish social and economic life. Among other studies, it produced materials on the 1926 Soviet census, the social structure of the Soviet Jewish population, unemployment among Soviet Jews, and other data. Some activities were discontinued. Contract projects focused on selected areas and selected services to industry and agriculture. The change in the size and nature of ORT activities was perhaps due to the fact that Soviet industrialization was expanding geographically. Fac-

TABLE 9

ORT-Supported Short-Term Vocational Training in the USSR
1931–1932

Type of Training	City	Duration (years)	No. of Trainees	Amount of Assistance (rubles)
Metalworking	Kiev	1	64	4,000
Bootmaking	Kiev	1	96	10,000
Metalworking	Dnepro-petrovsk	1	122	15,000
Woodworking	Belaia-Tserkov	2/3	112	5,000
Woodworking Instructors	Belaia-Tserkov	2/3	35	25,000
Sock-knitting	Moscow	1	150	3,000
Woodworking	Zhitomir	1/2	60	2,000
Various	Kharkov	*	*	3,500
Various	Shpola	*	*	1,200
Hatmaking	Evpatoria	1/4	*	*
Hatmaking	Odessa	1/12	*	*

*Figure not available

tories were being established near the sources of raw materials, frequently far from Jewish habitations.

In 1934, ORT followed the pattern established in earlier years. It provided assistance to Jewish colonies in the southern Ukraine and Crimea. Thirty-nine *kolkhozy* with 2,422 families (9,631 individuals) were receiving help in agricultural pursuits in the districts of Kalinindorf, Odessa, and Pervomaiisk.[20] In 1930-1936, 70 settlements with some 4,000 families benefited from ORT support. ORT was also instrumental in creating supplementary income for needy Jewish farmers by providing opportunities for the employment of women. These programs called for short-term vocational courses, conducted in 41 *kolkhozy*, including courses in tailoring, knitting, and toymaking. In 1934 the programs in the Crimea and Ukraine had 1,150 trainees in 50 *kolkhozy*; in 1936, 2,560 trainees in 58 *kolkhozy*.

The Lure of Birobidzhan

With industrialization proceeding at a rapid pace, activities on behalf of artisans and *kustars* were gradually reduced, but the programs in Birobidzhan were expanded. Established in 1928, Birobidzhan, situated in the far east of the USSR, was propagandized as a "Palestine" for Russian Jews. It was initially closed to non-Jews, but this restriction was later removed because Birobidzhan, located close to the Japanese (now Chinese) border, was, and is, of great strategic importance to the Russians.

Most of the Jewish Communists of *Evsektsiia* (which was dissolved in 1930) were opposed to the project, which they viewed as a return to Jewish autonomism but they were overruled. (The position taken by the Jewish Communists of *Evsektsiia* was incomprehensible to many Russian Communists, including Kalinin, head of the Supreme Soviet.) An ORT mission composed of Tsegelnitski, Weinstein, and Dr. Joseph Rosen of Agro-Joint, visited the area in 1934. Tsegelnitski prepared a report for the Central Board of the ORT

Union on the area as a possible place for Jewish settlement. ORT Union leaders debated the question at length. Syngalowski suggested a commission to collect information before presenting the question to the Central Board, and Lvovich proposed that Dr. Rosen be asked to make a presentation on the subject to ORT Union leaders.

Some experts had already suggested that Birobidzhan was not suited to Jewish colonization. Others, particularly some of the old territorialists, were sympathetic. Still others believed that Jewish refugees from Nazi Germany might find a haven there. At a meeting of the Executive Committee of the ORT Union on January 6-8, 1934, in Paris, Tsegelnitski enthusiastically endorsed the project. Dr. Rosen of the Agro-Joint was less enthusiastic, being aware that, aside from technical problems and a harsh climate, the project would require a substantial investment of funds.

All this, however, was too late. Tsegelnitski had already initiated ORT work in Birobidzhan in 1933, when he supported the preparation of plans for and later the construction of, a veneer factory there. It is not known whether he did this on his own initiative, but in 1933, Tsegelnitski, a Soviet citizen, did not have much choice.

Later, in 1935, ORT supplied machinery and equipment to various Birobidzhan factories, including a number of highly sophisticated electrical projects.[21] Birobidzhan thus became a regular part of the ORT program. An important activity was the preparation of technical projects for industrial enterprises. ORT also supplied raw materials not obtainable in Birobidzhan. It participated in colonization work, organizing short-term courses for would-be settlers, and training courses in occupations appropriate to the new location. In 1936 ORT concluded an agreement with KOMZET for the transfer to Birobidzhan of 200 individuals, the majority of whom were graduates of ORT vocational schools.

ORT also afforded direct assistance to Birobidzhan farmers in areas where their introduction to agricultural pursuits could be facilitated. It supplied tractors and other specialized machinery, selected vegetable and flower seeds, and helped farmers combat destructive insects. In 1935-1936 an ORT model farm served as an example of effective agricultural methods.

Adolf Held, who visited Birobidzhan in 1936, returned with mixed impressions about the Jewish opportunities there, but for some years Birobidzhan was propagandized by fellow-traveling circles in all the countries of the West. One of these was the Ambijan Committee, an American Communist-supported organization begun in 1934 and liquidated only after World War II. Today there is nothing Jewish in Birobidzhan except its purely formal status. The Jewish population is less than 10 per cent of the total.[22]

The Final Years

From 1934-1935 on, importation of machinery paid for by relatives of Russian Jews residing abroad, mostly in the United States, had decreased considerably. Many independent Jewish artisans were entering state employment, which was more lucrative and more secure. Individual skilled artisans were no longer appreciated in the Soviet planned economy.

The economic crisis in the United States had seriously affected Jewish families who would otherwise have been ready to support relatives in the USSR. This program never again achieved the importance it had in earlier years.

As of January 1, 1937, ORT programs in the industrial area included 126 producer-cooperatives, training workshops, and factories. Of the total, 53 were in urban localities and 73 in agricultural settlements. The total number employed in these projects was 10,054 men and women.[23]

In March, 1933, the ORT Union agreement with the Soviet Union was extended to May 1, 1938. On January 8, 1938, the ORT Union suggested to KOMZET a further extension, but was informed that the agreement would not be renewed and on November 24, 1938, the chairman of KOMZET, S. Chutskaev, personally informed Soviet ORT that the agreement would not be renewed. In the letter of Soviet ORT reporting this decision to the ORT Union it was emphasized that the Soviet Union did not need outside assistance. During the same period, under the pressure of the authorities, the activities of the Agro-Joint and of the ICA were liquidated.

The years 1937 and 1938 were somber years in Russia. A wave of purges—Stalin's Terror—convulsed the land. Among the victims were many Jewish party men, former leaders of *Evsektsiia*, including Merezhin, who had signed the Soviet-ORT agreement on behalf of KOMZET. Another was Liberberg, the Jewish head of Birobidzhan.

Sometime in early 1938, Tsegelnitski, representative of the ORT Union in Moscow and head of Soviet ORT, was arrested and deported to a camp in what has come to be called the Gulag Archipelago—according to some reports, to Kazakhstan.[24] There were unconfirmed reports that he had been sentenced to death by the NKVD while in the camp. One thing is certain; he disappeared along with other victims of the terror.

This was the end of ORT in the Soviet Union after some 20 years under the Bolsheviks and 58 years since its creation in 1880.[25]

Despite the ORT Union's request of June 1, 1938 to have a representative present in Moscow during the liquidation of its activities, Louis Boudin, a New York attorney and ORT leader, was refused a visa. According to Article 21 of the Soviet-ORT agreement, the liquidation of ORT was to be carried out in a stipulated legal manner, but this provision was not adhered to.

All work was stopped, and inventories, shops, equipment, and bank accounts in the Crimea, southern Ukraine, Birobidzhan, and elsewhere were taken over by the authorities. The ORT Union requested payment of about $264,000 accruing to it in accordance with the agreement (there were some problems in connection with exchange rates), but the Soviet authorities never responded to this request.[26]

Lord Dudley Marley, an ORT leader in Great Britain, who was in Moscow in September, 1938, wrote to Bramson on September 16 that "ORT, being international, had no governance to call upon" and was therefore in a situation much worse than that of Agro-Joint, which, as an American organization, could, upon liquidation, have recourse to the United States Embassy. Marley noted, however, that he had "every hope that we shall get a satisfactory result." He was wrong, but this can hardly be held against him.[27]

In 1938, in the Soviet Union, there was no reason to be optimistic. It was the time of *Ezhovhchina*,[28] the Stalin-orchestrated wholesale murder of millions of innocent Russian men and women. Who would dare, under these conditions, to speak for a Jewish international organization?

ORT in the Soviet Union should not be judged by its sad ending in 1938. Its work was a useful contribution to the productivization of a large number of Jewish men and women in both industry and agriculture. It was, as Syngalowski noted, a difficult task, but to the extent that it was not prevented by the authorities, ORT succeeded in helping the Jews of Russia in their difficult struggle to adjust to new conditions.

Midpassage: Fifty Years of ORT
A Note on Leadership, Program, and Ideology

In "65 Years of ORT (1880-1945)," Syngalowski divided ORT history into four periods: 1880-1906, 1906-1914, 1914-1919, and 1919-1945.[1] Our perspective today is broader than Syngalowski's of thirty-odd years ago. A look at the first fifty years supplies a more useful frame for bringing into focus ORT's essential character and meaning, and the principles that made it unique in the history of Russian and, later, world Jewry.

Created as a purely Russian organization, it became an international one. From the vantage point of fifty years we can trace the process of ORT's adjustments to new conditions and the resulting changes in both character and method.

Leadership Shift

The ORT leadership began to change in the mid-1920s. Spreading activities brought local Jewish leaders to the top councils when new people from countries in Eastern Europe joined the ruling group. The number of professionals work-

161

ing in the organization and sitting in its councils increased. During the early years in Russia, management was largely in the hands of Jewish individuals known as *obshchestvennye deiateli* (*klal tuers*, in Yiddish), which may roughly be translated as volunteer lay leaders.

It is difficult to provide a precise definition of these terms, connected as they were with special conditions in Russia. These individuals, in the main business people, financiers, or outstanding professionals, devoted their free time to communal affairs. They were in a category *sui generis*. As ORT activities expanded, the need of technical advice made this arrangement impractical. Complex technical problems required the special knowledge of experts who were on the job full time.

As activities spread to the West, the process of professionalization was accelerated. In sociological terms one might say that decision-making was more and more concentrated in the hands of staff professionals who, while they consulted with the lay leadership, were assuming the management of the organization, to a large degree replacing local volunteer-activists.

In many of the cities of the new Eastern European states, ORT-appointed representatives supervised local activities, dealing with local committees, but reporting directly to the Center in Berlin or, later, Paris. It should be noted, however, that the professionals managing the ORT Union were individuals whose work and, indeed, lives were entirely devoted to ORT. [2]

Sussya Goldmann has written about this period in his memoirs, and spoke about it in speeches at ORT assemblies. During these formative years, the future of the ORT Union was much in doubt outside the immediate managerial group. And it was this small group who, in their daily work, assured the continuation of activities. Despite the social breakdown following the war, lack of resources, inflation, and obstacles in connection with the newly established states, they succeeded in overcoming these difficulties. They also brought a new idea to the Jewish communities of the West which, rightfully proud of their status in society, did not always readily accept the unfolding work design of ORT.

Program Trends

ORT's traditional goal had been the promotion of industrial and agricultural labor among the Jews of Russia. A substantial part of its activities had been devoted to practical work— financial relief to needy artisans and agricultural settlers and the provision of needed machinery. In the period following the 1905 revolution, Jewish cooperatives were established and a plan devised for geographical distribution of Jewish artisans aimed at their rational resettlement in areas where markets were available. Vocational education was always an organic part of the ORT program, including schools and various systems of vocational training. Some of these tasks were peculiar, at least in certain aspects, to Russia and Eastern Europe. As time went on, programs were adjusted to accommodate new conditions, others were either abandoned or reduced in priority.

Looking back, a number of conceptions governing the practical work of ORT are clearly discernible. There were those who promoted assistance to individual artisans and farmers; and there were partisans of cooperative undertakings in both cities and agricultural settlements. An ongoing debate revolved on the social and economic advantages of cooperative enterprises versus reliance on individual enterprises.

There were lively discussions on the proper methods of teaching a vocation. Some ORT activists felt that priority should be given and resources devoted to the vocational training of Jewish youths who, after three or four years of schooling, would have no difficulty in obtaining employment.[3] For many of the old *maskilim* of ORT, training schools were a must, while others, particularly from the provinces and bringing their own experience to the discussions, argued that youths could be better trained in shops than in schools.

The proponents of the latter approach pointed to the substantial costs of maintaining a vocational school that provided for training in a maximum of three or four crafts and did little to develop a feel for the circumstances under which the future artisan would have to work. The debate, often heated, arose again and again in the newly established states, particularly in Poland.[4] To appreciate the background of these discussions, the special conditions existing in Tsarist Russia and in Eastern Europe generally should be borne in mind.

With the passage of time there was increasing concern about the general level of technical skill among the "great army" of Jewish artisans already gainfully employed. In the newly established Eastern European states, where the Jewish artisan had to fight for his economic position in the face of discriminatory rules and laws, this was a particularly serious problem.

A program appropriate for this specific clientele was therefore needed, and to meet this need the ORT Union pioneered a special response by instituting a broad program of evening courses, Sunday classes, and technical demonstrations in the use of modern machinery for Jewish artisans and apprentices. It was a considerable task for ORT and it required a great effort for those who had to find time for courses after a hard day of work and who had to meet family obligations. The Sabbath, naturally, could not be used for vocational pursuits.

In the countries of Eastern Europe, ORT maintained its traditional pattern well into the 1930's. As it enlarged its work outside Eastern Europe, new problems arose in dealing with Jewish communities structurally different from those in Eastern Europe. Direct assistance and cooperative undertakings were, in the main, abandoned. Vocational education and training adjusted to Jewish needs in the various countries were given priority.

Along with geographical changes, there were changes in programmatic approach, orientation, and perception. ORT now looked at its work from a Western perspective. The full impact of the change was to come later, when activities were

extended to many countries and the upcoming ORT generation tended to consider the first fifty years of ORT as a sort of
prehistory.

In retrospect, it is obvious that the 1930's were a watershed in the annals of ORT, not least because the time
called for new activities geared to Jewish refugees seeking
escape from unbearable conditions, or fleeing for their lives
from Nazi Germany.

Search for Ideological Meaning

Decades were to pass from the time of its creation before
ORT acquired a stable and definitive framework. These years
were a fateful period in Russian history, a time of intensified
revolutionary dissent. It was also a time of reawakening
among Russian Jews and the birth of Russian-Jewish
ideological movements.

Looking for an answer to the problems facing the impoverished Jewish masses, one sector of Russian-Jewish society (later to become the Zionist movement) urged emigration, including emigration to Palestine.

Another sector, including members of political groups
(one of which was later to become the Bund),[5] saw in the
political and social changes and democratization developing
in Russia a future for the Jews in that country. ORT was not a
political organization and it had no established ideology, but
in its programs and outlook it was plainly among those who
connected their future with Russia and preached *doigkeit*
("here-ness").

This emphasis on "here-ness" remained an ORT principle until about 1930. There were to be changes and adjustments later, when the world was faced with the unspeakable
events of the Nazi decade. Following the establishment of
the state of Israel and the radical change in the perception of
the Diaspora, the ORT position underwent further revision,
although this has not always been reflected in official ORT
materials. It was only after World War II that ORT went to
Israel, and acquired great significance there in the scope of

its activities and the place of Israel in the general ORT framework. (See chapter on ORT in Israel.)

Productivization had been viewed by many in Russia as a remedy for Jewish social and economic ills. Vocational schools had, in fact, been in existence long before the creation of ORT. A Jewish trade school in Kremenchug had been established in 1809, and the vocational school *Trud* (Labor) in Odessa, which was later supported by ICA, in 1864. From the beginning, however, and certainly as later refined by the "young Turks," the ORT program went beyond vocational training. Objectives may not have been clearly formulated, but they were sensed intuitively by most of those active in ORT and by its beneficiaries.

The early leaders of ORT did not think in broad historical categories. In proclaiming productivization as an essential goal they simply identified one of the important problems facing the Russian Jewish masses throughout the Pale. Productivization—labor not only in its technical sense, but as a way of life, and perhaps a way of living rightly and justly—was proclaimed as a means of changing the social and economic structure of the Jewish community.

It was this idea that made ORT so popular with those in the Jewish community who were unwilling to see emigration as the only alternative, accompanied, as it was to be, by social and personal disruption. However much it may have lacked a defined ideology, ORT offered something concrete to the Jewish masses—an attractive, practical program. Under the difficult conditions of Tsarist repression, Jewish mass emigration continued and, naturally, the number involved in ORT programs could not be compared with the much larger number of those who left seeking a new and better home. The majority of Jews, however, remained in Russia, seeking and hoping for a different solution.

Situation and Ideas

Most of the debates within ORT circles centered around the technical aspects of activities: To teach this or that craft, how to better train young students; how to find employment for them; should ORT assist individual artisans or focus on broader cooperative actions? Except for the "great debate" during the first decade of the twentieth century (see Chapter IV), in which the deeper meaning of ORT was touched upon, however indirectly, there was little discussion about the place of ORT in Jewish life, about—if one may use the term here—ORT philosophy.

Were ORT activists consciously avoiding such a deeper debate or was the avoidance due to circumstances? Whatever the reasons, the situation changed after ORT went abroad. Objective circumstances forced the leadership to reflect on ORT's place outside Russia and, perhaps, also outside Eastern Europe where the Jewish masses lived under special conditions. But was ORT needed in the West?

The Debate

Both Bramson and Syngalowski played a role in these discussions, but it was Syngalowski who strove to conceptualize the place of ORT in Jewish life.

The debate among ORT leaders concerning the meaning of ORT continued during the Twenties. Leaders in the West, free of the fear of Tsarist censorship, privately among themselves, at meetings, and often in connection with ORT activities in Soviet Russia, then at the beginning of its industrialization, were trying to arrive at a concrete formulation of the ORT idea.

The details of the debate, conducted largely in Russian, are, unfortunately, not altogether clear, and minutes of discussions are not available.[6] The debate came into the open only in 1930, when *Wirtschaft un Lebn*, the Yiddish-language ORT magazine, in its June issue, carried two articles, one by Syngalowski and one by Zylberfarb, the latter then president of ORT in Poland. These two important leaders, holding opposing views, tried to identify the ideological and sociological framework of their organization.

Zylberfarb held that from the beginning ORT had been

limited not only by Tsarist restrictions but by the inability of the ORT leadership to involve the Jewish masses in its endeavors. "ORT," said Zylberfarb, "is not an organization of the masses . . . but an organization for the masses . . . not unlike many other Jewish relief agencies . . . Hehalutz [sic] is a movement," he argued, "ORT is a society," and the character of its organization determined the narrow parameters of its framework.

Zylberfarb obviously viewed a "movement," as opposed to a "society," as a higher form of social engagement. To which Syngalowski replied that ORT was more than a "society" for specific purposes; it was, in fact, a "movement" of Jewish masses having multiple social and economic goals. "Among large and small movements . . . social and national, there is one called ORT, and its aim . . . is the salvation of the Jewish people through an increase among them of the number of toiling individuals."

It was "salvation," not "services," that Syngalowski stressed. He argued that the ORT movement went beyond the organizational form of the ORT Union, and that it should not be confused with the physical ORT organization which, due to many factors, did not enjoy the popular support that it deserved.[7]

Syngalowski and "ORTism"

It is obvious that the debate reflected a continuing search among ORT leaders for self-definition and a deeper exploration of the ORT idea. We are obliged to add that neither the Syngalowski-Zylberfarb debate, nor others with which we shall deal later, yielded a clear conceptualization of ORT as it developed from the 1880s on.

Yet the debates were important to the historical development of ORT, and Syngalowski's role in the ideological controversy should be especially remembered. His perception of ORT was broader and deeper than that of any of his colleagues. It might be said that in propounding his concept of an ORT "movement," Syngalowski tried to establish its distinctive character and to place it within the context of the great Jewish social and ideological trends of the late nineteenth and early twentieth centuries.

ORT had not been conceived as a worldwide instrumentality. It was, in fact, rooted in the conditions of Tsarist Russia. Bramson, Lvovich, and their colleagues pragmatically brought ORT into the areas formerly part of Russia, and then spread it to the West. But it was Syngalowski who tried to enlarge the ORT concept and, by constructing a broad ideological basis, afford a rational framework for its expansion throughout the Jewish world.

Gregory Aronson, the ORT secretary in Berlin from 1926-1931, in his unpublished *Notes of the ORT Secretary* (in Russian), emphasized the singular position of Syngalowski within the ORT hierarchy. "If anyone created ORTism," said Aronson, "it was Syngalowski . . . who enlarged the concept of Jewish national rights with the idea of Jewish economic emancipation."

An old-time socialist, Syngalowski viewed ORT and its programs as a means toward achieving a total transformation of Jewish society, a transformation leading to the Jewish socialist future that he had dreamed about in his youth.[8] For him, the work idea was intimately related to, and was perhaps even the essential precondition for, an existentially satisfying human life.

Although he thought in strictly secular terms, to Syngalowski labor was more than a way of earning an honest living; it was almost a Hasidic religious concept—work as creation. Like A. D. Gordon before him, and perhaps under Gordon's influence, he saw the modern Jew as leading an abnormal life through his loss of contact with nature and the land. ORT, he believed, offered a way out of this predicament.

Some forty years later, Nathan Gould, in the name of the Women's American ORT, presented to a colloquium sponsored by the World ORT Union a position paper entitled "ORT as a Movement in Jewish Life."[9] Although with some important differences, the paper followed the Syngalowski concept. We shall return to this matter later.

The practical achievements of ORT in its first fifty years fell short of the goals of its leaders. It would be a mistake, however, to think about ORT only in terms of practical results. To put ORT retrospectively in its proper place one must look also into the intellectual and ideological search unfolding among the Jews in Russia, mainly among the intelligentsia. In its early beginnings the Jewish labor movement was essentially politically oriented, and believed that priority should be given to revolutionary struggle against Tsarism, and the development of class consciousness among the Jewish poor. The ORT approach was a significant innovation.

By focusing on action keyed to the immediate pragmatic economic needs of the Jewish masses, it actually served as the catalyst of much contemporary economic thinking among Jewish activists of differing views. Its ways of dealing with the Jewish condition had an indisputable impact on Jewish social thought of the period, heightening the involvement of all Jewish political parties and, later, of Jewish social institutions in important economic aspects of Jewish life and fostering the crystallization of their economic programs.[10]

Chapter X

The Thirties–A Decade of Crisis

The decade of the 30's witnessed the nazification of Europe, along with anti-Jewish campaigns almost everywhere that ORT operated substantial programs. The situation was further complicated by a financial crisis, requiring sacrifices by both the ORT Union and local affiliates. It was a critical time, calling for strenuous effort.

From the early 1930's on, many of the Jewish communities of Europe were in a state of turmoil. A new climate was spreading over Europe. Where memories of the war of 1914-18 were still strong, there was a disinclination to acknowledge the threat coming from the Rhine.

The coming to power in Germany in 1933 of a party based on racial principles and an anti-Versailles Treaty platform attracted the ultra-reactionary and anti-Semitic groups active in the newly established states. The principle of economic autarchy, gradually accepted throughout the Eastern European countries, coupled with militant chauvinism, imposed increasing restrictions on Jewish commerce, Jewish industry, and Jewish crafts.

171

The Nazis in Power

An unparalleled movement of Jewish refugees followed upon the advent of the Nazis. The stream from Germany began in 1933. Following the 1938 Anschluss, there were added Austrian Jews and Jews from Czechoslovakia, that nation having fallen to Hitler after the Munich Pact and dismembered in 1939.

Of the 500,000 Jews in Germany, only some 240,000 were still there at the outbreak of the Second World War; of the 190,000 Jews in Austria, about 60,000 remained; and in Czechoslovakia, of some 390,000, 360,000 remained. Thus, from the time the Nazis came to power until the outbreak of the war in September, 1939, more than 400,000 Jews had left their homes in search of new ones.[1] Most went to the West—to Belgium, France, England, and the United States; some, by special arrangement, went to Palestine.[2]

Under these inauspicious conditions, the ORT organizations in the European countries began, in whatever limited ways they could, a fourfold action to help the Jewish masses withstand the assaults of the anti-Jewish elements in the local populations and within the respective governments:

(1) Vocational assistance to refugees from Germany, Austria, and Czechoslovakia;

(2) Intensified vocational training of youths and adults, with emphasis on quality education to reinforce the competitive potential of the Jewish artisan in the Eastern European countries;

(3) Assistance to artisans in need of machinery and those interested in agricultural resettlement, with special attention given to finding gainful employment for artisans and opportunities for farming;

(4) Constructive relief to declassed groups, that is, those that had been thrown out of their professions.

The Onslaught Begins

The 1932 German elections affirmed the swing to the right. Substantial sectors of the German population had clearly expressed sympathy with the extremist anti-Semitic NSDAP.[3] Changes began to come swiftly after January 20, 1933, when Adolf Hitler became Chancellor of the Reich.

The new government organized an anti-Jewish boycott; Nazi hoodlums attacked Jews and Jewish establishments wherever they could find them. Every kind of attack was mounted. Jews were dismissed from positions in government and the professions; within six months of the Nazi takeover some 5,000 Jewish public servants had lost their jobs. The 1935 "Nuremburg Laws" effectively isolated Jews from the rest of the citizenry. Some 10,000 Jews were expelled to Zbaszyn (Poland). Then came the "Kristalnacht"[4] destruction and more.

Some 500,000 German Jews (according to Jewish estimates) and additional tens, perhaps hundreds of thousands of half-Jews and quarter-Jews, the so-called non-Aryans, found themselves in a helpless situation with little possibility of earning a livelihood. In July, 1938, Jews were forbidden to engage in various commercial and financial occupations as well as the practice of medicine. These measures compelled German Jews to seek immediate emigration.

Action on behalf of Germany's Jews was urgently needed. There was a divided opinion on the advisability of emigration. Speaking at an ORT executive meeting in Paris in January, 1934, Dr. Wilhelm Kleeman, a banker and a prominent man in the Berlin office of the ORT Reconstruction Fund, suggested that in considering the question of emigration a distinction be made between "large and small German communities spread among the provincial cities. . . . Whatever happens, the large communities will continue to exist; only the small ones will disappear."

This opinion now seems outlandishly unrealistic, to say the least. Yet, who among the Jews of Europe or, for that matter, non-Jews, including Germans, could have foreseen, in the early 1930's, the horror of things to come?

On the Defense

German Jews, traditionally committed to caring for Jewish brothers in need, had now been transformed into a community itself in need of care. German Jewish organizations soon set up a comprehensive program of self-help. As early as 1933, a *Zentral Ausschuss fur Hilfe und Aufbau* (Central Committee for Aid and Reconstruction) had been organized. A coordinating body, the *Reichsvertretung Judischer Landesverbande* (Association of Jewish Provincial Communities) had also been formed.

Another agency, the *Hilfsverein*, dealt with the all-important matter of emigration. Emigration to Palestine, however, was in the hands of the *Palestina-Amt*. There were also specialized agencies for economic aid, loan *kassas*, and labor exchanges.

Various relief actions were initiated by German Jewish agencies in cooperation with JDC and other Jewish organizations.

The local German ORT, under Chairman Wilhelm Graetz and Secretary David Klementinowsky, and the Reconstruction Fund continued their activities. The local ORT, however, now addressed itself, as it had not at first, to the native Jewish communities.[5] Its efforts were devoted to vocational training, sometimes in cooperation with local Jewish communal centers.

Problems arose due to lack of adequate facilities. Nevertheless, between 1931 and 1934, ORT established seven vocational courses in Berlin providing training in woodwork, motor repair, and other crafts. Indicative of the desperate plight confronting German Jews is the fact that the students were some 200 unemployed former physicians, lawyers, and clerks. It was not until 1937, after two years of démarches by German ORT, and with the help of the World ORT Union, that the first ORT vocational school was opened in Berlin.

The establishment of the school at this particular time, aside from its practical importance, was a demonstration on the part of the remnants of German Jewry of their will to survive and resist.

The Berlin School

The school provided vocational training for Jewish youth who could not gain admission to a state or municipal trade school on the completion of their elementary schooling. It enrolled 101 students for training in woodwork and 13 adults in courses in gas and water plumbing.

Operating under the protection of a foreign organization (British ORT), the Berlin school survived the "Kristalnacht" and was still functioning in 1939, at which time it had more than 200 students. The local ORT society, under the chairmanship of Heinrich I. Michelsohn, was still in existence and, in fact, remained during the first years of the war.

In 1939, on the eve of the w̄ar, Col. J. H. Levey of British ORT came to Berlin where he succeeded in obtaining permission to remove the school, with its 135 students and ten teachers, to England. British authorities had indicated their willingness to accept the transfer provided the school plant was also transferred. At the last moment, the Nazis refused permission for removal of the equipment. Only days before the outbreak of the war the British gave their consent to the transfer of pupils and teachers without the equipment.

A total of 100 students and seven teachers and their spouses left Berlin for England in August, 1939, thus establishing the ORT school in Leeds. Some training programs were maintained at the school in Berlin into the war, but these were geared to adults. The school was liquidated by the Nazis in 1943.[6]

An experiment in vocational education of Jewish youths involved the utilization by ORT of facilities outside Germany, so that, probably for the first time in its history, ORT not only provided vocational training and retraining to meet local needs, but followed the emigrants to provide services for them in their new abodes, stable or transitory.

Classes for German Jewish youths who had emigrated to Liepaja (Latvia) and Kaunas (Lithuania) were organized in 1933. In an 18-month course of study, training was given in mechanics and electro-mechanics. In Lithuania, in addition to training in crafts, ORT provided agricultural courses in Ungaria, near Mariampol (1934) and in Kalinovo, near Kaunas (1935).

Later, the ORT Union negotiated with German Jewish organizations on a plan for settling substantial groups of Jewish skilled artisans in countries of Eastern Europe and

South Africa. Under the restrictive conditions prevailing at the time, little was achieved in this direction, although graduates of ORT schools were directed to South Africa and Latin American countries.

Since substantial outlays were always involved, Bramson made frequent visits to London to discuss various plans with Sir Herbert Samuel, at that time head of the London Council for German Jewry, and with Lord Marley, S. Lurie, and Col. Levey of British ORT. These negotiations were not always successful; long periods of time often elapsed before decisions were made by the Council in London.[7]

In 1936 the ORT Union concluded an agreement with KOMZET providing for the transfer to Birobidjan of 200 individuals, mainly ORT school graduates, including a number from Germany.

In 1938 an ORT delegation composed of Bramson, Lvovich, Lord Marley, and J. Sheftel, attended the Evian Conference exploring ways by which to enlarge their work on behalf of the victims of the Nazis. Like other Jewish representatives who had traveled to Evian, they came back disappointed. Indeed, the Evian Conference, convened by President Franklin D. Roosevelt to see what could be done for the refugees, heard the Polish government's astonishing proposal of mass emigration of Polish Jews from Poland.

Haven in France

With the advent of Hitler and the beginning of the refugee movement, ORT activities in France became functional. Because of its geographic location, and perhaps also because of traditional French hospitality to victims of political repression, the French Jewish community bore the brunt of the early impact of the refugee movement.

Beginning about 1933, ORT in France was radically reorganized. The new situation was a far cry from that of the 1920s. Officially ORT in France dates from 1921.

After the coming of the Nazis, Jewish international organizations were not wanted in Berlin, and the ORT Union had become an object of such constant harassment that it was unable to continue its activities or maintain communication with affiliates abroad. JDC had left Germany in 1933. In October of the same year the ORT Union was forced to transfer its offices to Paris where, some 12 years earlier, Bramson, Lvovich and a small group of their friends had initiated ORT outside Russia.

The transfer to Paris brought many new men to the top councils of the organization, among them Henri Bodenheimer (Chairman of the Central Board), Prof. William Oualid, the writer Edmond Fleg, and Dr. Zadock-Kahn, all of whom had been coopted to the Central Board. By 1934, only a small number (12 of 36 members) of the Central Board of the old Russian group were still active.

French Jews from both the native community (the *Consistoire*) and the milieu of the emigres (the *Federation*) were attracted to ORT.[8] Activization of the local ORT was systematically pursued by the ORT Union, which now had to build a foundation for its work out of Paris. Perhaps in furtherance of this goal—although there were other considerations—the Central Board decided in 1934 to hold its next plenary meeting in Paris rather than in Poland,[9] as had been suggested by the Polish ORT people who had felt this would be helpful to Polish ORT activities.

Refugee Service to the Fore

With tens of thousands of German Jewish refugees arriving in France, it was incumbent upon ORT to provide vocational retraining to help integrate them into French life or prepare them for occupations in other countries.

One of the important tasks fulfilled by ORT in France during the first years of the influx of refugees from Germany was to find jobs for them. It did this in conjunction with local Jewish organizations, particularly the *Comité National de Secours aux Refugies Allemands,* a French agency created to render assistance to refugees from Germany under the chairmanship of Baron Robert de Rothschild. The hiring of German Jewish refugees by Jewish and non-Jewish firms was especially helpful since they were able to arrange for the required special work permits.

At the same time, ORT began to enlarge its programs. In 1934 it conducted three vocational training courses for 75 students. In 1935 the number of courses rose to ten and the number of students to 306; in 1936 there were 13 courses with 380 students; in 1937 enrollment stood at 500; and by the end of 1939, during the first months of the war, ORT was training 1,428 students in Paris, Chelles, and Montmorency.

Most of the training was in fashion and sewing for women and in radio technology for men. A school for training mechanics was also established in Paris in 1939.

A determined effort was made to direct some refugees to agriculture. The intention was to bring to France a small group of German Jews as a nucleus for attracting others. With the help of Dr. J. Rosen of Agro-Joint, a committee of agronomists found a suitable area at the Farm de LaRoche in the district of Villeneuve, between Bordeaux and Toulouse in the Department of Lot et Garonne. The French government favored the program, and soon some 20 families were settled at LaRoche, ORT supplying the necessary equipment and technical guidance.

ORT not only attracted influential Jewish personalities to its work but went beyond the Jewish community, emphasizing the importance of its programs for the general economy of the country. In 1937 a Committee to sponsor ORT was created in the French parliament. Its first chairman was the scientist and statesman Paul Painlevé. After Painlevé's death, Edouard Herriot took over the chairmanship. For some years during the post-World War II period, Senator Justin Godard was active in these endeavors.[10]

Response in England

ORT in England dates from 1920, when two Russian Jewish emigres, Ida and Dr. D. Mowshovitch, with the object of

Farm cooperative in Bessarabia, Rumania, during the thirties.

ORT trade school for girls in Iassy, Rumania.

aiding ORT programs, organized a number of Russian Jewish families residing in England as well as some representative Anglo-Jewish families. Among them were the Beloff, Schalit, Halpern, Kallin, and Wolf families. Alexander Halpern, son of Jacob Galpern, who had been an ORT leader in St. Petersburg, served as chairman.

At the outset, the group limited its activities to fundraising and promotion of the ORT idea and its practical programs. It attracted to its activities the British Chief Rabbi Joseph H. Hertz, the Sephardic Chief Rabbi Moses Gaster, Lord Rothschild, and many non-Jews, including H. G. Wells and George Bernard Shaw. Good relations were established with governmental circles, and there was liaison with the Parliamentary Committee to Sponsor ORT, headed by Lord Marley.

Later, ORT in England incorporated the Reconstruction Fund and the Cooperative Supply Company. In 1938, British ORT collaborated with OSE in the Joint British Committee for the Reconstruction of Eastern European Jewry, headed by Lord Rothschild.

With the coming of the Nazis, British ORT expanded its activities. Refugee relief was now a central concern. Action was taken to obtain visas for German Jewish refugee families seeking new homes in whatever country.

Care was provided for the students of the ORT school in Berlin that had been transferred to England. The students were sent to Kitchener Camp, a reception center for refugees in Sandwich, Kent. The teaching personnel went directly to Leeds where, at the end of 1939, in the midst of the war, the school resumed its work.[11]

Poland on the Brink

With the destruction of the Polish democracy in 1930, the Jewish situation worsened. After Pilsudski's death in 1935, the reins of government passed to the hands of Marshal E. Smigly-Ridz, and the right wing had a firm grip. In the mid-1930's, pogroms and anti-Jewish riots occurred in many cities, with some 35 Jews killed and 500 wounded. To combat overpopulation it was proposed to rid the country of its Jews, whose number had declined from 10.5 percent in 1921 to 9.8 per cent in 1931. [12]

In the 1930's, Polish Jews were gradually being barred from major economic enterprises, particularly developing ones. As a result, Jews faced the danger of confinement to an economic ghetto. Systematic steps were taken to exclude Jews from the automobile industry in which, from the beginning, they had been pioneers and promoters. The same situation prevailed in radio, aviation, and many other fields. The state was trying to "make the economy Polish."

In some Jewish circles emigration was seen as the only way out of the situation, and a number of projects were proposed envisioning substantial Jewish departures from Poland. Polish ORT had no political position with regard to emigration. Its answer to the sharply deteriorating social conditions was to maintain its traditional programs and to increase its efforts, notwithstanding lack of funds.

Its program was adjusted to the needs of various regions, retraining workers in soft industries and providing them with updated technical skills, thus increasing their chances of obtaining employment. There was even discussion of introducing training in business administration.

In this connection it should be noted that in 1937, J. Jaszunski, a leader of Polish ORT, believed that, in the face of worsening conditions in all sectors of Polish Jewry, ORT should enlarge its constituency. He made what, for ORT, was a revolutionary suggestion: That ORT should abandon its negative attitude toward commerce and inaugurate a program of instruction for Jewish merchants. It was Jaszunski's contention that not every type of commercial activity should be considered non-productive. He rightly pointed out that if Jewish merchants were wiped out, Jewish workers would be dealt a hard blow. [13]

Like all new ideas, Jaszunski's proposal was at first received with skepticism and open opposition. Some steps in this direction were taken, however. The proposal required not only the approval of the ORT leadership, but considerable additional funds, then not available. Decades passed before courses in business administration and management were introduced in ORT schools and accepted as a part of a normal curriculum. Such courses are today seen as an organic part of ORT training programs. That initiative should be credited in the annals of ORT to Jaszunski.[14]

By 1936, ORT vocational training programs in Poland included 4,579 trainees in 66 institutions: 18 day schools (including the Technikum) with 1,824 students, 28 workshops for adults with 1,386 students, and 20 special courses for craft improvement with 1,369 students.[15]

The ORT schools and the schools operated by ICA and other organizations, of course, provided for only a small number of Jewish children in need of vocational training. Nevertheless, the ORT schools in Poland were highly respected. They conducted their own examinations, and certificates issued by them had the same validity as those issued by the state.

With the anti-Jewish campaign mounting, opportunities for Jews in the villages were severely limited. ORT nevertheless continued its assistance to and guidance of 61 Jewish agricultural (farming and gardening) units containing 1,300 families. With ORT assistance, some Jewish artisans working in the towns acquired small parcels of land in the vicinity of their homes, thus earning additional income. To assist Jewish farmers and prospective settlers, courses were established in Warsaw, Sosnowiec, in the vicinity of Bialostok, and near Vilna.

ORT continued to furnish legal assistance and material support to Jewish artisans who were required to have guild certificates permitting them to practice a particular craft. Training in crafts was given to Jewish apprentices, making it possible for Jewish workers to enter them. By the end of 1936, some 20,000 Jewish artisans had been qualified.[16]

As early as 1934, Polish ORT had established a committee of experts to study the situation of Jewish artisans and suggest measures for the rationalization of Jewish handicrafts and the creation of better marketing conditions. This committee, under the guidance of J. Lestshinsky, made a number of recommendations which, unfortunately, could not be implemented due to lack of funds. It was only in 1937 that ORT established a Consulting Bureau in Warsaw which continued, but with little success, the work of the committee.

This service was handled in cooperation with JDC, ICA, the Union of Jewish Artisans, and other organizations which established for the purpose a United Committee on Artisans that operated in several towns. In many places ORT represented the United Committee and, in fact, did its work.

In the Rumanian Anti-Semitic Milieu

While the economic condition of Jews in Rumania was relatively better than in other Eastern European countries, the anti-Jewish policy of the Octavian Goga government had created difficulties for them. In contradiction to the obligations assumed at Versailles, the authorities decreed a massive revision of the citizenship of Rumanian Jews, adopting complex procedures aimed at depriving Rumanian Jews of citizenship and, thus, the opportunity to earn a living. These hostile policies reflected the mood of substantial elements of the Rumanian people.

While the ideas prevailing in Nazi Germany were influential, there is ample evidence that anti-Jewish sentiments had been persistent in Rumania long before the Nazis came on the scene. Already in 1920, Alexander Guza of the National Christian League and, later, Corneliu Godreanu of the vitriolic anti-Semitic Iron Guard, had imposed many limitations on the Jewish community.

ORT activities in Rumania did not take on substantial proportions until the 1930's. Syngalowski had visited Bucharest in 1931, where he conducted an extensive educational effort on behalf of ORT[17] and succeeded in obtaining the support of Dr. Wilhelm Filderman,[18] president of the Federation of Jewish Communities, and Rabbi J. Niemirover, spiritual head of Rumanian Jewry. His appeal reawakened interest in ORT throughout the country—in Bucharest, in Kishinev, and in Cernauti.

ORT was experienced in coping with situations resulting from anti-Jewish legislation. This was applied in the midthirties by devoting much attention to the legalization of Jewish artisans in Bessarabia and Bukovina who, under the new industrial laws, risked losing the right to practice their crafts.

It was estimated that some 50 per cent of Jewish artisans in Bukovina were unable to furnish the citizenship documents required by the authorities. A local ORT committee dealt with this problem. In Bessarabia, similar efforts were concentrated in the Jewish Artisans' Society and in loan *kassas*.[19]

ORT managed to maintain its activities in all parts of Rumania, despite the increasingly anti-Semitic climate. In 1936 it operated 14 schools with 1,002 students, ten workshops with 401 adult students, a refresher course for 14 students, and six training centers with 262 trainees. Characteristically, the government, which recognized ORT schools, refused to honor their diplomas, whereas these diplomas were accepted in most other countries.

The Baltic Countries in the Between-War Years

The emergence of a new middle class, recruited mainly from the villages, had given rise to an increase in anti-Jewish feelings in Lithuania. Among the open anti-Jewish groups were the Traders and Artisans Association, which was trying to destroy Jewish competition. In spite of the anti-Jewish propaganda, the Lithuanian Jews generally succeeded in integrating into the country's economy and supplied much of the skilled labor. It was a situation that offered a natural field for ORT.

The ORT school in Kovno had been enlarged in 1932 and its curriculum expanded to four instead of three years. In addition to vocational training it provided general education at the level of the first four years of *gymnasium*. ORT educational standards were highly appreciated.

To satisfy increasing demands for admission to ORT schools and vocational training courses, and to provide better teaching facilities, ORT in Lithuania, in cooperation with the ORT Union, built a "house of Jewish Labor" in 1934. The Kovno school came to be considered among the best technical schools in the country and enjoyed the support of the state.

By the end of 1936, ORT vocational training courses had 196 students in three schools, 275 students in seven workshops for adults, and 57 trainees in three other facilities.

In a country where about 6 per cent of the Jewish population was engaged in farming and gardening, many activists, including Jacob Oleiski of Kovno, who was associated with ORT both before and after World War II and was an ardent supporter of Jewish agricultural labor, insisted that Jews had to prepare themselves for agricultural work.[20]

In February, 1934, the local ORT opened its first agricultural school, intended to provide practical agricultural knowledge, with some theoretical instruction, in a one-year curriculum. It had an enrollment of 30.

The Jewish situation in Latvia changed radically in 1934, when President Ulmanis abolished the Latvian constitution and created an authoritarian regime emphasizing nationalism and economic control. Jewish economic positions came under attack one by one. It became necessary to take steps to assure the continuation of Jewish crafts. ORT therefore concentrated on vocational training.

It conducted 11 training institutions with 452 students and five schools with 288 students, five workshops for adults with 136 students, and a refresher course for 28 adult artisans. The schools were located in Riga, Daugavpils (formerly Dvinsk), and Liepaja (formerly Libau).

Jewish farming was practically non-existent in Latvia, although the local ORT tried to promote agricultural training among the younger generation.

In Bulgaria

ORT began activities in Bulgaria in 1926. Its programs, coordinated with local Jewish communal institutions, was small. Three training workshops for 70 youths in woodwork, bookbinding, and tailoring, and a training course in textiles for 15 adults were established at the Jewish primary school in Sofia. This was an interesting beginning for ORT in a European Sephardic community; up to that time most, if not all, ORT activities had been oriented toward Ashkenazi Jews.

Following the enactment of anti-Jewish legislation in 1940, the ORT workshops in Bulgaria were closed.

Organization and Finance

The Fourth ORT Congress, which was to have been held in Berlin in 1929, did not take place until 1937 in Paris. At this Congress the structure of the ORT ruling bodies was strengthened, concentrating direction in a 14-member Executive Committee and a Central Board of 51. These changes in structure were duly recorded in the Bylaws of the ORT Union in 1938. Bramson was elected Chairman and Lvovich and Syngalowski became Vice-Chairmen of the Executive Committee. The membership of the Committee included, among others, Leonce Bernheim, Pierre Dreyfus, A. Berlant, and J. Meerovich.

In the early 1930s the ORT Union had intensified its fund-raising efforts in the East European countries—Poland, Rumania, Lithuania, and Latvia, which also were the beneficiaries of ORT activities—with the aim of offsetting the drop in income occasioned by worsening economic conditions in the West.

In 1933, Bramson returned to South Africa to organize a campaign on behalf of the United Committee of ORT-OSE-Emigdirect. He was succeeded there in 1936 by Syngalowski who remained for about a year. With the help of Richard and

Freda Feldman, ORT-OSE committees were established. ORT-OSE campaigns were also conducted in Australia, Egypt, India, England, Switzerland, and Holland. There were repeated visits to the United States, including tours of the country by Lord Marley and by Lvovich.

During the period 1930-1939, ORT Union income amounted to about $3,905,945: $999,140 from American ORT Federation and JDC, $349,782 from West European countries, $1,272,643 from local sources, and $1,284,378 from various other sources. Total expenditures during the same period amounted to $3,998,100.[21, 22]

Chapter XI

World War II and Catastrophe

World War II in Europe began on September 1, 1939. In the West it seemed, at first, a "phony" war, with no battles (all of which was soon to change). In the East it was quite different. Within a week Poland had been overrun. The Soviet-Nazi Pact had permitted Hitler to penetrate Poland from the west, and, on September 17, a Soviet army entered Poland from the east.

For the fourth time, Poland was partitioned, this time between Hitler's Germany and Stalin's Soviet Union. In June, 1940, the Soviet Union annexed Lithuania, Latvia, and Estonia, and in July of that year it took Bessarabia and northern Bukovina from Rumania. Freed of the danger from the east, Hitler attacked Western Europe. France fell in June, 1940.

Within nine months of the outbreak of the war the largest centers of Jewish life in Europe were occupied by the Nazis, and hundreds of thousands of Jews had to seek refuge. There were few channels of escape and only a small number were able to find temporary safety. There were few, whether among statesmen, generals, or the man on the street who had expected that the Nazis would advance so rapidly.

Plans Aborted

Did the leaders of the ORT Union take the coming war into account in preparing their plans? No doubt they did. But it was not easy to face up to the gruesome possibilities. Whatever their views about the war, they maintained, in their plans for 1939, an attitude of optimism and projected new and expanded activities.

One such plan for 1939 provided a series of courses to upgrade the skills of Jewish members of industrial trade unions in Poland under an agreement between ORT and the National Council of Jewish Trade Unions, the initiator of the plan. It was not normally the business of trade unions to undertake training. However, the fierce competition of non-Jewish labor had made such training a necessity. According to estimates of the Trade Union Council, some 30,000 Polish Jewish workers needed additional training.

The Jewish community in Hungary also approached the ORT Union for help in establishing a vocational retraining program which became urgent when anti-Jewish legislation made it impossible for many Hungarian Jews to practice their professions. This task was to fall to the newly created ORT Society in Hungary, which was to initiate an Institute for the Promotion of Jewish Apprentices.

Again, the 1939 budget noted that in various countries—Poland, Rumania, and to some extent Latvia—Jews were deprived of the right to acquire building sites in the border regions. Since ORT schools required buildings, it was determined to use all available means to construct them wherever possible. There was no hesitation at ORT headquarters; whatever the circumstances, the work had to go on.

The ORT budget for 1940, when the war was already in full progress, amounted to $1,475,000 (the 1939 budget had totaled $1,250,000). The estimate for 1941 was $1,375,000; for 1942, $1,225,000; and for 1944, with Europe completely under the Nazis, $653,000. There is no need to explain the drop in the budget for 1944.

Paris–Vichy–Marseilles

The situation in Europe soon took a turn for the worse. In France, at the outbreak of the war, many persons of means left Paris. A large number of businesses and institutions also fled the capital to the relative security of the French interior.

Jewish organizations, among them JDC and ORT, departed as well. ORT relocated in Vichy, where the house on rue Carnot soon became the center of Jewish life in that city, celebrated for the curative value of its water.[1] It remained in Vichy until mid-January, 1940. As the "phony" war went on with Paris not under attack, there seemed no reason for the office to remain in Vichy. And so it returned to Paris, where it remained until June, 1940, when, with the Germans approaching Paris, it again moved to Vichy.

Vichy, which after the armistice became the capital of the Pétain government, was not the best choice for a Jewish organization. In November, 1940, the ORT Union moved to Marseilles where JDC and HICEM, dealing with emigration problems, were also located.

War-Time Balance Sheet

On the eve of the war, the ORT Union comprised a network of 200 supportive and functional organizations in 17 countries, with responsibility for some 900 economic units in various areas of activity; a truly remarkable achievement. Under the conditions of war, with Hitler astride Europe, ORT organizations simply continued their operations.

ORT activities during this fateful period, when deportations, death in gas chambers, and the very will to survive were all part of an unending nightmare, should not be viewed only in terms of programs and goals. Orderly activity in a workshop or *atelier* was a means of salvation and a moral act, in its own way an act of resistance and self-defense.

In the Midst of the Holocaust

As the ghastly years went on, the Jews of the ghettoes of Poland, Rumania, Lithuania and Hungary gradually disappeared into Auschwitz, Treblinka, and Maidanek. If, under these conditions, there were still, here and there, efforts to maintain a functioning program, the motivations became so complex as to reach beyond mere narration of ORT history; their significance has to be read as part of Jewish spiritual and physical resistance to the Nazis.

The Jewish situation during the period of the war differed from country to country, depending on the degree to which Hitler's "final solution" was applied by the groups in power.

Under the German occupation, work, while under strictly determined conditions, was, at least, a partial passport to life. Not only did it bring additional food rations—at ORT workshops workers received a plate of soup and a hundred grams of bread—or a measure of self-sufficiency to the Jews of the ghettoes, they could "survive" for a time; the Germans used the labor of these Jewish workers who would later be sent to the death camps.

Emanuel Ringelblum, historian of the Warsaw Ghetto, repeatedly notes that the life of the Jew was predicated on his work permit, at least for so long as the Nazis considered him useful.[2] Thus, in many cities the *Judenrat* (Jewish Council established by the Nazis) was active in organizing producer cooperatives working for German military and civilian needs. Cooperatives and other work projects existed in Lvov, Cracow, Radom, and other cities, often in conjunction with people connected with ORT who had the necessary technical knowledge.[3] As an instance, the Hasidim of Aleksandrov, with the assistance of the *Judenrat* and ORT, in 1941 organized hosiery workshops.[4]

In October, 1939, after the fall of Poland but before the creation of the Warsaw ghetto in November, 1940, ORT was able to utilize available equipment and knowledge for setting up a tailoring workshop which provided employment for some 250 people. In 1940, an ORT workshop manufacturing undergarments functioned at the Jewish orphanage on Krochmalna Street, employing youngsters and adults. To the extent that it was able, ORT, out of its reserves, also supplied equipment to artisans outside Warsaw.

In July, 1940, however, Nazi Governor-General Hans Frank disbanded all organizations, Jewish and non-Jewish. In order to continue their activities, ORT and other Jewish organizations had to be incorporated into the apparatus of the *Judenrat* as part of its welfare services. Later, this restriction was modified, and ORT, TOZ (Polish counterpart of OSE), and some others were permitted to operate as autonomous agencies. In Warsaw, ORT was fairly independent of the *Judenrat* and operated within the framework of the so-called Jewish Social Self-Help (JSS), a Jewish organization working in some cities, particularly Cracow.

ORT tried to retain contact with prewar cultural activists, writers, and actors. In the ghetto of Lodz, it was part of the Jewish Cultural Organization, which included people from the Bund and YIVO. In October, 1940, Chaim Rumkowski, the head of the Lodz ghetto, disbanded the organization.

In August, 1940, the German authorities granted permission to the Jewish Council in Warsaw to conduct vocational training courses, with the proviso that the curriculum be devoted exclusively to technical training. The Commission for Vocational Training, which included representatives of the Jewish Council and Warsaw ORT, was accountable to the Nazi authorities.

By the summer of 1941 this program comprised 24 courses for 832 boys, 24 courses for 818 girls, and 16 courses with a mixed enrollment of 681, a total of 2,331 students. Later there were courses for nurses, with some 250 students working at the Jewish hospital.[5]

Among other programs, ORT supported agricultural training in Poland. Courses in gardening were established by TOPOROL (Polish initials of a prewar Jewish society) and ORT, with 224 full-time and 267 part-time students.[6] This activity was much appreciated in the ghetto, whose inhabitants hoped to create "green corners" to make the district more inviting. Under the severe conditions there was a high incidence of student dropout, most often due to Nazi terror.

ORT efforts were also promoted in many other provincial cities, including Rzeszow, Stanislawow, Grzybow, and Otwock. ORT engineers Chmelnik and Shmigelski, under the supervision of the Jewish Council, arranged for vocational education in the factories of the Bialystok ghetto. In the ghetto of Vilna there was an ORT school for youngsters.[7] ORT also supported farming. About one farming project, in Zarki, we have the testimony of Jaszunski.

The ORT group in Warsaw was liquidated in January, 1943, a few months before the destruction of the ghetto. Jaszunski, a long-time ORT activist and leader, was taken to Treblinka where he perished along with his family.

Elsewhere Under the Nazis

In the summer of 1940, Rumania dissolved its ties with defeated France, placing itself on the side of the conquering Germans. The new pro-Nazi government, invested by the King, made anti-Semitism the keynote of the regime. Mass brutality and outright murder of Jews occurred in areas around Bessarabia, soon to be taken over by Russia. By the fall of 1940, Rumania was occupied by the Germans and a network of Gestapo units was installed.

In December, 1940, the government, having already imposed harsh restrictions on Jewish professionals, decreed that trading certificates issued to Jewish artisans would not be renewed, and cancelled agreements between Jewish masters and Jewish apprentices. In 1941, anti-Jewish pogroms took place in many cities. Several hundred Jews were murdered in the city of Iassy. Forced labor battalions, deportations of Jews to the war-torn Ukraine, and other atrocities followed.

Less than half of the Jewish population of Rumania survived the Catastrophe.

Throughout, ORT organizations, operating under harsh conditions and suffering from lack of funds, strove to bring some measure of relief to the Jews of Rumania. Transfer of funds to Rumania was almost impossible. In 1941, the ORT school in Bucharest was vandalized by Rumanian Nazis. The program had to be transferred to another building. The Bucharest school which taught radio, sewing, and manufacture of lingerie to some 20 students in each field, functioned almost throughout the war—a remarkable example of carrying on against impossible odds.

Other ORT projects were maintained for various periods in Oradea Mare, in Cluj, and in Iassy. Valuable assistance was also given to Jewish artisans and merchants by some 80 loan *kassas* founded by the American Joint Reconstruction Foundation, a subsidiary of JDC.

Sporadic ORT efforts also were maintained in Hungary, which, in 1938, had annexed part of Slovakia and Sub-Carpathia in cooperation with Nazi Germany, contributing to the destruction of Czechoslovakia. Hungary later occupied the rest of Sub-Carpathia, and in 1940 was given northern Transylvania, taken from Rumania. In 1943, although not yet fully committed to Nazi policies, Hungary participated in the German invasion of Russia. In 1944, Hungary itself was occupied by the Germans.

From the beginning of the war, Hungary's Jews had been subjected to restrictions. Then came the deportations to the death camps which affected some 50 per cent of the prewar Hungarian Jewish population.[8]

During these years the recently established ORT organizations conducted small-scale activities in Budapest and a number of provincial cities. In Budapest it had two training schools for boys and girls; from a separate fund it also supplied equipment for tailors and carpenters. For a time it supported seven workshops for young refugees who had escaped from Yugoslavia and Poland, and conducted training programs in Misolc, Ungvar, Sarkad, and other cities.

Lithuania and Latvia faced a direct threat to their independence with the outbreak of the war. Geographic changes were imposed by the Nazi-Soviet pact. The great Jewish center of Vilna was attached to Lithuania, and remained so until the German attack on Russia in June, 1941.

ORT work in both Lithuania and Latvia continued during the short period up to July, 1940. There were ORT training programs in Vilna, Shavli, Vilkoviski, and Kovno (Kaunas) in Lithuania, and in Riga, Libau, and Dvinsk in Latvia, most of them geared to the needs of refugees from Poland. Programs included both trades and agriculture. In January, 1941, ORT institutions in Lithuania and Latvia were nationalized by the Soviets and ceased to exist as independent entities.

The German attack on Russia placed the Jews of the Baltic countries in a trap. Few succeeded in crossing the Russian border despite the fact that, formally, Lithuania and Latvia had by that time been annexed by the Soviet Union. Soviet border police returned Jews attempting to escape, most of whom were murdered by Lithuanian partisans. The Nazis began their rule in the Baltic countries by killing thousands of Jews and putting the rest into ghettoes.

In 1942, Jacob Oleiski, the veteran ORT Lithuanian activist, suggested to the Jewish Council of the Kovno ghetto that it set up a vocational school there. With permission of the authorities the program began in March, 1942. It offered training in locksmithing, dressmaking, and, later, carpentry, with an initial enrollment of 150 youths. In addition, it provided courses in construction for adults. Clandestinely, it taught general subjects.

The Kovno school was closed in August, 1942, but was reopened that November with a roster of 350 students. In early 1944 the ghetto became a concentration camp, and the number of students declined sharply. In July, 1944, the ghetto was liquidated.[9]

ORT-France Under Occupation

That ORT was able to conduct an extensive program in occupied France is explained by the fact that the ORT center remained in France for several years. Brutal as it was, the

Pétain regime, with its *Zone Sud* for a time not occupied by the Nazis, tolerated, to a degree, certain Jewish activities, among them ORT.

From 1940 to 1942 there were ORT facilities in some 20 cities, including Lyons, Toulouse, Marseilles, Nice, and Montpelier. In Paris, at the rue de Saules—formerly a shelter for the homeless—ORT conducted a program for 700 students. The infamous "great action" in July, 1942, when thousands of Jews were rounded up and deported, was reflected in ORT's 1943 enrollment which dropped to 500.

It is hard to believe, but ORT was able to conduct programs in the internment camps in Gurs, Rivesalte, Recebedoux, Brens, and Septfond, where activities involved the internees, at least to some degree, in productive occupations. As of 1942, some 2,240 individuals, including 730 internees, were benefiting from ORT support.

The ORT farm in the Department of Lot-et-Garonne merits particular attention. The project was a small one, involving about 80 families. But it was little short of a miracle that in occupied France it was possible for ORT to continue, until 1943, an effort originally begun as a project for German refugees. P. Minc Alexander, a labor leader later affiliated with the Bund in Paris, has told the story of the ORT farm in La Roche under the occupation. The farm was administered by D. Klementinowski, with the agronomist Osher Malkin, later the head of Mikva Israel in Israel, as technical director. La Roche became an oasis for many Jewish families who for a time found not only a refuge but a warm Jewish atmosphere in which they could even observe the Jewish holidays. Both Bramson and Syngalowski visited La Roche and participated in cultural evenings there.[10]

As deportations became more frequent Jewish refugees from France made their way to Switzerland, creating a substantial community of about 16,000. Because of legal and housing problems, refugees were housed in some 100 camps and internment homes.

Both the Swiss authorities and the Jewish organizations understood that when the war ended these people would not remain in Switzerland. Nevertheless, Swiss ORT saw the value of occupational programs and initiated some 150 vocational projects for young people who could not continue their schooling elsewhere. It burgeoned quickly and by 1944 comprised some 99 workshops, courses for adults, and schools. By the end of 1945 there were some 158 units with 2,023 individuals undergoing vocational training in preparation for eventual resettlement.

Following the Refugees

With the beginning of the war, the ORT school in Leeds, which had received the students and teachers from the school in Berlin, was enlarged as refugee youths from Czechoslovakia, Austria, and Poland added to the ranks of the escapees. Most of the funds for support of the project came from JDC in the United States. In 1942, some of the boys, lacking British citizenship, were interned in Australia.[11]

As the war dragged on, the geography of ORT changed considerably. Following the Jewish refugees, ORT programs, for the first time in the organization's history, went far beyond traditional centers in Europe.

In 1941 it was working in Shanghai, where 17,000 Jews had found temporary refuge from the Holocaust.[12] In 1941, ORT, on the initiative mainly of a group of Russian refugees, organized a vocational school with a student body averaging 150 to 200. The curriculum included bookbinding, fashion, and gardening.

There was much debate among the refugees about the advisability of conducting a school in a Chinese city with a large reservoir of labor. But the ORT people succeeded in convincing those who were opposed to vocational preparation. The school continued its work up to the time that the Jewish community in Shanghai dispersed in 1950.

ORT training programs were introduced during the war in the United States, Canada, and in several countries of South and Central America.

"Dom Sierot",Warszawa,
Krochmalna 92

Pracownia krawiecko-bieliźniarska "Ort'u" została otwarta na terenie
Domu Sierot przy ul.Krochmalnej 92 dn.10 marca 1940 r.Pracownia jest
czynna codziennie,oprócz sobót od 9 - 2,1 raz tygodniowo trój.T-wo
opłaca honorarium instruktorki,zaopatrzyło pracownię w 2 maszyny do
szycia,30 krzeseł i żelazko elektryczne.Dom Sierot oddał na użytek
pracowni 3 okienną,słoneczną salę,5 maszyn do szycia i całkowite
urządzenie.
Obecnie szyje 20 pracownic od lat 14 do 24 /przeciętny wiek 17 lat/.
Przeważnie wychowanki lub byłe wychowanki internatów: Dom Sierot i
Bursa - Krochmalna 92,Dom Sierot z Placu Grzybowskiego 7,Dom "Młodzieży
Twarda 27,dwie chałucki.
Stpień przygotowania:
4 uczęszczały do Ortu na krawiecczyznę od 8 miesięcy do 2 lat,
4 "   "   "   " bieliźniarstwo 8   "   " 2 "
1 absolwentka państw.seminarjum krawieck.w Wilniowcu,
1 roczny kurs konfekcji dziecięcej,
3 pracowały u krawcowych,
1 represzerka przy trykotażach,
1 kamiselciarka,
1 wytwórczyni przy ubiorach wojskowych,
2 terminowały w szwalni Domu Sierot,
2 bez żadnego przygotowania.
W czasie od 10 marca do 20 kwietnia r.b.uszyto na obstalunek dla "Ort'"

Dla "Domu Sierot" : kretonowych sukienek   61 sukienek,
                     spodenek cajgowych   17   "
                     majtek chłopięcych   20 par
                     koszulek   39 "
                                                13

Otrzymane z "Ort'u" pieniądze w sumie 305.- zł.zostały wypłacone pra-
cownicom za pokwitowaniem.Siedem pracownic jada na miejscu obiady,po-
krywając ten wydatek szyciem dla zakładu /obiad oblicza się po 1.- zł/.
Dziewczęta pracują z zapałem i robią postępy.-

                                        Zarządzająca Bursa

                                        /-/ St.Wilczyńska

Warszawa dn.5 maja 1940 r.

A report documenting a phase of ORT programs in Poland under Nazi
occupation.

The Orphanage
Krochmalna No. 92
WARSAW

The ORT workshop for the manufacture of garments and underwear was opened in the orphanage, 92 Krochmalna Street, on 10 March 1940. The workshops are open daily, excepting Saturday, from 9 a.m. to 2 p.m. A cutting course is given once a week. ORT pays the teacher's salary and has supplied two sewing machines, 30 metal chairs and an electric iron. The orphanage has placed at the disposal of the workshop a light three-windowed room, five sewing machines and all the necessary material. At present there are 20 seamstresses, aged from 14 to 24 (the average age is 17). Most of them are from the Krochmalna orphanage; the others are from the orphanage at 7, Gzybowskiego Street and from the youth home at 27, Twarda Street; two of the girls come from Hehalutz.

Vocational standard: 4 attended a dressmaking course from 8 to 24 months at ORT

4 attended an underwear making course from 8 to 24 months at ORT

1 is a graduate of the State seminary at Wizniowiec

1 attended a course for ready-to-wear childrens garments manufacture of 12 months

3 worked in dressmaking salons

1 worked in a knitting shop

1 worked in a shop manufacturing ready-to-wear vests

1 worked in a shop manufacturing military uniforms

1 learned dressing at the orphanage

2 had no vocational training.

During the short period from 1 March to 20 April the following ORT orders for the orphanage were filled: 78 cotton dresses for children, 20 pairs of trousers, 39 pairs of shorts for children and 13 chemisettes.

We have received 305 zlotys from ORT which were paid to the seamstresses against a receipt. Seven seamstresses take their lunch in the workshop and pay for it by their work (1 meal : 1 zloty). The girls work diligently and are making very good progress.

Warsaw, 10 May, 1940   The Director

(—) Stefa Wilszynska

Nr.226.   Warszawa,11.1.1941 r.

P.T.
Prezydium Ż.S.S.
K r a k ó w

Zasiłek dla Fermy Żarki.Tow.Ort uchwaliło wyasygnować dla
fermy rolniczej w Żarkach kwotę zł.2.000 i wysłało w tej
sprawie list według załącznika.Proszę honorować tę uchwa-
łę i wysłać do Żarek wspomnianą kwotę,ewentualnie przez B
legaturę czy też K.O.P.
Fundusz Kształcenia Zawodowego został już wprawdzie wycze
pany,lecz w czasie najbliższym mają nadejść pieniądze na
ten fundusz.Zresztą chodzi tu o stosunkowo drobną kwotę.

Przy tej sposobności proszę wypłacić miesięczny zasiłek
również dla Laciarni w Krakowie i ewentualnie w okolicach
na wniosek p.Dra Hilfsteina.

Majątek Stowarzyszeń.Nawiązując do dzisiejszego listu
Nr.225 o majątku Tow.Ort,proszę wznowić starania o przeka-
zanie Ż.S.S. majątku stowarzyszeń będących w likwidacji.
Sprawa ta staje się coraz bardziej aktualną.

                        Z poważaniem

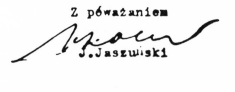
                        J.Jaszuński

                    ┌─────────────────
                    │ Wysłania data
                    │   12396

The photocopy of a letter written on 11 October 1941 by J. Jaszunski, member of the "Judenrat" and ORT director, to the Office of Jewish Social Mutual Aid in Cracow, which refers to ORT's agricultural work. In translation it reads:

Warsaw, 11 October 1941.

To the Office of Jewish Social Mutual Aid
CRACOW

Subvention for the Zarki farm

The ORT organization has decided to grant 2000 slotys to the Zarki farm; a copy of a letter advising the farm of this decision is attached herewith. Kindly carry out this decision and send this sum to Zarki, either by hand or by post. The funds earmarked for vocational training have already been exhausted, but new, though limited, funds should be soon coming in. I take this opportunity to request you to pay the monthly subvention to the garment menders in Cracow and its suburbs in accordance with Dr. Hilfstein's proposal.

With reference to my letter No. 225 of today concerning ORT property I request you to take further steps to transfer the property of societies in liquidation to the Jewish Social Mutual Aid. This matter becomes increasingly urgent.

Respectfully yours,
(signed) J. Jaszunski

»O R T«
GESELLSCHAFT ZUR FÖRDERUNG DES HANDWERKS UND DER LANDWIRTSCHAFT
UNTER DEN JUDEN
ABTEILUNG DEUTSCHLAND E. V.

FERNRUF: 44 51 39

TELEGRAMM-ADRESSE
„FÖRDERORT BERLIN"

POSTSCHECK BERLIN NR. 11029

BERLIN N 58, DEN 17. April 1941
SCHÖNHAUSER ALLEE 53

Z E U G N I S !
============================

Herr Dr. Arthur Israel F e i g e war vom 1.Mai 1937 bis
zum heutigen Tage als Lehrer für den theoretischen Unter-
richt an unserer
"Privaten Jüdischen Lehranstalt für handwerkliche
und gewerbliche Ausbildung auswanderungswilliger
Juden des " O R T " in Berlin"
vornehmlich in den Fächern: " Rechnen, Physik, Elektro-
technik und Zeichnen" tätig. Ausserdem war er lange Zeit
mit der laufenden Vertretung des Schulleiters beauftragt
und hat ferner bis zu deren offiziellen Beendigung die
"Elektrotechnische Abteilung" als deren Leiter betreut.
In dieser Eigenschaft war er der Schulleitung für die
Ausbildung von Elektrotechnikern verantwortlich.

Herr Dr.Feige hat sich als ein bedeutender, hochqualifi-
zierter Fachmann erwiesen und hat aus seinem reichen Fach-
wissen den ihm anvertrauten Schülern eine ausgezeichnete
Ausbildung vermittelt. Er hat seine Aufgaben mit pädagogi-
schem Talent gelöst, sich immer für seine Schüler mit ka-
meradschaftlichem Verständnis eingesetzt und sich bei den-
selben besonderer Beliebtheit erfreut.

Die vielseitige Einsatzmöglichkeit, die umsichtige Führung
der Arbeit und das stets hilfsbereite Wesen von Herrn
Dr.Feige haben so auch für eine ausgezeichnete Förderung
des "ORT"-Gedankens gewirkt. Ihm ist der erreichte Erfolg
der allgemein als ausgezeichnet anerkannten Ausbildung
mit zu danken.

Wir können Herrn Dr.Feige daher nur auf das Beste empfeh-
len. Wir bedauern sein infolge Eingliederung des Gesellschaft "ORT" in die"Reichsvereinigung der Juden in Deutsch
land" erfolgendes Ausscheiden.-

GESELLSCHAFT " O R T "
ABT.DEUTSCHLAND E.V.

Vorsitzender   Geschäftsführer

Heinrich Israel Michelsohn   Werner Israel Simon

In Berlin under the Nazis—certificate issued by the Berlin ORT to a
teacher, April 17, 1941, testifying to his competence.

France under Nazi occupation, 1942: the ORT farm in La Roche. D. Klementinowski is at left, next to Dr. A. Syngalowski, and agronomist Osher Malkin, with students.

Dress design and production in Perigueux, France, 1942, under occupation.

Struggle for Survival

During the war and the Catastrophe each ORT organization was on its own. There was little possibility of communication with areas under Nazi occupation, and even less with the Jewish populations enclosed in the ghettoes. For the second time in its history ORT experienced a World War condition in which it had to fight for survival. During the 1914-18 war, activities had been limited to the Russian Empire; during the Second World War they were spread across the globe. The World ORT Union center in Marseilles used every possible means to establish contact with and transmit funds to ORT organizations in Eastern Europe. With the United States joining the war in December, 1941, this was difficult, if not impossible.

Bramson, who had been ill for some time, died in Marseilles on March 2, 1941. Syngalowski and Lvovich, the latter then in the United States, assumed leadership of the ORT Union as co-chairmen. While under the circumstances this step appeared to serve objective needs as well as to satisfy personal ambitions, it did not turn out to be a good solution. By this time the two old friends and political comrades had become estranged and no longer saw eye-to-eye even on current ORT problems.

After the Allied invasion of North Africa, the unoccupied zone in France was taken over by the Germans. Anti-Jewish actions now made the Jewish situation throughout France utterly intolerable. Arrests and deportations were a daily occurrence. Not even a skeleton ORT staff could be maintained in France.

Syngalowski escaped to Switzerland in 1943 and transferred the ORT Union office to that neutral country. From there he tried to renew contacts with people in various countries while at the same time intensifying his efforts on behalf of Jewish refugees in Switzerland. He was aided in this by a group of local communal leaders, among them Armand Brunschwig, P. Dreyfus de Gunzbourg, Prof. Liebman Hersch, and Dr. E. Heymann.

Lvovich, in the United States, had for some time been trying to devise an institutional form for a working ORT group which could maintain the continuity of a central ORT apparatus until the end of hostilities and the liberation of Europe. He was not alone in his concern for the future of ORT. A number of ORT leaders who had come to the United States from European countries supported him. Ten of the 40 members of the ORT Central Board, and three of the 11 members of the Executive Committee, were then in the United States. It was understood that there was no way an ORT Center could function under the Nazis, and it was expected that Syngalowski would shortly join the New York group.

In the spring of 1942, Lvovich and a group of ORT leaders, including George Backer, Pierre de Guinsbourg, Louis B. Boudin, Alexander Halpern, Alexander Dolowitz, William Kleeman, Jacob Frumkin, Mendel Sudarsky, Solomon Frankfurt, and Murray Levine, established an Emergency ORT Committee for World ORT Affairs in New York, composed of "all members of the Central Board of the World ORT Union who are in or may come to this country."

George Backer was elected chairman. Lvovich participated *ex officio* in deliberations on all actions to be undertaken by the group. Much discussion ensued as to the character of the new ORT body and its designation as a "Committee for World ORT Affairs." Baron de Guinsbourg believed that no formal organization should be created in New York and that the New York group should limit itself to advisory functions. Dr. Sudarsky, on the other hand, argued that the Committee "should constitute itself the Central Committee [of ORT] in exile."

This radical proposal was in keeping with the prevailing pessimism about the future of Europe and the duration of the war. If adopted, it would certainly have opened a jurisdictional dispute with the ORT Center in Europe, wherever it was and whoever was at the helm. The proposal was rejected in favor of a more limited definition of the future tasks of the new body, which was, essentially, a caretaker entity for ORT activity outside the war areas. Nevertheless, with the continuing occupation of Europe, the Emergency Committee considered itself to a large degree *in locum tenens* of the legitimate ORT organ that might or might not be able to function in Europe.[13]

The decision to establish an Emergency Committee in New York, although fully justified by circumstances, was to create an additional cause of conflict within ORT. But this was to come later; for the time being, the jurisdiction of the Emergency Committee expanded. It represented ORT, it was in contact with the major Jewish organizations, and it received funds from campaigns conducted in the United States, Canada, Latin America, and, later, from specialized relief agencies.

The Emergency Committee was active in organizing and financing programs in Latin America, and ORT schools in, among other places, São Paulo and Havana. It initiated programs in Chile, Uruguay, Bolivia, and Canada. It was in contact with *Alliance Israelite Universelle*[14] in connection with a project for the establishment of vocational schools in Morocco and India. It even devoted itself to postwar planning.

Minutes of the Emergency Committee reveal that it considered itself competent to deal with problems involving fundamental policy. There were those who hoped that the end of the war would bring political changes in Russia. Lvovich, in fact, was working on a plan to revive ORT work there. In the spring of 1945, Louis Boudin was appointed chairman of a committee "to investigate and arrange for resumption of activity in Russia."[15] Naive on the face of it, this prospect was very much in the spirit of expectations entertained in some circles.

Syngalowski did not come to the United States. After his arrival in Switzerland in 1943 he requested transmission of funds from New York for ORT programs, but otherwise evinced no interest in the Emergency Committee. For him, ORT was a European organization, and supportive efforts undertaken overseas were welcome only to the extent they did not overstep their bounds, and did not engage in what he considered "interference from outside."

At War's End

These various attempts to assure ORT's survival resulted, when war ended in 1945, in three distinct ORT centers: one, headed by Syngalowski in Geneva; the second, under Lvovich, in New York; and the third, the de facto center in Paris, to which many members of the ORT administration and Executive Committee, appointed before the war by the Central Board, came after the liberation. It was not exactly the most efficient arrangement from which to begin the arduous climb toward renewal.

It was precisely at this time, when the end of the war had opened up broad vistas of activity, that there arose among the leaders of ORT a divergence of views as to the structure of the organization and its future, aggravated by a clash of personalities.

After the war, and perhaps already during the occupation, an open feud broke out between those two old comrades and coworkers, Syngalowski and Lvovich. Syngalowski resented Lvovich's role in the ORT Emergency Committee in New York, which, according to him, was "American" and "assumed authority" which it did not possess. A great deal of persuasion on all sides of the conflict, and perhaps some luck, was needed to arrive at a situation in which all parties could work together.

In the fall of 1945, Lvovich returned to Europe to discuss with the ORT leadership there the general ORT situation and the complex relationship between the separate ORT centers. The Emergency Committee had now been functioning for several years, and some of its members doubtless felt that the time had come to formalize the status of the New York Committee and perhaps make it the center of ORT, based on the claim that administration of ORT funds could be better managed from New York.

This attitude expressed the prevailing mood of the American Jewish community of the time. Many Jewish social workers who had served abroad were critical of the "inefficient" management of Jewish communal work in Europe. From their standpoint, Jewish agencies providing services to refugees and displaced persons in Europe needed to be modernized, and this could best be done by qualified American workers.

Needs in Europe were indeed mounting. Budgets of Jewish organizations working overseas reached unprecedented heights, and the American Jewish community, in an effort to increase income and cut overhead, was bent on amalgamating service agencies and fund-raising campaigns. Leaders from the industrial and financial world called for the introduction of business methods in the administration and distribution of public funds. A large part of ORT funds came from the United States where JDC was in the forefront of efforts to introduce "efficiency" to Jewish social welfare abroad. It was only natural that these considerations should influence the attitude of the Emergency Committee.

Lvovich's trip to Europe was thoroughly debated. Boudin prepared a memorandum for Lvovich's discussions in Europe. In it he put forward the idea, though not in so many words, that ORT would be better off with greater American input in its management. However indirect on this point, his memorandum was precise with respect to the areas that the Emergency Committee wished, for the time being, to reserve to itself: "Jurisdiction of the Emergency Committee during the interim [before a final decision of a convention or conference to be held that summer] includes the Western Hemisphere, the British Empire, Germany, Austria, Italy, the liberated countries of Western Europe, North Africa, Egypt, and Palestine, with the understanding that if France prefers to work under the supervision of Switzerland, it may do so; also, that if North Africa prefers to work under the supervision of France, it may do so. The liberated countries of Eastern Europe are to be supervised from Switzerland."

He had always emphasized that "the financial center during this interim period is to be in New York City," and "all financial reports [are to] come here directly."[16] Boudin's insistence on financial reporting to New York inevitably led to a misunderstanding between the Emergency Committee and ORT in Europe. While Boudin and his colleagues talked about temporary arrangements, everyone knew that "temporary" often has a long duration.

Boudin's proposals, couched in dry, legal language, whatever their rationale, were received as an unfriendly act by most of the leadership in Europe, and especially by Syngalowski. While appreciating the role played by the ORT group in the United States, the European leadership could not accept the principles underlying Boudin's proposals. In their view, these proposals put the character and direction of ORT at risk, divorcing its beneficiaries from their organization in Europe, with the further hazard of converting ORT into a charitable agency, American style, and possibly under American control. It was a serious confrontation involving basic perceptions, in a situation where a rational discussion was not always possible quite aside from differences in point of view.

ORT now faced not only the staggering task of rehabilitating survivors but also the problem of unifying its leadership and putting its house in order. The latter was doubly important since a new idea had been born among JDC people in the United States, a plan to assume overall guidance of reconstruction efforts in liberated Europe. ORT, to put it plainly, had to be on guard.

The importance of ORT programs was universally recognized, but there were those who believed that its work could be done more efficiently and at less cost by other hands.

The First Postwar Conference and Its Aftermath

In this atmosphere, further complicating a difficult situation, "peace" between the factions and individuals involved was not achieved swiftly. The ORT Conference, held in Paris in the summer of 1946, accepted elements of the so-called American Plan after much discussion and bickering. The American delegates at first argued that ORT headquarters should be established in Paris, where there would be a major Jewish community. In the end, all participants agreed that the Geneva offices could not be liquidated immediately.

Center of the World ORT Union since 1943, Geneva was not only the site of many international organizations, general and Jewish, it was also a city where Syngalowski had developed intensive activities and generated important support from its Jewish communities, and from the Swiss authorities as well. Besides, Syngalowski refused to move to Paris where, in 1946, conditions were, in fact, unsuitable for the efficient functioning of ORT. It was later decided to establish one headquarters in Geneva under Syngalowski, and another in Paris, under Lvovich, the Paris unit to be a "political and public relations" center.

The "American Plan," however, contained another demand, already mentioned in the memorandum prepared by Boudin for Lvovich's discussions in Europe, to wit, the establishment of a financial and accounting office in New York as the overall financial control center.

The idea of a financial center in New York, highly distasteful to the Europeans, had a history of its own. In 1943 the Council of Jewish Federations and Welfare Funds, a national agency located in New York, through its Budget Research Committee, had engaged Prof. Mark Wischnitzer to make a study of ORT budgeting, accounting, and reporting procedures with regard to funds distributed overseas. Wischnitzer's study was conducted while the war was still in progress and much of the material on ORT activities in Europe was not readily available. Wischnitzer was, of course, aware of the limitations of his study, particularly with respect to individual ORT projects such as schools and training units. He felt, nevertheless, that the data collected would be useful to the Council of Jewish Federations in assessing its allocations to beneficiary agencies.

Whatever the Council's reaction to the report, the general

impression was that it was critical of ORT, particularly of its administrative procedures and statistical and financial reporting. In 1946, Boudin, Murray Levine, and others cited the Wischnitzer study as justifying their recommendation to establish an ORT financial office in New York.

Without detailing the situation as it developed after the 1946 decision, there was now an added element of dissension. In addition to the conflict between Syngalowski and Lvovich there arose a dispute between the American delegates, led by Boudin, and the ORT co-chairmen, Syngalowski and Lvovich. Syngalowski, in particular, resented the tone of the demands made by the Americans. Boudin had obviously come to believe that both Syngalowski and Lvovich, whatever their past achievements, were at this stage a hindrance to ORT development.

In two reports,[17] one to the ORT Central Board and the other to American ORT, Boudin indicated his negative opinion of both old ORT leaders. "Knowing Lvovich as we do, it was inconceivable that we should turn over the operations of ORT to his management," Boudin wrote. As for Syngalowski, ". . . he has become even more brazen in the statement of falsehoods" which, according to Boudin, Syngalowski had been making all along.

Boudin stated that ". . . it [was] clear that neither the members of this group nor the American ORT Federation can keep on sending money to our managers [read Syngalowski and Lvovich] without making themselves privy to the irresponsible and unscrupulous use of the funds. Also it is clear that we cannot put funds at the disposal of our managers without inviting public scandal of the worst sort." Further, Boudin noted, "The utter callousness with which ORT money is wasted by those who try to impose 'economies' on others is shocking; and its seriousness is only exceeded by their sabotage when it suits their political purposes."

Boudin cited cases of bad administrative judgment, lack of attention to administrative detail, questionable statistics, and the like—in short, what he considered mismanagement.

Boudin was obviously determined to present valid information to the American Jewish community engaged in fund-raising and, good lawyer that he was, he detailed all the shortcomings of European ORT with great force and logic, pulling no punches in his language.

It was a sorry situation, and more or less a one-sided affair. *Audiatur et altera pars*—but Syngalowski, although he replied in letters and cablegrams, did not feel obligated to engage in protracted polemics with Boudin. He did not, as Boudin knew, "recognize" the existence of any authority other than Geneva's, of which he was the legitimate head.

As we look back at this confrontation, it becomes clear that, at bottom, the dispute was a question of who was to control the re-established ORT. It is equally clear that the personality of the principals was a significant factor.

To view the conflict in perspective one must take into account that it erupted after several years of war and occupation in Europe. During the war, the Nazi occupation, and the DP years immediately following the cessation of the war, it had been impossible to conduct ORT work in a "business-as-usual" manner. Currency difficulties aggravated the problems. Little communication with local communities or groups had been possible, and ORT activities had been essentially clandestine.

From time to time the ORT center had been able to transfer funds to beneficiaries, but it had not always been possible properly to account with exactitude intricate transactions involving confidential and often risky arrangements. Like all other Jewish organizations, local if they existed and American if they were there, ORT in Europe had to work under prevailing conditions. The emphasis had been on rendering assistance and not the kind of record-keeping, however important and legitimate, required by organizations engaged in fund-raising in the United States.

As the war and occupation came to an end, ORT leaders in Geneva and Paris had had to think about activating programs among DPs in Germany, Austria, and Italy, and the

Jewish survivors of the camps. Precise administrative procedures sometimes succumbed to the exigencies of trial and error. Perhaps there were other ways of handling the different situations, but as the needs presented themselves to the individuals responsible for physically saving the survivors, there had been no time to choose, and assistance had sometimes been given without taking the preliminary steps that would ordinarily have been taken.

Nonetheless, the question of proper reporting forms became a continuing dispute between Geneva and New York. Methods, not substance, were at issue. Below the surface it was a struggle for control.

In 1947, following the 1946 decision, the ORT Union established a financial and accounting office in New York. There was some uncertainty about the functions of this office. The Americans understood that the office would control all financial transactions. But Lvovich, in a letter to Boudin dated May 13, 1947, referred to it as an information center for the American Jewish public. Louis J. Walinsky, who during the war had worked in Washington and was later in charge of ORT work among DPs in Germany and Austria, was engaged as director. (ORT work among DPs was the subject matter of another dispute dividing Boudin and the Europeans—see Chapter XIII.)

According to Boudin, efforts to bring order and regular procedures into the administrative apparatus of the ORT Union met with "stubborn resistance of a few persons who found themselves in control of the ORT operational machinery."[18] Among other things, Boudin made an issue of the financial and statistical forms prepared by Walinsky.

The need for regular reporting was also emphasized by Aaron B. Tart and Edward L. Sard, successive executive directors of the American ORT Federation. According to Boudin, ORT's managers in Geneva and Paris did not cooperate in the introduction of this administrative reform, although adequate reporting was a prerequisite of successful fund-raising.

An Episode of Transition

This wrangle might have had a readier solution had this legitimate request and Boudin's other suggestions been presented in a more acceptable way. Alexander Halpern, a leader of British ORT, and himself a critic of the Syngalowski administration, nevertheless wrote Boudin: "You have invented a bogey of 'irresponsible and unscrupulous managers' [who] deliberately intend to sabotage the entire American program." And, "I may not agree . . . with quite a lot of what has been done either in Geneva or in Paris, but I am unable to accept the method which you have chosen to remedy these deficiencies."

Eastern Europe was still in upheaval. Germany was a "cigarette economy," where one could buy anything or, so to speak, anybody, with so many Chesterfields or Lucky Strikes, and many Europeans felt that this situation had not always been taken into account by American critics.

There is no question but that the personalities of the individuals in the conflict played a significant role. Boudin, the cold, brilliant lawyer, an American Socialist militant accustomed to political fighting and infighting, was an immensely stubborn and arrogant man who took small account of mitigating circumstances. Syngalowski, essentially a man of letters, not much of an administrator, was self-centered, not always sure of the meaning of rules and regulations, and jealous of his prerogatives and role in ORT. By now he had come to view ORT, if not as his creation, somehow as his exclusive preserve. His administration could stand improvement, but the impetus could not come from the "outside."

Both men, it need hardly be said, were dedicated to ORT, each convinced of his position. There was no petty ill will in either of them. They brought to their conflicting positions different backgrounds and, indeed, different cultures. The conflict was non-ideological, but it went deep, breaking up some old friendships.

The actors in this drama of transition from ORT-at-war to ORT-in-peace are now gone. Looking back, past the intensity of time and emotion, the episode reduced itself to just that—an episode in the revival of post-Holocaust ORT, the last pangs in the birth of a new postwar ORT. [19]

Chapter XII

The American Anchor

ORT was organized in the United States in response to an appeal made by Bramson and Syngalowski, who came to New York in 1922 as delegates of the recently established World ORT Union. Russian ORT, as indicated earlier, had made contact with the United States both before and during World War I. That this initiative was the beginning of a development that would to a large degree determine the destiny of ORT was beyond their perception at the time.

American Jewry contributed generously to ORT finances. But its role in the evolution of the organization involved more than financial support. Indeed, in the post-World War II world it provided the very foundation for the continuity and development of World ORT. To understand the significance of American ORT one must bear in mind the profound changes that had taken place in Jewish life after millions of Russian Jews had been isolated behind the Iron Curtain by the Soviets. The catastrophe of the 1940's brought to an end the centuries-old hegemony of the Russian-Polish Jewish center in Jewish life. There has been a historical symmetry in Jewish life, with the youngest large Jewish community of the Diaspora becoming the new social, religious, and cultural center of Jewish life.

The Jewish historian Simon Dubnow, in his classic work, envisaged the grave responsibilities of the Jewish community in the United States and the voluntary efforts of various Jewish groups there. He anticipated a new world Jewish center in the Western Hemisphere that would replace the defunct Jewish center in Russia. He predicted that American Jewry would establish a close relationship with Palestine (Israel), and this, in his words, would be "a blessing for the people as a whole."[1]

In fact, the American community has had a special distinction. It has become the focus of attraction for other Jewish communities. More than that, and unlike the earlier center in Russia and Poland, it has become a community wielding substantial influence in American life in general.

A parallel judgment applies to American ORT. For not only has ORT in the United States become a substantial local institution, it has been transformed by history, as it were, into a directing force. In partnership with ORT organizations in many countries of Europe, Africa, South America, Canada, and with Israel since its birth, American ORT has maintained and stimulated the programs of the World ORT Union. In the very nature of things it made a particularly significant contribution when Europe and European Jewry were enduring the critical war years and their aftermath.

Early Roots

ORT in the United States was formally established on June 22, 1922, at a meeting in the headquarters of HIAS of representatives of *landsmanschaft* societies, labor unions, and the Workmen's Circle.

On his arrival in New York, Bramson had contacted Herbert H. Lehman, then chairman of the JDC Reconstruction Committee. Nevertheless, both he and Syngalowski made their major appeal, everywhere they went, to Jewish fraternal and labor groups, who represented the mass of Yiddish-speaking immigrants, whose relatives and friends were, in large measure, still in Europe.

It was a time when the Jewish immigrants were going through the difficult process of Americanization. For a long time they continued to see themselves as part of that European Jewish community from which they had escaped. On the American Jewish scene, ORT's natural allies were the groups centered around the People's Relief Committee, one of the three constituent agencies of the Jewish Joint Distribution Committee.[2]

The first ORT president in the United States was Jacob Panken, later a Municipal Court judge and still later a judge of the Domestic Relations Court. A lifelong Socialist, he had represented the Socialist Party at the Congress of the Second International. He was active in every field of Jewish labor— the International Ladies Garment Workers Union, the Amalgamated Clothing Workers of America, the Workmen's Circle, and the Jewish *Daily Forward*.

Among those attracted to ORT then were such men as the Socialist writer and lawyer Louis B. Boudin, and the Poale-Zion militant and journalist Baruch Zuckerman. The most important member of the early group was Baruch Charney-Vladeck, a Socialist militant and writer who, during the days of the 1905 revolution in Russia, was known as the "Yiddish Lassalle." A Russian-Jewish revolutionary activist and a brilliant Bundist orator, Vladeck was known to both Bramson and Syngalowski from his Minsk days. Vladek was to shape the first decade of ORT on the American scene and to leave his mark upon it for years to come.

In April, 1923, following an ORT campaign throughout the United States, a national ORT conference was convened at which ORT merged with the People's Relief Committee, creating the People's Relief ORT in America. Although the new ORT organization was clearly a part of the democratic labor movement, it nevertheless successfully appealed to all groups of the Jewish community—labor, industry, and intellectuals. This approach, followed by Bramson and Syngalowski in full agreement with the American leadership, was to prove highly significant for the path ORT was to take. From November, 1914 on, the American Jewish community had responded in a unified way, through JDC, to the plight of their Jewish brothers during World War I.[3] The broad appeal of ORT fit neatly into this pattern.

Ups and Downs of the 20's

The drive launched by People's Relief ORT in 1923 was not successful. As a consequence, the organization was dissolved in 1924. During the same year, however, at a conference of some 130 Jewish organizations, unions, and Workmen's Circle branches arranged by a provisional ORT committee, a new American ORT was created which considered itself a continuation of the original 1922 initiative.[4]

Soon after its creation, American ORT launched an ORT Reconstruction Fund (see Chapter VII). The campaign was supported by American Jews from the world of business and finance—Adolph Lewisohn, Nathan Straus, Paul Baerwald, David Sarnoff, Julius Rosenwald, Paul Felix Warburg, Howard S. Cullman, James H. Becker of Chicago, and Morris Wolf of Philadelphia; also, Dr. Cyrus Adler, Jacob Billikopf, and Joseph M. Proskauer.

Henry Moskowitz served as liaison with the largely assimilated upper-class Jews, while Vladeck, Panken, Boudin, and Adolf Held represented labor. The campaign was successful, bringing in some $300,000. More important, ORT was able to conclude a three-year agreement with JDC, freeing itself, for that period of time, of the need to conduct independent campaigns.

ORT work in the United States was conducted in cooperation with Bramson and Syngalowski, both of whom had returned to the United States in 1923. In 1924, Syngalowski left for Berlin. He was replaced by Lvovich who, with Bramson, remained in the United States until mid-1925.

Tool Campaign and Landsmanschaften

At the same time, Jewish labor groups began the People's Tool Campaign, headed by Vladeck and participated in by

Held, Nathan Chanin, and Joseph Baskin. Known in the Yiddish milieu as the *Gezeig* (in Yiddish, instruments, machines) campaign, this was probably one of the most imaginative initiatives undertaken in the name of ORT.

Later, the ORT Tool Supply Corporation (see Chap. VII), which for years had been procuring equipment for Jewish artisans, became the channel through which relatives, friends, and *landsmanschaft* societies were able to send equipment to designated artisans in Soviet Russia, Poland, and elsewhere.

The interested party in the United States—individual, family, or society—paid the cost of a specific item, which was then sent to an individual in Eastern Europe. The *Gezeig* idea of providing the instruments of work was a dignified and meaningful way of assisting artisans, quite different from charity. This work, which involved a great deal of technical know-how, was conducted in cooperation with ORT services in Berlin, and was well understood by the Jewish masses.

According to Alexander Dolowitz, a leading ORT activist, more than 10,000 applications for *Gezeig* from relatives in the United States were received and acted upon between 1928 and 1931. The applications came from 480 cities "from the Atlantic to the Pacific."[5]

For American Jews, the situation of their brothers in Eastern Europe was always of immediate concern, and American ORT leaders frequently visited the "old home." In the 1930's there were visits by Held, Boudin, Vladeck, and others to the USSR to observe ORT work there and to learn something about the Birobidzhan project. They were impressed mainly by the profound deprivation still widespread in Soviet Russia.

The success of the People's Tool Campaign led to its merger in 1932 with American ORT, under a new name, People's ORT Federation. It was an important event because it submerged a conflict that in one way or another has persisted between the *Forward* group (associated with the Jewish Socialist daily newspaper, *The Forward*) and those opposed to the *Forward* line. Though Panken was very much a *For-*

ward man, he brought the opposing sides together. In 1936 the name was changed to American ORT Federation.

The JDC Connection

During the next ten years, ORT either benefited from JDC grants or conducted independent drives in which it made direct requests to welfare funds in Jewish communities. There were many problems involved in the fund-raising efforts of Jewish groups competing for a share of what was collected. Separate fund-raising by ORT was strongly discouraged by JDC. It is difficult to get at the root of the ambivalent relationship between JDC and ORT in those days. JDC contributed significant subventions to ORT though it did not look with favor on the repeated visits of ORT leaders from Europe whose appeals could not but affect JDC's own campaigns.

In any event, it appears that in March, 1938, JDC, in material prepared for public release, pointed out that during the preceding year its contributions to ORT had represented 67 per cent of the latter's budget, and that separate ORT fund-raising efforts were therefore not necessary. The material, however, was not released.[6]

From 1938 through 1946 ORT received its allocations from local Jewish Federation and Welfare Funds and refrained from making independent public appeals except in Chicago and in New York, where Max D. Steuer, Edgar Salinger, Judge Edgar J. Nathan, Jr., Lazarus Joseph, and David Roisenstein actively participated in the ORT campaign. It was not until 1947, after the war and under pressure of the massive needs in liberated Europe, that ORT entered into an agreement with JDC whereby a minimum of $2,000,000 in the year 1947 was provided by JDC for World ORT programs.[7]

This agreement has been renewed annually. In the late 1970s, allocations were between $3,000,000 and $3,500,000. From 1947 to 1979, grants to ORT have totaled $70,000,000.

Not everyone in ORT circles has been happy about this arrangement. Some have pointed out that under the agreement ORT accepted a subordinate status. It would serve no useful purpose to speculate on what the alternatives might have been had ORT terminated its contract with JDC. More to the point, the ORT-JDC agreement has reflected the post-war mood and trends in the American Jewish community.

The '47 Pact

The 1947 contract, signed by George Backer, then American ORT president, and Moses A. Leavitt, then executive vice-president of JDC, stipulated that "the parties deem it in the public interest that public fund-raising within the United States be unified as far as practicable," and that "the work of the World ORT Union . . . should be coordinated with the vocational overall program of JDC in Europe, and that so much of JDC's program as involves direct vocational training should be turned over to World ORT Union."

In turn, ORT and its affiliates undertook an obligation to "refrain from any public fund-raising in the United States," but reserved the right to "continue [their] membership, organizational and educational activities." While JDC vocational programs were turned over to ORT, ORT assumed the obligation to "consult with Dr. Joseph J. Schwartz [JDC European head] on the overall programs and budget of ORT, and for this purpose will make available to Dr. Schwartz full information concerning the world budget of ORT."

The agreement also stipulated that "all new or enlarged programs should be discussed, in the first instance, with the respective JDC country director involved, and, thereafter, if necessary, with Dr. Schwartz and a mutual understanding arrived at."

To understand the background of this agreement it must be borne in mind that it was concluded during a period when JDC contributions, as well as funds collected in the United

States, represented over 80 per cent of World ORT income. The balance came from South African Jewish communities. Moreover, the American Jewish community was then in the process of coordinating its various service activities domestically. The JDC was simultaneously expanding its efforts to cover all areas of social services abroad, creating a Medical Department (World OSE Union notwithstanding) and a Reconstruction Department whose activities overlapped the work of ORT. Within this context, the '47 pact was a compromise. While ORT agreed to refrain from independent fund-raising, JDC was forced to recognize ORT's special purpose and refrain from unnecessary duplication of services. The time was right for delineating the differing spheres of responsibility, helping to remove the considerable confusion that existed as to who was doing what for the Jews of Europe.

Having accepted a compromise on the division of services, JDC nevertheless won the right to control American ORT activities and, more important, the ORT budget. As time went on, the positions and attitudes of the two organizations underwent changes. Perceptions concerning past differences were altered. New tasks arose for the two contracting parties, and a mutually satisfactory relationship replaced old, and now forgotten, recriminations.

But this came later. In the late 1940's, many ORT people, among them Syngalowski and his immediate coworkers, did not look kindly on what they considered an "unjustified interference" in ORT affairs.

Schools for Refugees

At the beginning, ORT efforts in the United States were intended to be supportive of ORT programs in Eastern Europe, and eventually wherever ORT spread its activities. After the Nazi invasion of Europe and the resulting stream of refugees arriving on American shores, American ORT took on additional responsibilities in 1940. Through the efforts of

Bramson ORT Training Center in garment trades for new arrivals, established in New York in 1942.

Bramson Division of Technology, Electronics Laboratory, established in New York City in 1977.

Shelley Appleton shown at inauguration of the Bramson ORT
Training Center, Division of Technology, in New York City,
September 6, 1977.

the American and European Friends of ORT, an ORT school was established in New York for the training of refugees from Europe in technical crafts. In 1957 it was transferred to Israel, where it bears the name of the old ORT activist from Russia and France, Abraham C. Litton.

A second ORT school, initially sponsored by European Women's ORT chapter, the Leon Bramson (later Leon and Vera Bramson) School was opened in New York in 1942 for training in needle trades. In 1942, American ORT also conducted eight training workshops in the Fort Ontario (Oswego, New York) camp established for some 900 refugees brought from Italy. Later, during the years of large influx of DPs, the ORT schools operated in three shifts daily.[9]

Thus, during the years of the war and its aftermath, the United States was put on the ORT operational map in addition to preserving, indeed substantially increasing, its supportive role. It was not until 1977, 55 years after ORT's founding in the U.S., that an ORT school was established for American Jews, thanks to the vision of Women's American ORT.

The Federation Concept

American ORT developed along the lines of a multi-group federation. Mention should be made of some ORT groups that have played, and continue to play, a significant role in ORT activities in the United States. Among these the earliest was Labor ORT, which began its activities in the 1920's; in 1938, it became the American Labor ORT division of the American ORT Federation. This was accomplished under the leadership of Vladeck, who passed away during the same year. Adolf Held and Mrs. David Dubinsky were active in this work.

Some 100 unions participated in ORT appeals. Among them were the International Ladies Garment Workers Union, the Amalgamated Clothing Workers of America, the Furriers Union, the International Leather Goods Union, the

Plastics and Novelty Union, the United Hatters, Cap and Millinery Workers International Union, the Retail, Wholesale and Department Stores Union, the Bakers Union, the Restaurant Workers Union—all embracing large Jewish memberships.

The Jewish labor movement has remained a basic element in ORT activities. Labor was active during the Second World War and in reconstruction work after the war. David Dubinsky, Sidney Hillman, and Jacob S. Potofsky enthusiastically supported various ORT projects. Dubinsky not only helped to obtain substantial union contributions, but for years participated personally. Since 1941, Samuel Milman, the ORT veteran from Poland, has been in charge of Labor ORT.

Women's American ORT

Women's American ORT was destined to become not only the largest ORT organization anywhere but to play a major educational and social role in the American community as well as in ORT. This organization established ORT as the major factor in solidifying ORT ideas in the American Jewish community.

Founded in 1927 under the leadership of a group including Anna Boudin, Mrs. Alexander Dolowitz, Mrs. Jacob Panken and, later, Ray Harris, Naomi Finkelstein, Gertrude Kaphan, and Jeanette C. Gayl, by the 1970's it had a dues-paying membership of more than 135,000, organized in 1140 chapters across the country.

WAO's financial support of various ORT programs—school buildings, training, scholarships—has grown substantially over the years, rivaling JDC support. By 1979, WAO's contributions to the World ORT Union over the postwar years totaled $42,000,000. In recent years, Women's American ORT has, in effect, redefined its purpose and strategies from what they had been by intensifying its participation in a broad spectrum of Jewish and non-Jewish communal activities, notably on matters of career education and the fight against anti-Semitism. As a mass organization, another aspect of WAO deserves particular attention. WAO alone among ORT groups has sought for the deeper meaning of ORT. Nathan Gould, in his writings in the name of WAO, has returned to the idea of ORT as a movement responding to Jewish social needs and asserting its Jewish identification. Discussion of this question will come later, but it should be noted here that the ideological examination of the meaning of ORT has, so to speak, been reopened. With the American Jewish community now the center of Jewish life in the Diaspora, ORT in America has taken up the search for a definition begun decades ago in Europe.

With regard to the place of WAO in ORT and American Jewish life, a significant achievement of WAO has been its success in identifying with upcoming Jewish American generations. It has been responsive to their aspirations, with respect to specific Jewish interests and issues that concern American society more generally.

In the late 1940's, the American ORT Federation instituted a membership system that, by the 1960s, had become a considerable factor in maintaining the democratic character of the organization. Among others, Joseph S. Spivack of Cleveland, Harry H. Platt of Detroit, and Chaim Miller, Jacques Zwibak, Victor Plavin, and Morris Olshina of New York have brought to their constituencies the message of ORT. In the late 1970's, ORT membership numbered some 18,000, distributed among some 100 chapters throughout the United States.

Among American ORT Federation chapters there is the American and European Friends of ORT, organized in 1940 by wealthy Russian refugees who had escaped the Nazis in France and settled in the United States. Most of them had been connected with or supported ORT efforts in France, Germany, and even in Russia. While the group brought to ORT considerable financial support, historically it should be viewed from a different perspective. Whereas in the 1920's Bramson had appealed to Russian-Jewish emigrant workers, the newcomers from Hitler-torn Europe, among whom were such men as A.C. Litton, represented the wealthy Russian Jewry who, in style and tone, reflected the old-time Russian ORT and the traditions and social ways of the Russian-Jewish bourgeoisie. The group was small in numbers but, like their less affluent brothers decades before, they fulfilled their social responsibility to care for those in need. They became part of the American ORT Federation and continued their efforts for two decades. As the old generation left the stage, the men of the middle generation, Jacques Zwibak, Simon Jaglom, Leon Najda, and others, continued the good work. ORT will be well served if their sons preserve this interesting Russian-European effort in the United States.

Different Times—Different Ways

As the position of American ORT both in and outside the United States changed, so did the character of the American ORT Federation. From a largely labor-emigrant-oriented body, it became a broad membership organization embracing many sectors of American Jewry throughout the country. Its appeal has permitted the mobilization of a large number of individuals attracted by ORT vocational programs in and outside of Israel.

While future development cannot be predicted, in the late 1970's American ORT, on the initiative of Women's American ORT, and through the persistent efforts of Nathan Gould, established a second Bramson school in New York after a long discussion in the organization.

The new Bramson School, designed by B. Wand-Polak, Latin-American ORT director, and at the level of a community college, provides young adult students with courses in modern technology and business management in addition to courses in Jewish studies. It is too early to judge if this marks the beginning of an operational ORT program in the United States, but the initiative represents a significant change in its relation to the American Jewish scene.

The American ORT leadership, among whom William

Haber, Harold Friedman, Judah Cahn, Roland Moskowitz, Alvin L. Gray, John Davidson, Shelley Appleton, Charles F. Bensley, Bruce B. Teicholz, Sidney Leiwant, and Mrs. Ruth Eisenberg and Beverly Minkoff of Women's ORT are prominently represented, has recently succeeded not only in bringing into the ORT orbit the various Jewish groups and social elements they represent, but in moving ORT toward greater integration into the American Jewish community.

As always, the road has not been without obstacles and development has been accompanied by a slow changing-of-the-guard. Haber, who comes from academia, helped raise ORT in the eyes of the community. He was instrumental in moving the organization out of its isolation and closer to the community mainstream. Friedman, who succeeded to the American ORT Federation presidency in 1975, brought to its councils experience and connections with many of the basic community structures—UJA, JDC, HIAS, and the Council of Jewish Federations. Haber and Appleton have actively participated in World ORT affairs, each bringing to it his own competence. Appleton came to ORT with long experience in the labor union movement and management of large labor bodies.

Since 1948, for more than thirty years, Paul Bernick, in addition to his duties on behalf of the World ORT Union, where he plays an active role in the formation of overall policy, has had professional responsibility for American ORT. Among other things, he has been in charge of relationships with the United States Government and public bodies.

ORT work, as it grows, must be presented and interpreted constantly to the Jewish community, which is perhaps most attuned to appeals for relief, not always aware of the specific tasks of the ORT movement and its worldwide system of vocational schools. Jack Rader, author of much of the material disseminated about ORT and its programs, together with a staff of specialized professionals, has seconded Bernick's efforts.

As we observe ORT in the United States during the course of some 58 years of existence, we cannot but conclude that it has a special place in the world ORT movement. While all autonomous national ORT organizations are in principle equal, the facts make some more equal than others. While some ORT organizations could no doubt continue their work and survive without American aid, others could not be maintained without such aid, nor, without it, could the world ORT continue to grow. Like much else in Jewish life in the 20th century, this is a result of historical change; for the time being, at least, matters cannot be otherwise.

Chapter XIII

The Survivors

The wholesale destruction brought about by the Nazis came to an end in 1945. It was only then that the scope of the Jewish catastrophe became apparent. Of the 9,000,000 Jews in Europe in 1939, some 5,700,000, more than 60 per cent, had been murdered by the Nazis with the help of various native anti-Semitic groups.[1]

The great Jewish community of Poland was no more, and the old Jewish communities of Rumania, Hungary, and Czechoslovakia had been reduced by 50 to 80 per cent. While on the whole the West fared better, some of its Jewish communities had been largely obliterated. Of the approximately 3,300,000 Jews who had survived in Europe, some 2,000,000 were in the USSR, isolated behind the Iron Curtain. The remaining 1,300,000 in the West and East included those who had been placed in camps for displaced persons, the so-called DPs.

The D.P. Era

DPs represented a postwar phenomenon, involving individuals forcibly removed from or compelled to leave their

232

native countries because of the war, the occupation, and the ensuing events.[2] Following the collapse of the Third Reich there were approximately 12,000,000 DPs of all nationalities residing in the enlarged territory of Nazi Germany and other countries. Within six months after the end of the war, some 6,000,000 had been repatriated, after which the process of repatriation slowed down.

Repatriation did not significantly affect the status of Jewish DPs. In certain parts of Europe, very little of Jewish communal life remained; not only had Jews been killed, but Jewish institutions—buildings, schools—had been destroyed. Most of the Jewish survivors who returned to their native cities and towns soon fled their not always hospitable native lands which had been transformed by Hitler into mass cemeteries and where anti-Semitism was still rampant.

The new Jewish migration reversed the old geographic pattern, intensifying a movement that began with the great migration at the turn of the century. Now, after many centuries, the movement was from east to west. From Poland, whose borders were still unstable, Jews, including those repatriated from Russia, began to move to the West—to Czechoslovakia, from Czechoslovakia to Austria, from Austria to the Western Zone of Germany and to Italy.

Jewish migration into the Western Zone of the former Third Reich and into Italy continued long after the end of hostilities, reaching a peak in 1946-1947. There was constant movement between Germany, Austria, and Italy, and from those countries, through the illegal *Bricha*, to Palestine.

At the end of 1945 there were about 90,000 Jews in Germany, Austria, Italy, and Shanghai. In the latter city there was a small group of refugees from Germany and Austria who had joined the Polish Jewish refugees and the Russian Jews who had fled after the Bolshevik take-over in Russia.[3] Some 250,000 displaced Jews were located in Czechoslovakia, Hungary, Rumania, Spain, Sweden, Switzerland, and the Soviet Union, to where, at the beginning of the war, Jews from Poland, Lithuania, and Bessarabia had been forcibly deported or had fled seeking safety. It was a constantly shifting population in search of new homes.

By 1946, the influx into the DP camps from Poland had subsided. There followed a wave of Jews from Rumania and other countries. It became apparent that under the existing emigration restrictions, Jewish DPs would have to remain in the camps for prolonged periods. Thus there came about the unique phenomenon of Jewish displaced persons—people without a country and without legal status.

The war over, the governments of the victorious countries paid scant attention to the displaced victims of the Nazis. In addition, European authorities had a negative attitude toward those who "did not want" to be repatriated to their country of origin. Such persons became "stateless." Jews, needless to say, being not only stateless but unrepatriable, were in this category.

The table below shows the distribution of Jewish DPs between 1946 and 1949:

TABLE 10

Jewish DPs, December 1946– July, 1949

Area	End of 1946	End of 1947	Mid-1948	Mid-1949
Germany	142,847	154,600	100,120	34,582
Austria	29,158	26,000	16,511	5,845
Italy	25,000	25,400	18,249	5,578
Other	—	—	8,056	6,393
Total	197,005	206,000	142,936	52,398[4]

By 1947, more than two years after the end of the war, the movement out of the camps to permanent homes had been insignificant. ORT leaders were, of course, aware of the situation, and especially aware of the peculiar demography of the Jewish camp population. The majority of the survivors in the camps were young people between 16 and 24 years of age. Trapped at an early age by the advent of Nazism, few had had any education.

Human Renewal

It was no accident that already in 1945, immediately after the liberation, the first vocational school for DPs was set up in

Landsberg, Bavaria. It was begun by Jacob Oleiski, former director of the ORT school in Lithuania. He had survived the horrors of the Kovno ghetto and the Landsberg camp, his vitality after all this a wonder to his coworkers.

Oleiski's project was initiated in the American Zone. Later in 1945, a vocational training unit was organized in the Bergen-Belsen camp, in the British Zone, by former ORT teachers.[5] This beginning of ORT programs in the DP camps represented more than the introduction of organized vocational training for Jewish men, women, and children who happened to be there; its particular importance lay in the fact that it brought to Jewish survivors the realization that they had regained their freedom of choice and would now be able to make plans for the future.

At the first postwar conference of the World ORT Union in 1946, ORT leaders, having decided to intensify their activities, adopted, among others, the following resolution:

"Considering the tragic situation of the Jewish displaced persons in Germany, the Conference recognizes that, in view of the prolongation of the stay in German camps of these human masses, the problem of productive employment and professional training becomes ever more acute, be it considered from the point of view of their future or in regard to their present moral condition . . . The Conference . . . requests . . more funds for the professional training of tens of thousands of surviving Jews (*Sherit Hapleita*) in Germany, Austria and Italy and for equipping them with machinery."[6]

Steps had already been taken. Toward the end of 1945, Lvovich had been sent to the camps to organize ORT programs there. In the spring of 1946, Vladimir Grossman came to Germany as director of activities in the British and American zones, and ORT activities soon began in earnest.

General rehabilitation efforts were coordinated by UNRRA (United Nations Relief and Rehabilitation Agency) and, later, in 1947, after UNRRA had been liquidated, by the IRO (International Refugee Organization). The first head of UNRRA was Herbert H. Lehman, for years a devoted friend and supporter of ORT.

On the local level, however, the necessity of dealing with UNRRA and IRO presented problems for ORT. In addition, the presence of American, British, and French military authorities in the three zones meant a mass of bureaucratic detail that often interfered with practical work, such as shipping supplies and installing training facilities.

Lvovich entered into an agreement with UNRRA under which, with the latter's blessing and under its sponsorship, ORT agreed to provide training for 10,000 Jewish DPs.

In late 1946, UNRRA requested that ORT undertake programs in Austria, where the reactivated Jewish community was dealing with an increasing number of new arrivals, mainly transient Jewish refugees. A few months later, ORT work was initiated in Italy.

While the UNRRA-ORT agreement was especially important in that all activities in the DP camps required prior UNRRA approval, agreements were also concluded between ORT and JDC, and between ORT and committees of Jewish DPs in the relevant western sectors of occupied Germany under which the exclusive competence of ORT in matters affecting the vocational training of Jewish DPs was recognized.

Camps Without End

The matter of the status of Jewish DPs had by now become a major concern of Jews everywhere. American Jews had hoped that once the Nazis were defeated, vigorous action would be taken on behalf of Jewish survivors. This did not happen. The Jewish DPs remained in the camps. Their number was steadily increased by the arrival of refugees from Eastern Europe.

Oleiski and his colleagues in the Jewish DP organization did everything they could to further ORT efforts in the camps, trying to sustain hope against all odds. The organization of schools under the chaotic conditions that surrounded the camps was a Herculean and sometimes frustrating task.

We cannot here go into the complex social and psychological aspects of the situation.

The DPs felt that they had been abandoned by the world, misunderstood by their fellow Jews, with little being done to relieve their misery. Dr. Zalman Grinberg, a physician and survivor of the Dachau camp, later chairman of the Jewish Central Committee for Displaced Persons, noted:

"Now that the problem of food no longer exists and the fear of death has been removed . . . even if these people [the DPs] lived under conditions far more livable, there would still be the need of creating a psychological milieu wherein work would be a form of therapy," and "the demoralization [in the camps] came during the period after liberation,"[7] when camp inmates were left for months and years in a state of enforced idleness.

Conflicting Perspectives

Difficulties within the internal structure of ORT itself created other problems. At the time, ORT management was divided according to geographical zones: Lvovich, out of the Paris office, was in charge of the DP program; Syngalowski, out of Geneva, was in charge of other areas, including Eastern Europe.

This arrangement, although it did not make for efficiency, could not be avoided, since the relationship between the two men was at a low point and respective responsibilities had to be precisely delineated. One outcropping of the feud between the two men involved the exclusion of the Geneva ORT Central Inspectorate, created in 1947, from ORT schools in Germany which, under an agreement between the two leaders, had been entrusted to the Paris office.

It was under these circumstances that the ORT program in the camps became an additional source of contention between ORT Union European leaders and the Americans headed by Boudin (see Chapter X). Again the Europeans were accused of inefficiency and incompetence. It should be noted that Syngalowski himself was not entirely happy about Lvovich's administration of the DP program, but, faced with the criticism of the Americans, he stood by Lvovich against "external interference." Boudin not only criticized the "managers" for lack of organization and inefficiency, but used harsh language about several DPs who had been active in ORT efforts.

Undoubtedly, there was much in ORT's work in the camps that might have been improved. There was more involved, however, than efficient administration of the myriad daily details and reports required by the military authorities. Above all, there was the need to deal with the deep psychological dissatisfaction that colored the lives of the DPs and slipped over into their perception of the service agencies, Jewish and non-Jewish, active in the camps.

There were American ORT leaders visiting Germany who felt the American social workers and administrators could bring new and better methods into ORT work there. One such was Julius Hochman, an American labor leader and ORT activist familiar with problems of work organization. The Americans contended that American Army authorities preferred to deal with American personnel and that the presence of American personnel would facilitate day-to-day reports involving supplies, technical arrangements, and similar matters.

Working Within Instability

The point must be made that ORT faced difficulties not encountered by relief organizations. It was not dealing with food packages and cash relief, the management of which could readily be improved by well-supervised personnel with technical knowledge. ORT's function was to build schools and organize training units in addition to managing whatever other elements were involved in these programs.[8]

Jewish DPs were housed for the most part wherever the

In the DP camps. Carpentry workshop in Landsberg, Germany; first of the ORT programs for DP's.

Machinery sent from the United States to equip training workshops for displaced persons in Bergen-Belsen.

military could find places for them. Under these shifting conditions it was difficult to find appropriate places for introducing vocational classes.

And, having found a place for a school, what educational standards should apply to persons who had spent years in concentration camps or had survived the occupation? Guidance counselors, psychiatrists, and spiritual advisers were needed, not to speak of time, stable conditions, and confidence in the future—all of them essential elements of a carefully planned program.

Despite the many obstacles presented by bureaucratic strictures, lack of understanding, and jealous feuds, ORT operations in Germany, Austria, and Italy reached considerable proportions.[9] By late 1947, ORT was providing 597 courses in various trades and subjects in 78 training centers employing 934 instructors.

Recruitment of competent teaching staff was an especially thorny problem during the initial period. Such people were not to be found in the camps. Although in the beginning some former ORT instructors, administrators, and graduates of prewar ORT schools who had survived the Nazis were attracted to ORT schools, their number was limited and only a few were able to undertake such work because most were hoping to leave at the first opportunity.

In many cases it was necessary to employ German non-Jewish instructors, some of whom had had experience in teaching in German vocational schools. Refresher courses had to be organized for training instructors in modern methods of teaching their trades. Such courses were particularly needed in radio and electronics. Four seminars for instructors were organized in 1948. A comprehensive seminar attended by 30 instructors was held in Sweden. Other, shorter seminars were held for teachers of radio, electronics, tailoring, and dental mechanics.

Early in 1948, the technical office at ORT headquarters in Munich issued a number of practical textbooks geared to the curricula of ORT programs, including draftsmanship and technical manuals.

There was much experimentation to determine the best opportunities for vocational training which made it necessary for ORT to conclude agreements with private factories and with German authorities. Thus, one ORT school was established in Munich. The Bavarian Ministry of Interior put a large building at ORT's disposal where, in cooperation with IRO, JDC, and the Central Committee of Jewish DPs, ORT created a vocational school.

Frequent use was made of industrial plants outside the camps, and DP students were sometimes placed in private factories where, under ORT instructors, they learned their trades. This arrangement was of mutual benefit to DPs and factory owners when the factories that supplied the raw materials could retain the finished product.

Machines, instruments, and tools had to be obtained from the United States, Canada, Switzerland, Sweden, England, and France through the World ORT Union. Some machines had to be rented in Germany. Arrangements for procurement required technical expertise, knowledge as to the possibilities of performing repairs locally, availability of parts, and, of course, the financial dealings incident to the transactions.

ORT had to arrange for the use of two warehouses, one the central warehouse of the World ORT Union in Schleissheim, near Munich, from which supplies were distributed through the American and British Zones and Austria, and another serving the U.S. Zone in Munich proper.

Mention should be made of the currency reform in Germany in June, 1948. The initial impact of the reform on the voluntary agencies, including ORT, was plainly negative. ORT was paying salaries to hundreds of instructors, and DMs were not available. A special arrangement was effected whereby ORT personnel were put on the Burgomaster's payroll. ORT, however, undertook to reduce its personnel by some 30 per cent, which it did by October, 1948. Later, ORT made an agreement with IRO under which IRO took over responsibility for all ORT employees attached to IRO-sponsored ORT projects. IRO approval was given to ORT schools that complied with IRO-established standards of curricula, equipment, and other requirements for students receiving at least 40 hours of instruction per week. Within a short time, some 60 per cent of ORT schools had achieved the required standards.

Much effort went into adjusting programs geographically to the divisions set up by IRO and JDC. An office of inspectors was set up in the camps to control the work and make suggestions for improvement. As the ORT grew in size and complexity, the ORT administration was often unable to cope with the technical and managerial tasks. Much patience was needed to reach an effective level of operation.

A Large Enterprise

In its work of training DPs, ORT was called on to perform some special tasks not usually encountered in its programs, because of the particular needs of the DP population. It had to be sure that graduates of its courses had received training adequate to qualify them for employment, whether in Palestine or the United States. It had also to maintain contact with organizations dealing with emigration—the Jewish Agency for those going to Palestine, and JDC and HIAS for those going to the United States and elsewhere.

There was also the matter of choosing a trade. About half of ORT trainees were in the traditional Jewish needle trades.[10] Concentration on the needle trades reflected the composition of the Jewish DP population, and perhaps also it was relatively simple to provide.

ORT teachers tried to direct trainees away from the needle trades and into the electrical or metalworking trades which promised better opportunities in their future homes. These efforts involved planning at the policy level.

More than 40 trades were taught in ORT schools in Germany, including knitting, lingerie, leatherworking, electro-mechanics, watch-repairing, hat-making, shoemaking, optics, auto driving, corsetry, locksmithing, dental mechanics, masonry, construction, and manufacture of strings for musical instruments. Of special interest was the school for maritime trades in Neustadt (Holstein), a radical departure from the traditional training provided by ORT.

The ORT DP program was a large economic enterprise on the move; in terms of sheer logistics it might be compared to the operations of a state authority.

Toward the end of 1945, ORT programs in the U.S. Zone included 895 students; in January, 1946, the number of students was 1,895; during 1947 enrollment increased everywhere at a rapid pace. There was a decrease in 1948 that reflected the effect of the U.N. decision on Palestine, reached on November 27, 1947. At the beginning of 1948, the so-called Mobilization for the Holy Land attracted a number of young people, and *Aliah Beth* also had an impact on the plans of the DPs.

TABLE 11

Enrollment in ORT DP Programs
1947–1948

	Jan. 1 1947	July 1 1947	Jan. 1 1948	Apr. 1 1948
Germany-U.S. Zone	2,500	5,855	8,412	7,426
Germany-British Zone	470	704	2,219	1,535
Austria	—	390	1,037	1,215
Italy	—	956	1,613	1,892
Total	2,970	7,905	13,281*[11]	12,068

*Estimates, compiled by Financial and Accounting Office, World ORT Union, quoted in Gringaus, *ORT Economic Review*, No. 6–9, 1948.

The actual management of ORT programs at various times and in various zones was in the hands of directors, inspectors, and, at the training level, specialized instructors. In 1946, ORT staff in the U.S. Zone numbered 178; in February, 1947, it numbered 427; by the end of 1947 it stood at over 900.

Those Who Served

We cannot record here the names of all of the individuals who contributed to ORT work in the DP camps. They contributed not only technical knowledge, but patience and understanding of the special conditions under which they worked. Among the administrative personnel were Oleiski, Rabinowitch, Schachnovsky, Vladimir Grossman, Samuel Steinberg, Mrs. Horowitz, O. Dutch, B. Branton, S. Solun, Dorothea Green, Bernard Wand-Polak, and Mrs. I. Mowshovitch.

Dissatisfied with the situation in the camps, Boudin persuaded Cylvia Margolies of Women's American ORT to go to Germany as director of the U.S. Zone and liaison officer with UNRRA and the U.S. Army. Mrs. Margolies remained in Germany and Austria for nearly a year.

Later, the World ORT Union invited Louis J. Walinsky to become director of ORT programs in the U.S. Zone and, later, director of all ORT operations in Germany and Austria. Walinsky had the advantage of being both an American and an able administrator, and he succeeded in improving relations between ORT and IRO, which contributed greatly to the development of ORT work in the camps.[12] He was already serving as director of the Financial and Accounting Office in New York, and for a short time was also Secretary General of the World ORT Union. He could, therefore, take over management of the DP program only on a temporary basis; he served from May 1947 to September 1948.

During his service abroad the burdens of the New York office fell on Edward L. Sard and the old ORT activist, Jacob Frumkin, the latter acting as adviser and dealing particularly with tool and machine supplies for the DP area.

The matter of bringing American personnel to the DP camps was a subject of much discussion among the American and European ORT leaders that engendered bad feeling. Involved were diplomacy, management practices, and respect for the needs of the liberated survivors.

As in other disputes between the Americans and the Europeans, there was exaggeration and uncalled-for belligerency on both sides. In retrospect, it can be said that the foreign personnel brought into the ORT operations extensive knowledge that the local personnel, after years of German occupation, did not have, and undoubtedly contributed to the progress of ORT work in the DP areas.

The End Begins

The establishment of the State of Israel in 1948 and, to a lesser extent, the U.S. Displaced Persons Act of 1948, provided new outlets for emigration and resettlement. At the beginning of 1949, only some 50,000 persons remained in the camps; three years later, in 1952, there remained only a hard core of some 15,000.

ORT's DP programs provided systematic training to an estimated 40,000 to 45,000 trainees. Many more than this enrolled, but either soon left or did not complete their training.[13] J. Donald Kingsley, Director General of IRO, wrote to Syngalowski on October 31, 1951, expressing IRO appreciation of the ORT programs.

He noted that, at its high point, ORT training covered "approximately 12,000 students at one time." IRO had throughout provided generous financial aid, which was terminated with the closing of IRO operations in October, 1951.

Chapter XIV

After the Nazi Scourge

By the early 1950's ORT work in the DP camps had come to a close. ORT followed the DPs to Palestine and, later, Israel, but that is a story to which we shall return.

Quite a different task emerged. JDC and ORT had to turn their attention to the settled communities, which now included refugee elements who were slowly being integrated.

Thus, ORT took on at the same time the task of vocational education in the Moslem countries, areas where it had not previously operated, while at the same time enlarging and transforming programs in Latin America, where numbers of Jewish refugees from Europe had settled during the war years.

In Europe the end of the war and of the Nazi occupation brought revolutionary changes in all aspects of social and economic life. The war had speeded up social and technological changes. The new societies emerging everywhere were undergoing a transformation that could not but affect the Jews.

With the establishment of the State of Israel, the image of the Jewish world changed and the perception of the Dias-

pora was altered. It became obvious that the existence of a
Jewish state in its historical setting would not mean the disappearance of the Diaspora. Jewish life in the foreseeable
future would be maintained at two centers, one in Israel and
the other in the Diaspora. Creation of a *modus vivendi* between the two, and the fostering of a mutually beneficial
relationship between them, would require great effort.[1]

It was a new ORT that responded to Jewish needs of the
postwar period. With the death of Bramson ORT had not
only lost an administrator par excellence, but its last link
with its Russian founders.

Like other Jewish social instrumentalities, ORT had to
adjust its aims and methods to find adequate approaches to
the realities of the post-Nazi era. The character of the needs
of the Jewish populations in the countries of their present
residence had changed substantially.

Hundreds of thousands of Polish Jewish artisans and
small businessmen had disappeared in the Nazi crematoria.
Western economy was moving toward a service base. In
Eastern Europe the question was how to retrain Jewish
workers to meet the demands of a planned economy. Different types of training and different types of schools were
needed to prepare Jewish youth for higher levels of technical
proficiency.

Redefinition of Jewish Education

On numerous occasions, Syngalowski had spoken about the
problem of Jewish education, a subject that acquired special
significance after the Holocaust. ORT schools of the Tsarist
and World War I period had devoted attention to Jewish
education. Local ORT groups, closely connected with the
Yiddish-speaking communities, were especially interested in
the matter.

But with the loss of six million Jews, the disappearance of
the great Polish Jewish community, and the establishment of
the State of Israel, Jewish education came to be seen in a

different light. Emphasis shifted to religious elements and the Hebrew language. Partly as the result of a general post-World War II trend, and partly as a conscious stand, the ORT school system dealt not only with vocational training, but very much with Jewish education.

The Hitler experience had heightened feelings about Jewish identification among some Jewish intellectuals. This was hardly necessary with Syngalowski, who throughout his life had been a strongly committed Jew. While not perhaps religious in the formal sense, his commitment to Jewish values and Jewish continuity was total, and he had a clear vision of what Jewish education should be.

For him there was a difference between a school for Jews and a Jewish school. Nor was ORT an agency for subsidizing vocational schools for poor students. *"Rachmones"* was not its motivation, and "philanthrophy" was foreign to its aims. Syngalowski believed that in striving to improve the Jewish condition economically, ORT should address itself to the community rather than to the individual. In educating a new Jewish generation in a Jewish school, ORT was creating a Jewish milieu, a national Jewish framework within which a Jew could live his life with moral satisfaction and pride in his work.

Syngalowski was not a Zionist in the classical sense, or even in the sense that Ahad-Haam understood it; he believed that a full Jewish national existence could be maintained in the Diaspora provided that the young generations acquired the essential economic and cultural tools.

New Times–New Ways

With all the reservations called for, it is from this perspective that the development and character of ORT schools after World War II should be considered.

During the post World War II period there took place a reformulation of ORT aims that was later reflected even in the constitution of the World ORT Union. The old ORT in Russia and Poland had striven to spread vocational training among Jews, and this goal had been maintained through the period following the first World War and the establishment of the World ORT Union in the 1920's. (The acronym ORT, in fact, includes the words "artisan labor"—in Russian, *remeslennyi trud.*) Post World War II ORT, however, spoke about the "amelioration of the economic and social status of Jews through vocational training and technical education in countries where the need exists."

The concept of technical education could be taken as including the vocational training provided by ORT, except that the framers of the new formulation clearly enunciated the view of technical education as distinct from and complementary to vocational training; and they cited both as the goal of ORT. It was a major adjustment in the breadth of ORT responsibilities, an adjustment to economics increasingly attuned to high technology.

Under the new formulation, programs provided by ORT schools covered the entire scale from basic training to the highly specialized, permitting graduates to continue their education at the university level. Vocational training in the narrow sense was not abandoned, but by the late 1960's ORT programs included automation, numerical controls, skilled service areas, and computerization as parts of ORT school curricula. ORT schools were graduating technicians who had no difficulty in adjusting their specializations to the needs of advanced industrial society.

Speaking at the ORT Congress in London in 1960, William Haber, President of the Central Board, placed the problem in focus: "Powerful technological forces are at work, not only in the economically advanced countries but also in those just launched on the road to industrialization. They demand . . . considerable knowledge and skill . . . Automation is altering the nature of human work, shifting the content of labor from manual to mental and demanding from the worker far greater scientific and general training.

"What we teach will be drastically affected. . . . It will

require great sensitivity and flexibility to respond to these revolutionary changes and to be constantly aware that we are training not only for today but for a period whose outline is still dim in the future."

In the late 1970's the problem still exists. It will no doubt continue to do so.[2]

A Revolution in the ORT Idea

These radically extended aspirations received still another twist in tune with the times as ORT gradually turned to career education, embracing all types of technical professions, including highly practical engineering. "Career" presupposes opportunities for advancement and covers endeavors of higher professional and social import than the occupations visualized by ORT's founders. ORT men and women of earlier generations had viewed vocational requalification essentially in terms of manual labor, although they saw intellectual pursuits as possibly going along with manual occupations.

The change in approach represented a revolution in the thinking of ORT. It reflected the debate over liberal arts versus career education that ORT tried to resolve from its own point of view. A significant factor was the constant search for improvement in technical education that engaged the attention of the ORT administration in Geneva and to which specialists in local schools have had a substantial input.

In the transmission of accumulated knowledge, experience, and tradition which is the proper role of an educational institution, structures and programs must be periodically re-evaluated to accommodate new ideas and concepts geared to the social and psychological needs of future generations. This is not an easy task, and it is the great merit of the ORT movement and its teaching staff that they have had the vision and courage to accept, and anticipate new directions.[3]

The Central Training Institute

Under the conditions prevailing in the liberated Europe of the late 1940's, the establishment of ORT schools depended to a large extent not only on the availability of financial resources, but above all on the availability of qualified teaching personnel. Already during the war years and in the midst of the Nazi terror, Syngalowski, in Geneva, was thinking about establishing a school for the training of ORT instructors and administrators to replace the more than 3,000 who had perished at the hands of the Nazis.[4] He envisioned that such a school would open opportunities for an important new career, that of Jewish educator, and whose graduates could then work in the ORT educational system the world over.

Recruitment of instructors had been a problem practically throughout ORT's existence. More often than not, ORT instructors, some of whom had learned their trades under a master-artisan arrangement, lacked the theoretical knowlege of their *metier* and the broader background needed to impart adequate education to aspiring students. As early as 1915, during World War I, ORT activists had insisted on strict technical preparation of ORT inspectors, who could then be helpful in improving ORT training programs.[5]

In 1946, the ruling bodies of ORT approved the Syngalowski plan, and early in 1949, after troublesome negotiations involving acquisition of a large estate, the Central Institute for the Training of ORT Instructors was opened in Anieres, near Geneva. Swiss experts assisted in the formulation of the curriculum. The two-to-four-year programs, which included theoretical studies and practical work in Swiss factories, was sufficiently elastic to accommodate students coming from different backgrounds and different cultures.

The curriculum covered general and Jewish studies, including Hebrew, English, history and literature. In time, the program was enlarged to include training of teachers from the developing countries and research in and testing of new techniques in vocational education. An arrangement was made with *Ecole Technique Supérieure* of Geneva whereby selected students were able to take courses leading to the degree of engineer-technician.

Max Braude devoted much attention to introducing new learning techniques in ORT schools—a particularly important matter since, during the occupation, little had been done by European specialists in this field. Prof. Robert Silverman of New York University, a specialist in educational psychology, participated in an ORT seminar on programmed instruction and the use of teaching machines. Dr. Marvin Feldman, then with the Ford Foundation, assisted in designing a curriculum.

At a seminar celebrating the 20th anniversary of the Institute in 1969, subjects under discussion included econometric methods of social diagnosis and the newest audio-visual instruments and closed circuit television as tools of education. Prof. P. Jaccard of Lausanne University spoke on problems of social and occupational forecasting, matters naturally of great interest to ORT.

While from the start, the Institute had attained an important place in the ORT school system, Alexander Magat, later ORT director in Argentina, who succeeded Lucien N. Volski, oriented the Institute toward a more advanced level. The present head of the Institute, Joel Szajn, is himself a graduate of the school.

In the course of some 15 years, through 1968, the Institute graduated about 250 instructors specializing in various fields, including electro-mechanics, radio, and industrial design. Students came from 19 European countries, Africa, Asia, and America. As of 1978, about 30 countries benefited from the activities carried out by the Institute. The Institute was also helpful in ORT programs in Israel, for whom accelerated courses were organized for mechanics from kibbutzim and moshavim to familiarize them with new techniques in their field. Refresher courses were provided for a selected group of Israeli plant sub-managers. The latter project was organized by ILO in cooperation with the Israeli Ministry of Labor, Histadrut, and the Swiss government.

A graduation ceremony at the Central ORT Institute.

The educational level of the Institute may be gauged by the status of its students in 1975. In that year, 19 students took their fourth year courses at the *Ecole Technique Supérieure* and received diplomas as engineer-technicians, six of them graduating as nuclear engineers.

Daniel Mayer, Chairman of the Executive Committee of World ORT Union, speaking at a 1969 seminar celebrating the Institute's 20th anniversary, stated that its importance was due to the fact that it had united in its program a constant interest in technical education, a feeling for change in pedagogical methods, and a deep concern for the development of human qualities of future ORT cadres.

Following the initiation of ORT technical assistance programs in countries of the underdeveloped areas, numbers of students came to the Institute from Guinea, the Ivory Coast, Mali, Zaire, and other countries. In the process, they also learned to respect and appreciate their Jewish fellow-students and teachers.

No special historical insight is needed to visualize the path traversed by ORT from its beginnnings in Russia to the establishment of the Anieres Institute. Bakst would certainly have protested the introduction of this new type of training into the ORT program. But ORT had changed, and the Institute represented only one step in this evolution.[6]

An Unrealized Vision

Toward the end of the war, Syngalowski was working on a 25-year plan for the economic rehabilitation of the European Jews. His idea was that after the war Jewish workers in all areas should be integrated into the various sectors of national economic life, industry as well as agriculture, and that this should be done on a pro rata basis relative to their number in different countries.

He believed that Jewish emancipation and equality depended on the degree of Jewish equalization in terms of employment. He remembered the restrictions on Jewish labor in Eastern Europe, but his conception of Jewish labor, perhaps not entirely developed, was theoretically not limited by geography. The plan, of course, could be effectuated only with the help of the respective governments, and Syngalowski appealed to Jewish leaders the world over to approach their governments in an endeavor to integrate Jewish demands into the general peace proposals then being elaborated everywhere.

Syngalowski's plan was in agreement with his longheld view of ORT's role and character (see Chapter IX). In retrospect, considering the actual developments in postwar Europe, it might be considered naive and premature. In 1943-44, the full extent of the Catastrophe was still unknown, as was the future political division of Europe, with Stalin taking all of the East and even some parts of the West. Perhaps Syngalowski was pursuing the dreams of his socialist youth, dashed by the not-so-generous reality of the post-Hitler era. In fact, the Holocaust notwithstanding, the governments of European countries were not as ready to tackle the Jewish question as Syngalowski had expected.

Nevertheless, his plan was useful. It drew the attention of Jewish leadership to the need to think not only of bringing relief to Jewish survivors, but of constructive long-term assistance in rehabilitation through training. Many years later, at its 1977 Congress held in London, ORT returned in a way to Syngalowski's preoccupations, when Shelley Appleton presented a report of the Long Term Planning commission. This was, however, an effort to "perceive the future," and was intended, not as a guideline, but as an attempt to identify areas of possible need, and to outline the framework of possible ORT activities.[7]

New Leadership

At the fifth ORT Congress, held in Paris in August, 1946, George Backer of New York was elected President of the World ORT Union. Backer and Judge Leon Meiss of Paris, newly elected President of the Central Board, occupied the two top lay posts in ORT.

Backer, a publisher and realtor and President of the American ORT Federation, was active in politics. He was a New York City Councilman serving out the unexpired term of the late Charney Vladeck. Judge Meiss, of the Court of Appeals in Paris, was a member of the Representative Council of French Jews and of the *Consistoire Central des Israelites de France* since the occupation and was active in French ORT.

The position of President of the World ORT Union was a new one, perhaps more symbolic, in terms of power, than real. It was an innovation that was not to continue long. In the 1950's, the positions of President of the Central Board and Chairman of the Executive Committee were re-established.

The new organizational set-up reflected the relative positions of the leading forces within the World ORT Union—the greatly increased importance of the American Jewish community and the enhanced status of France, the largest Western Jewish community on the Continent, then in the process of reconstruction.

The day-to-day management of affairs remained in the hands of the Executive Committee, with Lvovich and Syngalowski as co-chairmen. The seat of the Executive Committee remained in Paris, but a smaller Administrative Committee consisting of seven members was set up in Geneva, where Syngalowski had developed intense activity since his arrival there in 1943.

In mid-1947, the Executive Committee appointed two Executive Secretaries of the World ORT Union, E. Gordon of Paris and V. Halperin of Geneva. The arrangement was a complex one, created, apparently, with a view to satisfying the dual management of Lvovich in Paris and Syngalowski in Geneva. But it reflected a fragmented leadership that was not only inefficient but fraught with danger. It created separate centers of power, each with followers holding competing views. This situation continued for some time, engendering bad blood and interfering with the normal progress of daily operations. This was happening at the top, after years of war and occupation, while at the level of program and operation, ORT had taken an unprecedented step forward.

It was not until 1949 that the central office of the World ORT Union was definitely set up in Geneva. Measures had been taken to reinforce the administrative work there. In 1948, A. D. Kovarsky, Secretary-General of French ORT, was appointed Administrative Director of the Geneva central office. The Paris office was transformed into the Public Relations Department, to which, in 1950, was added a purchasing division handling procurement for Israel and North Africa programs.

In 1949, the New York office, with its accounting and financial responsibilities, was reorganized and its major functions transferred to Geneva. The New York office continued for some years to perform limited functions, including transfer of JDC allocations to Geneva and dealing with ORT campaigns in Latin America. It also dealt with purchase and shipment of supplies on instructions from the central office. In 1949, at the ORT Congress in Paris, it was resolved that "all ORT tasks in the United States in which the World ORT Union is interested be carried out by the American ORT Federation . . . in consultation and cooperation with the World ORT Union."

Lvovich, who, as co-chairman with Syngalowski of the Executive Committee, shared the management of ORT affairs and headed the Paris office, passed away on August 17, 1950. His death was a severe blow. The Paris office now came under the direction of F. Schrager, who had joined ORT in France after the liberation. Schrager was primarily entrusted with public relations responsibilities; later, at the request of the central ORT office, he made several trips abroad to lecture on ORT.

In 1951, Max A. Braude joined the central office in Geneva as Director of Administrative and Organizational Work. Problems of internal organization were gradually resolved. The Geneva office, headed by Syngalowski, became the sole governing center. From that time until his death on

October 7, 1956, Syngalowski was the undisputed leader of ORT; in fact, among the younger generation, he *was* ORT.

With his death, ORT lost the last of the three great men of ORT—Bramson, Lvovich, and Syngalowski—who, except for brief intervals, had at different times been at the helm of the ORT movement since the death of Bakst in 1904.

Shapers of the Last 25 Years

Following the death of Syngalowski, a new generation and a new team came in to carry on the work.

Fresh forces joined the ORT organization. Among those on the new team was William Haber, who in 1955 had been elected President of the Central Board. After Syngalowski's death this position acquired greater importance. Syngalowski had been both lay leader and professional, a *klal tuer* (see Chapter IX). It was becoming imperative to separate the functions of the lay and professional leadership.

Haber, a professor and dean at the University of Michigan, labor arbitrator and prolific writer on economic affairs, came to the ORT chairmanship after having served for some years as President of the American ORT Federation. He had long been associated with Jewish affairs, having served on the boards of the Hebrew University in Jerusalem, B'nai Brith, American Jewish Committee, and other organizations; he had a particular affinity for ORT and its vocational programs. Haber was the first head of the National Refugee Service created during the peak of German-Jewish emigration.

The assumption of the chairmanship of the Executive Committee by Daniel Mayer in 1958 was another move toward reinforcement of the lay leadership. Mayer, a long-time French Socialist leader, Minister of Labor in the Leon Blum government in 1946 (and others afterward), had been a member of the *Conseil National de Résistance* during the occupation. He resigned from the French parliament in 1956 and assumed the presidency of the prestigious *Ligue de Droits de l'Homme*.

A man of considerable political stature, a friend of Israel, a journalist and writer, Mayer was especially impressed by the philosophical aspects of the ORT movement and its emphasis on the dignity of labor.

The new lay leaders of the World ORT Union, Haber and Mayer, chairmen, respectively, of the Board and Executive Committee, represented an interesting personal combination. Haber, the arbitrator, sought almost instinctively to moderate and find consensus, while Mayer was a man of strong ideological leanings. In a worldwide forum embracing ORT men and women from all five continents, a multiplicity of cultures and languages, they complemented each other in the difficult task of ORT governance.

The appointment of Max Braude to the post of Director-General, a new professional position, took place in 1957, some four months after Syngalowski's death. For the first time in World ORT Union history a professional man was entrusted with responsibility for managing ORT's worldwide programs. In practical terms, Braude succeeded Syngalowski in the management of ORT, its organizations, direction, administration, and policy initiation and implementation.

Braude had served as Chief of Camp Operations and Maintenance for IRO in Germany. In this capacity he negotiated an agreement with ORT covering its schools for the DPs. During World War II he had been Chaplain of the U.S. Seventh Army in Europe, a post that he resigned in 1947 with the rank of Lt. Colonel. Previously he had been Chaplain at Fort Knox and later Director of the chaplaincy school at Harvard University.

At the same time, Dr. Vladimir Halperin, a great grandson of Baron Horace de Gunsburg, one of the founders of ORT, who had joined the World ORT Union in 1943 as Executive Secretary under Syngalowski, became Director of the World ORT Union, second to Braude in the administration. A small Administrative Committee consisting of Armand Brunschwig of Geneva as Chairman and Renzo Levi of Rome, Otto Heim of Zurich, and Haber as members, was formed to assist in dealing with current matters.

Era of Large Expansion

The new leaders signaled the coming to leadership of people of Western origin.

Under the guiding hands of Haber and Mayer, with the support of ORT leaders elsewhere, the conflicts that had divided ORT were eventually resolved.

The mid-1950's were a watershed in terms of the style in which ORT would spread its work throughout the world. Braude, with his IRO experience in dealing with complex international organizations, streamlined and rationalized ORT internal administration along modern lines, introducing separate departments of operation, administration, and financing, as well as programming.

He gave particular attention and emphasis to the pedagogical aspects of ORT education which he believed needed improvement. For the next quarter of a century, Braude was at the helm, managing ORT, and making it a world-wide instrument of Jewish social change. His high aspirations for ORT, judging by the results, have been justified.

The growth in ORT operations has been remarkable. From $4,400,000 in 1957, its budget rose to $78,000,000 in 1979.

A significant aspect that had been developing for some time was the relative decrease in financial participation by the U.S., although financial support from JDC, Women's

TABLE 12

Estimated Budgets of World ORT
Union, Comparative Total and Local Contributions (in Dollars)

Year	Total	Local	% of Local Participation
1957	$ 4,400,000	$ 1,628,000	37
1960	6,125,161	2,768,161	45
1970	19,058,000	12,230,000	64
1974	34,187,400	22,600,000	66
1979	78,000,000	58,000,000	73

American ORT, and the American ORT Federation continued to be substantial and even increased. In the 1970's, some two-thirds of the ORT budget came from local sources, including government subsidies. This has been particularly true with respect to France and, of course, Israel, where ORT programs in the 1970's reached considerable proportions (see Chapter XVII).

Speaking to the ORT Congress in London in October, 1960, Braude stated that "By 1959 over 75 per cent of French ORT's expenditures were met with local funds, over 60 per cent of Italy's, 90 per cent of Austria and Germany, while Holland continued to support itself entirely."

In addition to U.S. contributions, funds came from ORT organizations and various other bodies in Australia, Canada, England, South Africa, Switzerland, Germany, the Netherlands, Latin and South American countries, Scandinavia, and other countries. The Jewish Colonization Association, the Baron de Hirsch Fund, the Canadian Jewish Congress, and the South African Jewish Appeal have all contributed to ORT programs. Some contributions were earmarked for selected programs in various countries.[8]

Chapter XV

Renewal and Growth
Eastern Europe-Western Europe-Latin America

With the war at an end, ORT not only resumed its activities in the areas where it had operated before the Nazi destruction of the old Jewish communities of Europe, but spread its activities to new areas. While many Jews of Eastern Europe sought refuge in the West, others remained and attempted to reestablish their lives in their native countries.

It was only natural that ORT should resume activities in the traditional areas of its operations, but it did so in full realization that it faced a different Eastern Europe, an Eastern Europe bereft of most of its Jews and under Soviet domination. While work under Soviet conditions was beset with obstacles, these were not considered insurmountable.

Lvovich, in the United States at war's end, was "working on plans to revive ORT's work in Russia," and the New York-based Emergency ORT Committee asked Louis Boudin to go to Mexico City to discuss with the Russian Ambassador Umansky there[1] possible resumption of ORT work in Russia, despite the fact that there were some ORT leaders who had doubts about working under the Soviets.

While Lvovich and Syngalowski had substantial differences of opinion about many ORT concerns, both were interested in resuming work in now-Sovietized Eastern

Europe. For Syngalowski especially, Eastern Europe was a natural base not only of ORT but of Jewish life itself, the Yiddish language, and Jewish creativity. In the later division of functions between Lvovich and Syngalowski, Eastern Europe came under the latter's jurisdiction.

In the West Jewish life had also changed. Many of the great historic Jewish communities were gone. France, however, became a focal point of renewed Jewish immigration, and it was here that ORT programs developed most conspicuously. The geographic development of ORT programs was really conditioned by the continuing movement of Jewish populations looking for permanent homes.

What follows is a description of ORT's various postwar activities.

IN EASTERN EUROPE

Poland—A Revolving Door That Closed

Notwithstanding the still fluctuating character of the Jewish population and the prevailing anti-Semitic mood, ORT returned to Poland immediately after the liberation.[2] Between 1945 and 1949, it developed a network of schools and vocational workshops. Much of the work, which was supported by JDC, was geared to youths, although there were some retraining courses for adults. Of particular importance during this period were the radio school in Dzerzionow and the textile school in Bielsko.

All this was of brief duration. In 1949, the Polish government changed its policy with respect to foreign relief agencies. JDC was forced to leave, and ORT activities ceased. We know now that the liquidation of ORT activities in Poland, and, later, practically everywhere in Eastern Europe, was not due to an accidental zigzag in Polish policy but originated in the anti-Semitic line fostered by the Kremlin.

In 1948, the well-known Soviet Jewish actor and Chairman of the Jewish Anti-Fascist Committee in Moscow, Michoels, was murdered by the secret police during a visit to Minsk. The Jewish Anti-Fascist Committee was disbanded, almost all of its members were arrested and disappeared into camps and prisons. In 1949, the Soviets initiated a systematic anti-Jewish campaign directed against so-called "cosmopolitans," a euphemism meaning Jews, who were considered an unpatriotic element.

Stalin endeavored to establish a "unified" Jewish policy in both Russia and his empire outside Russia. The new anti-Jewish line spread to the Soviet satellites where the ravages were deep, both within the Communist apparatus from which Jews were purged, and within the Jewish community. Under these circumstances, ORT, connected as it was with an international Jewish organization, was suspect and not to be tolerated.

AN ABORTED POLISH SPRING

It was only after Stalin's death in 1953 and Gomulka's accession to power in Poland in 1956 that Warsaw approached the ORT Union in Geneva with the suggestion that it reestablish its program in Poland. In September, 1957, an ORT Union delegation composed of Joseph Chorin, a member of the ORT Executive Committee, and Dr. Vladimir Halperin, the World ORT Union Director, made an on-the-spot survey of the vocational needs of the Polish Jewish community. In addition to Warsaw, they visited Lodz, Wroclaw, Katowice, Lignice, Krakow, and Dzerzionow. The delegation recommended resumption of work in Poland.[3]

Although some ORT leaders, enlightened by experience, had doubts about the possibility of developing an adequate program under the rigid controls prevailing in the Soviet area, it was decided that ORT must, under any circumstances, service the Polish Jewish communities, provided that it could maintain its own independence in doing so.

A second ORT group, which included World ORT Union Director-General Max A. Braude, David Alberstein, later in charge of World ORT Union operations, and Joseph Chorin of the earlier mission, visited Poland in November, 1957. Out of this emerged a broad program especially geared to repatriates from the Soviet Union.

Following the 1957 agreement between the USSR and Poland, which was later extended through June, 1959, more than 18,000 Polish Jews had returned to Poland from the Soviet Union. About 12,000 of them remained in Poland, the rest having gone to Israel. Additional repatriates arrived in July and August, 1959. The Jewish community, then numbering some 40,000, sought to integrate into the Polish economy. Qualified craftsmen were needed.

It was at this time that the Jewish producer cooperatives, composed of Jewish artisans, developed substantial operations. In July, 1958, a law had been enacted regulating the issuance of artisans' permits and allowing for the operation of small private enterprises. Some 12 per cent of the Polish Jewish population were artisans. Here was a natural field for ORT activities.

The program initiated in 1957, had, by 1959, been extended to 21 cities and some 4,000 individuals in a variety of trades. Vocational classes were introduced among pupils of the Jewish schools then existing in Poland. The official slogan was productivization, and ORT was there to make it a reality for the Jews.[4] David Slobodkin, an oldtime ORT worker, became the executive head of the program. As of 1961, four years after the resumption of work in Poland, 7,482 individuals had received vocational training.

THE LAST CHAPTER

Unable to solve Poland's economic problems, and unwilling to grant a modicum of freedom to the Polish people, Gomulka, erstwhile leader of the "liberal" opposition, turned to the old and tried method of calming the rebellious mood. He found the culprit who was making it impossible for Poland to solve her problems—disloyal Jews and Zionists. Anti-Semitic hysteria mounted and thousands of

Jews, including many loyal Party members, were forced to emigrate, seeking friendlier homes.

At the end of 1967, the Polish Ministry of Health and Social Welfare liquidated the welfare programs supported by JDC. Jewish producer cooperatives were soon disaffiliated from the Jewish Cultural and Social Union and integrated into the state system, thus losing their Jewish character. There followed the dissolution of ORT and the termination of its program by the Polish authorities.

Rumania—A Moment of Hope

More than 400,000 Rumanian Jews survived the Holocaust. The changed social conditions in the country were particularly difficult for the Jewish community. Most of those who returned from deportation and those who had survived in their native cities had to think about new ways of earning a living.

The Communist regime did not favor private enterprise, and the only way open for Jews to integrate into the new economic order was through productive trades. The threat was especially great since, in the early 1940's, about 50 per cent of the Jewish population had been in professions now considered superfluous, or even hostile, to the state.[5]

Rumanian ORT resumed its activities in March, 1945, under its former leaders W. Filderman and A. Weiss. Conditions were unstable, with Soviet army units still present.

HAZARD, ENCOURAGEMENT AND DEMISE

Any attempt to establish contact with the ORT center in Geneva was dangerous. Nevertheless, toward the end of 1945 a small number of vocational courses for the training of young men and women in radio, lingerie-making, and other

skills were established in Bucharest. There were special difficulties in some places; e.g., in Iassy, the Jewish population of
30,000 included some 12,000 orphans, victims of pogroms
and deportations, many of whom had returned after long
stays in Transnistria[6] where they had suffered the horrors of
that infamous place.

Toward the end of 1948, delegates of Rumanian ORT, at a
meeting with leaders of the World ORT Union in Geneva,
elaborated a plan for enlarging activities in Rumania. In the
meantime, with the help of JDC and OSE, various measures
had been taken to alleviate the misery of the orphans and
children with some surviving family members.

In late 1948, Syngalowski visited Rumania, where, in
1931, he had assisted in launching the ORT program. As a
result of this visit, programs were enlarged and training
units initiated or broadened, not only in Bucharest, but in
Iassy, Galatz, Botosani, Cluj, Oradea, Arad, and Timisoara.
Some 3,400 students were in training. However, as in many
other countries, the programs had to deal with continuous
departures for Israel of students who had not completed
their training.

The importance of the work in Rumania may be recognized in the fact that members of the government repeatedly
evidenced their positive attitude toward it. Useful as they
were, ORT's activities in Rumania did not continue long. In
1949, as in Poland, and for the same reasons, the government liquidated ORT activities. They were taken over by the
Jewish Democratic Committee, a Communist front.

Bulgaria

Although ORT work in Bulgaria was reestablished after the
war, it was only after a delegation of Bulgarian ORT members—Eduard Arie, A. Haravon, and Nathan Grinberg—
had consulted with the Paris headquarters in 1946 that it took
on significant proportions.

In October 1947, a technical school in Sofia was opened. Some teaching had occurred there earlier. A school also functioned in Plovdiv. Syngalowski visited Bulgaria in 1948. As in Rumania, representatives of the government expressed their admiration of ORT work.

Some 40,000 of the Bulgarian Jewish population of 50,000 emigrated to Israel, but ORT maintained its program for the remaining community up to the end of 1949, when the authorities demanded its liquidation. All told, some 2,000 students benefited from ORT training.

Like the Berlin school some years earlier, which was transferred to Leeds, the Sofia school was transplanted, with its teachers and students, to Jaffa, Israel where it became one of the first ORT training units in Israel, a root from which a number of ORT schools in Israel grew over the years.

Hungary

Perhaps because of its Western background, the Jewish community of Hungary preserved, even under the Soviets, more of its traditional character than did the Jews of other satellite countries. The Budapest community to this day maintains a rabbinical seminary, the only such institution in all of Eastern Europe.

From 1944 to 1949, Hungarian ORT functioned as a national organization integrated into the larger community. In Budapest, ORT operated a technical school for boys and a trade school for girls. In 1947, a training unit was established at Debrecen, and in 1949 further ORT workshops were set up in Miscolc, Gynongyos, Bekeszaba, and Szeged.

Educational work was under the supervision of the Hungarian authorities and ORT diplomas were recognized by the state. A small farm project was initiated in Bonyhad. Among the students were individuals preparing themselves for farming in Hungary. Others were training with a view to emigration to Israel.

Czechoslovakia

ORT efforts in Czechoslovakia were confined to the brief years of 1947 to 1949. The February 1948 coup transformed the country into a Soviet satellite. All institutions and organizations were taken over by the government. ORT was then conducting some 32 vocational courses providing training for about 650 students.

The program was not a productive one, involving, as it did, an unstable population of diverse backgrounds who were seeking emigration. Some units were closed because students had left the country before completing their training.

IN WESTERN EUROPE

France—Resurgent Jewry

After the war, France became a center of immigration for thousands of Jewish families who were unwilling or unable to return to countries in Eastern Europe. The newcomers joined the French Jews who survived the Holocaust in the underground or had returned from Switzerland, Spain, and other countries. France quickly became one of the important Jewish centers of Europe.

ORT-France had drastically reduced its activities during the last years of the occupation. Under the Nazis and Pétain's regime there had been little choice, and ORT was, in the words of Judge Leon Meiss, "half asleep."[7] With the liberation in December, 1944, ORT's first postwar conference at Voiron (Isere), was convened.

THE YEARS OF RECONSTRUCTION

French industry then faced a shortage of skilled manpower for reconstruction. ORT graduates helped to fill the ranks of the French labor force depleted by the war and occupation. Soon ORT-France was operating a substantial network of institutions in 17 French cities: Paris, Marseilles, Lyons, Nice, Grenoble, Aix-les-Bains, Cessieu, Limoges, Moissac, Toulouse, l'Isle Adam, Henoville, La Roche, Gambe de Pujols, les Angiroux, Boulogne-sur-Seine, and la Malmaison.

The program included 1,225 trainees, 151 of them in agriculture. Enrollment rose to 2,925 in 1948, but fell off in 1949 and 1950 due to departures to Israel. A number of training units were established, some for youths and others for adults, as well as a number of special programs, including one for maritime training. Special mention should be made of the model vocational center that was established in Montreuil-sur-Seine, a Paris suburb, which was made possible in 1948 through the efforts of David Dubinsky and a grant from the International Ladies Garment Workers Union of the U.S.

Accelerated training courses intended for individuals needing adjustment to the new technological conditions were introduced. Adults were taught specific operations that would permit them to hold industrial jobs. The French Ministry of Labor was especially interested in this type of training.

ORT-France devoted particular attention to the needs of Jewish artisans trying to reestablish themselves in their crafts. They were provided with tools and other forms of help, including, when necessary, financial assistance. The French Union of Jewish Artisans requested and received help in training and retraining job applicants whom they could not retrain themselves because of lack of special facilities and equipment.

ORT was called upon not only to provide vocational training but financial assistance through scholarships for those in apprenticeships with private masters and through providing tools for many of the apprentices. Women's American ORT rendered substantial assistance in this program by "adopting" ORT pupils, sending them food and clothing. ORT centers provided medical services, canteens, and even vacation colonies.

FARMING

In the late 1940's, ORT-France was faced with an increasing number of applicants for agricultural training at the three ORT farms in La Roche, Cambes de Pujols, and Gars. Its agricultural program provided assistance to Jewish farmers already working on farms. Under an agreement with the Intergovernmental Committee for Refugees, later IRO, and the French Jewish loan *kassa*, ORT was entrusted with examining applications for loans made by Jewish farmers.

It arranged also for agricultural training (*Hachsharah*) of young *halutzim* preparing for emigration to Israel. This work was done in cooperation with the Jewish Agency, which assumed the costs of farm operations and maintenance of the *halutzim*, ORT assuming program budgeting.

The signal place of ORT in Jewish life in France in the years following the liberation is illustrated by its sponsorship of the Museum of Jewish Popular Art, which was inaugurated in May 1949. The originator of the project was L. Frenkiel, at that time Director of ORT Technical Instruction Services. He had been associated with ORT from the early days of the Vilna Technikum in the twenties. The museum was for many years a significant element of Jewish cultural life in Paris.

The growth of ORT-France was enormously facilitated by an increase in local income, which included subsidies for selected projects from the Ministry of Labor and receipts from the "apprentice tax" paid by enterprises employing a certain minimum number of workers and intended to encourage vocational education.

IMPACT OF NORTH AFRICAN ARRIVALS

In the mid-1950's and early 1960's, ORT faced a new task resulting from the political changes in French North Africa. It was during this period that Tunisia, Morocco, and later, Algeria became independent states. The ancient Jewish communities in these countries were severely affected. Tens of thousands of Jews from Mahgreb, Western North Africa, unsure of their future in the new states, emigrated to France or to Israel. Already in the late 1950's, before Algeria became independent, large numbers of Algerian Jews, French citizens by virtue of the 1870 Cremieux decree, had departed for the metropolis.[8]

The North African Jewish migration and the influx of Jews from Eastern Europe changed the Jewish map of France. Its Jewish community, which had been depleted by deportations, became the largest in all Europe, numbering some 650,000 in the 1970's. New Jewish settlements have emerged throughout the country, particularly in Paris and its environs, around the port city of Marseilles, and in Toulouse. Newcomers of course had to undergo a process of adjustment to the new country and the very different society in which they now sought haven. (See ORT in North Africa, below.)

ORT-France mobilized for the new task of the mid-fifties and sixties. The old *Ecole de Travail* in Paris, taken over by ORT, grew to include preparation for a variety of modern skills. Schools in Lyons and Marseilles were reorganized and transferred to larger quarters. The Strasbourg school, with its boarding facilities, created a better climate for deep-rooted Jewish life. Perhaps the tradition of the Strasbourg community facilitated the kind of Jewishness which imbued this school. The school at Villiers Le Bel, with its dormitory for young adults, attracted young men without a place to live.

In Toulouse, an interesting institution was brought to life in the 1970's with the cooperation of religious elements—a yeshiva where, in addition to the regular curriculum of religious studies, students received vocational training in various technical fields. This was not the first time that ORT had engaged in education uniting Torah and Technology, but the Toulouse project, *Yeshiva Torah et Technique*, was a significant innovation in the south of France, where many Jewish communities had recently received newcomers from North Africa.

BROADENED SCOPE

Assisted by French Women's ORT, ORT devoted much attention to basic educational needs, which were important for North African Jewish children who, during the years of crisis, had been unable to receive schooling in their native countries. Much was done to compensate for the education they had missed; for example, visits to museums and exhibits (not typically part of an ORT school curriculum) became a part of the program. Many young people required psychological guidance, and a service for this purpose was created in Paris.

A separate ORT department dealt with apprentices who needed help not only while in training but in finding appropriate jobs after completing their training. Courses were developed for children, youths, and adults of both sexes. Occupational training at a high level included courses in electronics, mechanics, computer operation and programming, plumbing, and tailoring, as well as accounting, communication, secretarial work, and other white-collar skills.

Students were prepared for the C.A.P. (certificate of vocational aptitude), the B.E.P. (certificate of vocational studies), and a technical baccalaureate, granted by the Ministry of National Education. Adult trainees worked toward certificates of technician or skilled worker, both issued by the Labor Ministry.

In scope and variety of activities, ORT-France occupies second place only to ORT in Israel. It achieved its high status because it succeeded in integrating its schools into the French system of vocational and technical education, including in its student population some non-Jewish students.

The high level reached by French ORT may be attributed to several factors, not least among them an imaginative local leadership and capable administration. The post-liberation leadership team has included, among others, Leon Meiss, Daniel Mayer, Roger Nathan, Pierre Dreyfus, Ruben Grinberg, Louis Kahn, Jules Moch, Guy de Rothschild, Robert

TABLE 13

ORT Trainees in France—1950–1977

	Trainees
1950	1,746
1957	3,294
1960	3,170
1962	4,002
1966	5,389
1971	5,737
1973	5,778
1977	6,966

Source: F. Schrager's report in the ORT history files
and W.O.U. reports covering the period.

Blum, and Mme. L. Roubach. For many years the professional head of ORT-France was Feivel Schrager who, after
retirement in 1972, remained active in ORT councils in Paris
and at the center. After Schrager's retirement, George
Melamed took over the directorship, later succeeded by Jules
Bloch.

Great Britain—from Program to Organizaton

ORT in England did not fare well during the war years
when vocational training was being increasingly taken over
by the government. There may also have been a lack of
strong leadership.

In 1942, in the midst of the war, ORT schools and hostels
were without funds and had to close their doors. A. Halpern, Chairman of British ORT from the early 1920's, who
was then in the United States, returned to England in the
summer of 1943 where he found the ORT situation confused. Following his discussions with Lord Rothschild,
Chairman of the British Board of Deputies Selig Brodetsky,
and the old ORT leaders Mr. and Mrs. Mowshovitch, it was
decided that the work of the practically defunct ORT society
should be revived.[9] The joint British ORT-OSE Committee
was no longer interested in educational work, and it was felt

that no purpose would be served in restoring it. In 1946, the Joint Committee was disbanded and the partners went their separate ways.

Initial focus was on the restoration of the vocational center in Chesham, Buckinghampshire. A new ORT training center was soon opened in Old Brampton Road, South Kensington, where courses in dressmaking and designing were conducted for DP camp survivors lodged in London hostels. Another initiative was the opening in London of a maritime course, an innovation in Jewish vocational training. In 1947, in cooperation with *Hechalutz*, an ORT farm was established at Goldington, Bury, in Bedfordshire, which provided preparation for *Aliyah*. This program, supported mainly by contributions from abroad, was plagued by lack of funds.

The Kensington school, which trained some 200 young people, mainly survivors of the Belsen camp in the British DP zone in Germany, was closed in 1950. The last school to operate in England was the dressmaking unit at Belsize Lane, Hampstead.[10]

In the late 1940's, British ORT participated in the vocational activities conducted by the World ORT Union among Jewish DPs in the British zone in Germany and in Palestine, under the British administration until the establishment of Israel, by contributing supplies and instructors. Lady Rose Henriques, a leading member of British ORT and British Women's ORT, visited Jewish DPs in camps in Germany and actively participated in ORT efforts on their behalf.

In the meantime there had occurred a change of guard in the ORT organization in Great Britain.

A GENERATIONAL CHANGE

As in France, the Russian founders were leaving the stage and being replaced by Britons. The Mowshovitches, the Wolffs, and others, who represented the old ORT tradition of work in the Diaspora, were considered in some circles to be unsympathetic to Zionism and perhaps unable, under the changed circumstances, to create the necessary climate for the growth of an ORT organization.[11]

Whatever the case, all concerned, in both England and Geneva, believed that British ORT must make a vigorous effort to reestablish itself. Halpern resigned from the British ORT chairmanship in 1955. In 1956, Master A. S. Diamond, a British jurist, took over the leadership, along with a group of concerned Jews, among them Prof. Norman Bentwich, Sir Keith Joseph, Sir Leon Simon, Lord Silkin, Lady Rose Henriques, and Mr. and Mrs. H. H. Wingate.

Despite some ups and downs, activities were revitalized, essentially in terms of supporting general ORT programs. British Women's ORT, started by Mrs. Wingate and including, among others, Mrs. S. Beloff, Mrs. Renee Soskin, and Lady Rose Henriques, helped to bring ORT back to the Jewish community through public meetings and publicity.

In the 1950's, after much discussion, and perhaps prompted by Geneva, British ORT decided to further change its strategy. In 1956 it appointed a professional, Hilary Goldberg, to direct its activities, but it took some years to get things going. An effort was made to enlarge the constituency through groups representing the professions and special interests.

Gabriel D. Sacher, who had led British ORT efforts since 1961, was elected a vice president of the World ORT Union. During his tenure, British ORT's financial contributions to World ORT programs rose substantially. The ORT School for Agromechanics at Natanya in Israel was one of the institutions endowed by Sacher. By mid-1970, British ORT membership numbered 5,000, among whom were many of the younger generation, who provided a healthy basis for future activities.

The road has not always been upward. In the early 1970's, England was beset with economic troubles, rising inflation, and difficulties on the Stock Exchange, all of which had an impact on fund-raising.

In 1975, David Young, a lawyer and banker, took over the chairmanship of British ORT. Since 1974 he has been Chairman of the Commission on Organization and Fund-Raising of the World ORT Union. At the same time, Lord Goodman, a leader in many public endeavors in England, was elected President of British ORT, a position that had been vacant for many years.[12] These organizational changes have borne good fruit.

THE JEWISH COLONIZATION ASSOCIATION

ICA, the Jewish Colonization Association, continuing a tradition dating back to Tsarist Russia and located in England since World War II, has made substantial contributions to various ORT programs. Cooperation with ICA has involved many projects in Iran, North Africa, and Latin America, and some projects in Israel. It has also involved artisan loan programs. ICA directors, J. Mirkin, Louis Oungre, V. Girmunsky and, later, Joseph Neville, were helpful as was the veteran Jewish communal worker, David Schweitzer.

Switzerland—Postwar Profile

ORT work in Switzerland reached a peak in 1945, when some 2,000 pupils were in training in Geneva, Zurich, Basle, and other cities. Local activities were reduced, due to the departure of refugees after the war. The number of Jewish refugees actually decreased from some 20,000 in 1945 to about 6,500 in 1946 and to 3,000 by 1949.

Swiss ORT, however, continued to perform special services arising from the Holocaust aftermath. Buchenwald survivors, on being freed from the camp, went to Switzerland for physical rehabilitation or cure of their ailments. Some were permitted to remain for courses in vocational training. At the end of 1947, in Davos, two training workshops were opened for cured tubercular patients and patients still in treatment but able to work. One workshop had 17 young girls and women in dressmaking; the other, 35 young people

Classroom in the ORT Technical Institute in Buenos Aires, in its enlarged and updated quarters.

Computer center at the ORT Institute in Buenos Aires, established in the late seventies.

In a community school in Mendoza, Argentina, one of many in which ORT programs were established in the 60's and 70's.

Rio de Janeiro ORT Institute of Technology, Laboratory in Electronics, established in the 1970's.

In the Jewish community school in Santiago, Chile. Photo taken in the late 1970's.

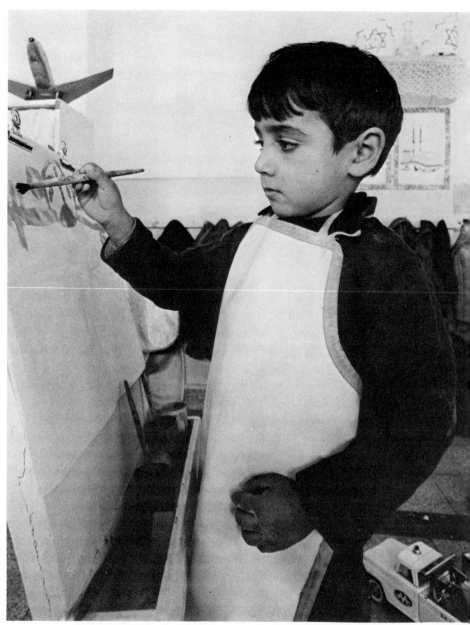

ORT kindergarten for Soviet Jewish children in Rome, 1978.

Language laboratory at the ORT Technical College in Business Administration in Milan, Italy, 1977.

English language laboratory for Soviet transmigrants at the Rome ORT School.

Plumbing course in the ORT Ecole de Travail, Paris, 1956. This is one of the earliest vocational schools in Western Europe.

ORT Technical School in Toulouse, established in the 1950's and greatly enlarged in subsequent decades.

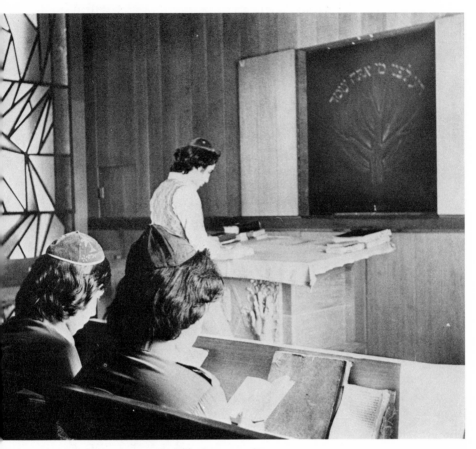

Synagogue service at an ORT school.

EVREI,

Salvaţi pe copiii voştri, înscriindu-i la cursurile Asociaţiei O. R. T.

O. R. T. are ateliere echipate cu cele mai moderne instalaţii.

Diploma O. R. T. dă o existenţă sigură în orice timp şi în orice loc.

O. R. T. ajută pe elevii merituoşi şi dă gratuit instrumente absolvenţilor.

Locurile fiind limitate, înscrieţi pe copiii voştri, dela 14 ani împliniţi, la următoarele cursuri:

MECANICĂ
STRUNGARIE
LACATUŞERIE
SUDURA - AUTOGENA
CEASORNICARIE
RADIO TECHNICA
ELECTRO BOBINAGE
TAMPLARIE
CARTONAGE
LEGĂTORIE

Dupa doi ani de studii vor avea drept de exerciţiul profesiunii.

Inscrierile au loc la sediul din Bucureşti, strada Episcopul Radu 31. Telefon 2.23.25 (Tram. 1, 16, 17 staţia Ardeleni şi Toamnei).

Poster announcing first ORT programs in Rumania after World War II.

in leather work. All, former camp inmates, had spent time in Davos sanatoriums and had to remain in the mountains until cured. The vocations selected were, according to expert advice, suited to these physically handicapped individuals.

In 1949, 209 pupils were still being trained in Basle, Montana, Davos, Zurich, St. Gal, and Bea. From the beginning in 1943 through 1950, about 5,000 men, women, and young people were trained in Swiss ORT schools. Beside local programs, Swiss ORT, as well as the Swiss authorities, had given support to the Anieres Institute (see above).

Nor was organization neglected. As of 1950, the Swiss ORT dues-paying membership, in a population of 22,000, numbered more than 4,000. ORT has sustained its community activity. Its active supporters have included, among others, Claude Bigart, Mr. and Mrs. Armand Brunschwig, Hans Baer, Otto Heim, and Dr. Berthold Wyler. For more than a decade, Mrs. André Maus was president of Swiss Women's ORT and Swiss ORT.

Germany and Austria—Phasing Out

After ORT activities in Germany and Austria peaked in the late 1940's, the situation in these countries underwent a change. In 1951, a substantial group of remaining Jewish DPs left for the United States, Canada, and Australia. The phasing out of IRO activities had a discouraging effect on Jewish efforts.

During the 1950's, the ORT school in Hamburg, in the British zone, closed, as did the schools in Frankfurt, Furth, Stuttgart, Wiesbaden, and Passen in the American zone. While the DP problem had, in the main, been solved by 1951, there was still one camp, Fohrenwald, in Bavaria, that was not closed until 1957.

The military authorities continued their support of ORT work and were helpful in facilitating relations with the German administration. ORT benefited by close cooperation with JDC, HIAS, and the Council of Voluntary Agencies.

At the end of 1950, only two ORT schools were functioning in Austria, one in Vienna and the other in Hallein, with some 280 students. In addition, there were classes in Hebrew and English. As in Germany, IRO cooperated with and encouraged ORT efforts.

Facilities for work among DPs, which had been coming to a close, had to be revived in the late 1950's when a substantial number of Hungarian Jews, fleeing the repression and lawlessness that followed the 1956 revolt in Hungary, came to Austria.

At the request of the U.S. Escapee Program (U.S.E.P.) some 2800 non-Jewish students were served by ORT, the cost being borne by the United States. Other programs of vocational training were undertaken in cooperation with the U.N. High Commissioner for Refugees.

Italy

Since the beginning of 1950, ORT activities in Italy had shifted from assistance to DPs to training of indigenous Jewish youth. There was a need, however, for vocational training among "settled" refugees who, in the early 1950's, represented almost 25 per cent of the Jewish population of Italy. Later, there was an influx of additional Jewish refugees from Egypt, from Libya (some of them Italian citizens), and from Hungary, following the 1956 revolt.

As the result of a visit by Syngalowski who, together with Renzo Levi, the Chairman of the Executive Committee of Italian ORT, elaborated a number of measures to promote local activities, the program in Italy assumed new dimensions. A conference was held in Rome, under the chairmanship of R. Cantoni, to discuss efforts on behalf of local needs.

The new Italian program had its unique problems. One was the necessity of teaching in different languages, Italian for the local people and Yiddish, Rumanian, and Polish for the refugees. At various times schools functioned in Rome, Leghorn, Milan, Turin, Florence, Venice, Trieste, and

Cevoli, and a training farm in collaboration with Italian *Hechalutz* operated at Cevoli San Marco.

At the request of IRO, vocational training had been introduced for the physically handicapped in the JDC sanatarium at Merano and at the Grottaferrata center. The significance of this IRO-supported work went beyond the immediate aims of vocational rehabilitation; it was of great value as a booster to the health and morale of the trainees.

The Italian government recognized ORT activities as a means of combatting continuing unemployment. In the mid-1950's, nearly all ORT students over 14 years of age received monthly government unemployment checks. This was a great aid in financing the program, at the same time integrating it into state efforts to combat unemployment.

Particularly noteworthy was a dental mechanics school in Milan, whose standards were such as to lead local dentists to seek admission. The television training course in Milan was a great attraction for Jewish youths, providing an opportunity for upward mobility; graduates had no difficulty in finding well-paid jobs and their status was respected.

As time went on, by the mid-fifties, ORT programs in Italy, unlike ORT work in the two other DP countries, stabilized and the schools gradually acquired prestige in the community. The new five-year *Lycee Scientifico* and the Business and Language Schools in Rome and Milan are considered an important part of the Jewish school system, providing both general and Jewish education. ORT-Italy also has assisted the Jewish communities of Venice, Genoa, and Florence with Hebrew teaching.

SOVIET TRANSMIGRATION

Toward the end of the 1960's and early 1970's, Italian ORT, led by Bruno Jarrach, suddenly came face to face with a situation, unlike any faced before—the arrival in Italy of emigrants from Soviet Russia.

While these migrants had visas for Israel, many decided

to go to the United States, Canada, or Australia. They did not have visas to these countries and had to go to Italy to obtain them. This involved waiting periods in Italy of varied duration. JDC took over refugee care and maintenance, while HIAS dealt with legal and other aspects of emigration. ORT undertook to provide language instruction.

In time the project reached substantial proportions as an increasing number of Russian emigrants were opting for the West. In the late 1970's, nearly 1,000 individuals at a time attended 25 courses for 15 hours a week of instruction. Facilities at an elementary level were provided for refugee children. The program for English courses and Jewish education was later concentrated in Ostia, where over 90 per cent of emigrants were housed, and in Rome, where the beneficiaries were mainly physicians preparing for medical examinations and adults living in Rome. While language instruction is technically not vocational training, the ORT undertaking in this aspect has nevertheless proved an important service to emigrants using the waiting period in Italy to acquire the knowledge of English they would need in their new occupational pursuits.[13]

Benelux at Several Stages

ORT has been active in all three Benelux countries. Its work was a postwar initiative that essentially followed Jewish refugees and DPs seeking new homes.

Belgian ORT was established in 1946 under the leadership of Alfred M. Ginsberg, Chairman of ORT in Antwerp, R. Van Prag, Chairman of the Executive Committee of Belgian ORT, and P. Philippson. From the beginning, Belgian ORT has maintained close contact with the Unemployment Relief Fund of the Belgian Ministry of Labor, which engages in rehabilitating unemployed workers and was interested in the vocational training provided by ORT.

One of the first tasks of Belgian ORT was to provide for Jewish children who had returned from camps or places of refuge and who had not had sufficient education to enable them to enter general schools. At the same time, ORT provided training for adults, most of whom, like the children, had returned from camps.

As of 1949, some 1,500 persons had been trained in seven vocational schools and 20 training workshops in Brussels and Antwerp, more than half of whom were under 18 years of age. In the summer of 1946, a training farm for *Aliyah* groups was founded at Kessel-Loo. Most of the 160 students later emigrated to Israel. After the closing of the local *Aliyah* home, ORT established an agricultural center at Rouquieres.

In 1947, Belgian ORT concluded an agreement with JDC whereby ORT pupils were given cash assistance to cover their immediate needs. Financial support was provided also by Women's American ORT which sent food and clothing parcels and also provided furnishings for the schools.

With the departure of many refugees for Israel and the stabilization of conditions, attendance in ORT courses dropped. In 1951, some five years after the establishment of the program, 444 students were being trained in electromechanics, dressmaking, and fashion design; in 1958 there were 966. The program came to an end in the mid-1960's.

In Holland ORT began in 1946 under inauspicious circumstances. Of the 150,000 Dutch Jews, 120,000 had been deported by the Nazis. The remaining 30,000 included returnees from Nazi camps and several thousand children who had been hidden during the war. After their gruesome experiences many Dutch Jews did not wish to remain in Holland and prepared themselves for *Aliyah*. It was the task of ORT to provide the would-be emigrants with skills that would be helpful in their new homes.

Modest beginnings were made in Amsterdam in 1946 where a course was provided in cutting and dressmaking for women, most of them refugees who needed vocational requalification. Of particular importance were the workshops for children, most of them orphans and some of whom had never had an opportunity to attend any school. Later, therapy was provided in homes for the aged.

In 1950 there were 24 vocational courses and training workshops, and in 1951, 33 with 22 instructors teaching 17 trades to more than 700 students. Part of the cost was paid by IRO, which covered outlays for DPs brought to Holland with the permission of the authorities. In time, the ORT program became self-supporting.

Among ORT leaders in Holland were Dr. A. Vedder, I. Rafalowitch, and Dr. A. Polak.

ORT in Luxembourg was limited to supportive activities. The small Jewish community has maintained its efforts on behalf of ORT projects. Membership in 1975 was 100.

*Greece**

After the liberation, and the departure of many of the survivors for Palestine, the Jewish population of Greece numbered 9,000 to 10,000. ORT was founded there in 1948, but, before the creation of ORT, JDC, aware that the survivors needed vocational readaptation and that the youth needed some kind of training, had set up lingerie-making and cutting courses for some 80 to 90 people.

ORT continued some of these projects and added a machine shop for boys, and evening classes in mechanical drafting. All told, some 120 trainees participated in the program, which was established to provide skills that would be useful in either Greece or Israel, to which there was considerable migration. A welding course started earlier was closed in 1951-52, when the seven graduates left for well-paid jobs in Israel. The program in Greece was terminated in 1956 due to lack of students.

However, Greek ORT has maintained a program of material assistance to students in vocational training in private and public trade schools. Some later continued their training at the ORT Central Institute in Anieres, Switzerland.

---

*While Greece is, technically, in Eastern Europe, it belongs, geopolitically, to the West.

LATIN AMERICA
—SEARCH FOR A ROLE

From Paris before the war and from New York during the war, ORT had tried to develop programs and organizations in Latin America, sometimes in cooperation with OSE. During the war, in fact, a Latin-American ORT-OSE Confederation had functioned in Buenos Aires. In the early 1940's, the New York Emergency Committee endeavored to create among the 600,000 Latin American Jews a base for financial campaigns and a vocational training program.

The first ORT delegate to Latin America was Ilya Trotzky. Dr. Moise Merkin joined the work there during the war, and in 1941, Dr. Boris Surovich went there. Latin America was a natural place for ORT since during the pre-and postwar periods streams of refugees had sought to reestablish in Latin America the lives that had been broken by the Nazis and the war.

Latin America came under concentrated ORT study and exploration by the mid-fifties.

In 1957, Schrager visited Argentina, Brazil, and Uruguay, where, along with the local leadership, he investigated the possibilities of opening new ORT projects. William Haber, Paul Bernick and Samuel Milman of New York, Max A. Braude and Dr. Vladimir Halperin of Geneva, and many others came later. Women's American ORT's interest intensified, particularly in the '60s, with numerous delegation visits.

In 1966, Bernard Wand-Polak, who had served in France, North Africa, and Israel, was appointed Director of Latin-American Operations for the World ORT Union, and with his presence on the scene began a new and more intensive chapter of ORT on the continent.

Initial Steps in Argentina

The first ORT school was opened in Buenos Aires in 1941. The initiative was a welcome one since it addressed itself to a community enlarged by an influx of refugees from occupied Europe. In addition, the country was in need of skilled workers and local industry was clamoring for the reinstitution of the apprenticeship system.

Local leaders, among others, included Moses Arenburg and Jacob Wengrower, President and Secretary-General respectively of the South American ORT Federation in Buenos Aires, and Arnoldo Taubenschlag, Chairman of ORT in Argentina.

In 1942 the school conducted a three-year course for 231 students and had applications from an additional 400 who could not be accepted because of lack of space.[14] It provided a fairly high level of education, including trigonometry, algebra, chemistry, and Jewish studies. There were also evening courses for adults under a 12- to 18-month curriculum.

It is interesting, and perhaps due to the presence of the refugees, that in an inquiry as to preferred language of instruction, 72 per cent of the students chose Yiddish. A large majority of the students had come from Poland and Germany and most were from poor or low-income families.

The Women's ORT Committee of Argentina provided a much-appreciated cafeteria. By war's end, some four years after its founding, the school was providing technical instruction to some 150 students, in addition to courses for apprentices.

Activities spread to provincial areas. A school for agromechanics in the ICA settlement at Dominguez acquired new agricultural machinery through grants from ICA and the World ORT Union. In Dominguez and Clara, courses were conducted in sewing, knitting, and design. A workshop was opened in primary training of children of Jewish farmers.

SOPHISTICATED EDUCATION TAKES HOLD

By the mid-sixties, ORT schools in Latin America, with Buenos Aires in the lead, underwent a change.

The innovative Buenos Aires Technical School attained

an enviable reputation. It became an important educational center recognized by the government, attracting students from all social groups, including the well-to-do. It is now under a six-year curriculum.

In 1975 its 676 students were divided into 21 classes in training for careers in electronics, chemistry, and data processing and other subjects. The course in data processing was the only one in the country. Programs, although prepared by ORT experts, require approval by the state. ORT graduates are qualified to pursue further study at the State Technological University, which grants diplomas in engineering.

Of the 48 hours of general weekly instruction, six are devoted to Jewish studies, including Hebrew, Jewish history, and literature; the Jewish studies program includes celebration of Jewish holidays and Israeli folk dancing.

Evening courses, in radio and T.V., recognized and subsidized by the government, had some 150 students in 1975, most of them adults looking for advanced training.

An interesting initiative was vocational training organized at the girls' religious Shuba Israel School. Attended by girls from orthodox Sephardic families, the school has about 50 students.

An Institute for Educational Technology was established in Buenos Aires in the mid-'70s to study the application of modern teaching methods in ORT schools in Argentina and other Jewish institutions. The Institute organized seminars on apprenticeship for instructors of the ORT Technical Schools. A seminar on creative education was conducted for teachers at Chaim Weitzman College in Santiago, Chile and still others at the *College Estado de Israel* in Asuncion, Paraguay, and the Max Nordau School in Mendoza, Argentina. ["Weitzman" is, of course, local spelling for Weizmann.]

In 1975, ORT conducted creative education programs in 11 Jewish communal schools for 3,292 pupils. These schools have manual education workshops and some are equipped with science laboratories. ORT encouraged the conversion of Jewish academic schools to comprehensive education.

In addition to annual grants from the World ORT Union

and Women's American ORT, the ORT school system in Argentina has benefited from government allocations to cover a part of teachers' salaries, and AMIA (the communal coordinating center) has included allocations to ORT in its grants to schools with Jewish study programs.

Uruguay—the Montevideo Community

The Uruguay Jewish community has consisted mainly of immigrants from Poland and Rumania between the wars and German refugees during the Nazi period. The community was open to the idea of professional training for the younger generation, and ORT representatives were welcomed.

An ORT committee headed by Dr. Shmul Kobrin was organized, and the first school was established in Montevideo in 1943, with some 100 trainees pursuing a three-year course for youths and a one-year course for adults seeking occupational requalification. Up to 1949, enrollment remained stable at around 100.

The school opened in rented premises, but later acquired its own building. Local contributions covered operational expenses; the World ORT Union subsidized the purchase.

Deterioration in economic conditions, increasing inflation, and general instability in the country led to Jewish emigration to other parts of the continent and other areas. The school has, however, maintained its program and even enlarged it by including courses in preparation for the baccalaureate.

In Brazil

Work in Brazil began in 1943, during the war, when Dr. Merkin came there as a representative of the South American ORT Federation. ORT societies were organized in Rio de Janeiro and São Paulo. The Klabins, a local family, were very helpful in establishing the ORT program.

In São Paulo, courses were given in mechanics, electricity, knitting, and diamond-polishing. São Paulo ORT, due to social and economic conditions, closed its training program in the mid-1950's.

In Rio de Janeiro the situation was different. Under the strong leadership of a group of ORT activists, including Shmuel Malamud, Waldemar Chindler, Israel Steinberg, Israel Saubel, and Martin Sztern, ORT attained a substantial place in Jewish education.

A school was established in 1945, the first ORT school in Latin America to function in a building of its own. In 1951, a bequest from Szymon Raskin and financial support from the local community permitted enlargement of the building. The school provided training courses at elementary and advanced levels in addition to courses in Jewish education. In the mid-1950's, courses in television were introduced.

In 1968, the school moved to another site, at the same time enlarging its curriculum to include electronics, chemistry, business administration, and data processing. All told in 1975, ORT programs, including training in the primary school, covered over 900.[15]

In Chile—Santiago

Jewish refugees arriving in Chile during the Nazi period doubled the Jewish population there, and it became of the utmost importance to provide them with vocational education and vocational requalification courses. Dr. Merkin visited Chile in 1943 and was instrumental in creating a local ORT committee, of which Samuel Goren was Chairman.

The ORT school in Santiago is officially recognized by the government. Its curriculum in mechanics and electricity corresponds to that of a technical high school. An ORT diploma qualifies a graduate to apply to the State University for Industrial Engineering. The school has an excellent reputation and many non-Jews are eager to send their children there. Classes in mechanics and woodworking were organized for boys and girls in *Hechalutz*.

In 1976, ORT concluded an agreement with the local *Vaad Hajinuj* involving the introduction of the ORT programs in science and technology. Such teaching had already begun in the Weitzman [*sic*] and Ben-Gurion schools.

In Bolivia

The population of the Jewish community of Bolivia rose from some 500 in the late 1920's to some 8,000 by the early 1940's. An ORT committee had been created in La Paz as early as 1941 which had the support of the community and in which the government, concerned with the need for technically skilled manpower, was interested. In La Paz courses were given in mechanics, and in Cochabamba, short-term mechanical training courses. In the late 1940's, when the Jewish population had been drastically reduced by emigration, the program had to be closed.

In Cuba—Havana

A program was introduced in the early 1940's in Cuba, where some efforts had been initiated as early as 1935, when an *ORT Komitet* was organized by local Jews.[16] It was not until 1943, however, that a school was established to help meet the needs of newly arrived Jewish immigrants. It was closed at the end of the war when many of the refugees went to new homes. In 1947, following a visit by Philip Block, former Executive Director of American ORT Federation, a vocational center was opened in Havana where courses were provided in watchmaking, dressmaking, and leather work. This project, while popular, was closed in 1959 due to political changes in the country and a dwindling Jewish population.

In Mexico

An ORT committee was organized in Mexico as early as 1935, when a large number of Jewish refugees with United States visas came to Mexico to await their "numbers" (entry permits).[17]

Among them were Jewish tailors, shoemakers, carpenters, and electricians who needed machinery and equipment if they were to earn a living and not become a burden to the community. ORT initiated a campaign, not unlike the U.S. *Gezeig* campaign of the 1920's, that was greeted enthusiastically by all concerned.

The Central Committee, the coordinating communal agency of Mexican Jews, created an ORT commission, underwritten by the World ORT Union, to conduct this constructive project.[18] The Mexican Jewish community has continued to respond to ORT appeals, and ORT delegates have maintained liaison with ORT friends in Mexico. Among the delegates have been Milman of New York, and Jacob Oleiski and Joseph Harmatz of Israel.

Elsewhere in Latin America

A supportive ORT committee is functioning also in Lima, Peru where, in addition to fund-raising efforts, it collaborated with the local Jewish school in introducing a creative education program. There were also ORT committees in Quito and Guayaquil in Ecuador, and in Venezuela and Trinidad.

ORT representative Dr. E. Barak visited Colombia, Panama, Costa Rica, Nicaragua, Honduras, San Salvador, and Guatemala, bringing to the Jewish communities in these countries (and others he visited) the ORT message.

Supportive and functional activities of ORT in Latin America have been of major significance. Of special importance has been the evolution of ORT schools toward higher standards of training. From relatively small and minor programs providing job skills, the schools have become sophisticated, high-standard institutions providing the equivalent of junior college education on a level to attract students seeking careers and upward occupational mobility.[20]

SUPPORTIVE GROUPS

In many countries, ORT has developed supportive organizations which provide the means for work elsewhere. Funds for these efforts have come from many sources. In the raising of these funds some smaller Jewish communities have played an important role. Seven of these are mentioned here: the Scandinavian countries, South Africa, Australia and Canada.

There is no need for ORT schools among the small Jewish communities of the Scandinavian countries. Nevertheless, the Jews of Sweden, Denmark, Norway, and Finland have assisted ORT programs elsewhere. Mention should be made of the fact that ORT activities have elicited a favorable response from official circles in Scandinavia.

Among others, Daniel Mayer, F. Schrager, V. Halperin, and S. Milman have visited the Scandinavian area and helped in the promotion of local efforts.

Sweden

Vladimir Grossman was sent by the World ORT Union on a mission to Sweden and, later, returned to Stockholm to continue his educational and organization work. ORT representative Ilya Trotzky has also worked there.

Highly industrialized Sweden has responded to ORT by allocating government funds for the acquisition of machinery for ORT schools in Israel. In 1972, an ORT study group consisting of Joseph Harmatz, I. Goralnik, and David Alberstein visited Stockholm, their visit having been made possible by the Swedish Engineering Employers' Association in cooperation with the Swedish Board of Education.

In 1977, the Swedish Internal Development Authority made a grant to Swedish ORT to be used for scholarships at the central ORT Institute in Anieres for future teachers in developing countries.

The local Swedish ORT leadership, among whom are Olaf Lamm, Guimar Josephson, Ivar Philipson, David Kopnivsky, and Margot Friedman, have propagated ORT ideas among interested groups, and been well received.

Denmark

Danish ORT obtained grants for ORT projects from the National Committee for Refugees. Leo Fischer, Dr. Sophus Appenheim, and Ludwig Trier, among others, have been active on behalf of ORT. The importance of their efforts may be gauged by the fact that, in the 1970's, Prof. Isi Foighel, who had been Chairman of the Jewish Community in Copenhagen and President of the Danish Refugee Council, was elected a Vice-President of the ORT Central Board.

Norway

In Norway, a committee to support ORT activities, created in 1960, has a non-Jewish majority and was presided over by the Bishop of Trondheim. It was instrumental in obtaining support for special ORT projects, including a grant for the language training program for Soviet Jewish emigrants in Rome and elsewhere. It contributed to the construction of the ORT school in Marseilles, as well as to other projects.

Finland

In the early 1950's, a new ORT organization was set up in Finland, led by I. Davidkin of Helsinki, and a fund-raising campaign was conducted there by Dr. E. Haskin, a delegate of the World ORT Union.

South Africa

ORT activities in South Africa have been limited to vocational guidance. As we have pointed out earlier, this began following Bramson's visit in 1927; an ORT-OSE Committee was formed in 1936.

Between 1940 and 1950, the ORT Occupational Bureau in Johannesburg and its branch in Cape Town counseled and placed some 1,200 individuals in 80 different trades. South African ORT has conducted a farming center for Jewish youths, which also provides a *Hechalutz* program for those planning to go to Israel. It has also maintained an ORT Bursary Trust which has provided scholarships to individuals wishing to study at technical colleges and universities and whose parents are unable to assume the expense.

Despite changes in the composition of the Jewish group and in the economic situation, ORT in South Africa has maintained its significant support of ORT activities elsewhere. Students at the Anieres Institute have appreciated the radio laboratory established through a donation from Abe Shaban.

In 1975, ORT membership in South Africa stood at 7,500, about eight per cent of the Jewish population. In the 1970's, David Sussman, Bazil Winick, and Richard Goldstone led the organization. Mrs. Freda Feldman of the ORT founding family was still active in ORT efforts.

Canada and Australia

In 1943, ORT organized a vocational school in Canada. Earlier, it had introduced vocational courses in the internment camps for German-Jewish refugees. In Canada, as in South Africa, the essential role of the organization has been fundraising for general ORT activities.

ORT in Canada was accepted by the government through its Federal agency, CIDA (Canadian International Development Agency), and several provincial governments as the only Jewish organization eligible for matching funds in developing countries. Among the founders were Mr. and Mrs. Leon Crystal. For over fifteen years the leading personality in Canadian ORT was Dr. Lou Harris. In recent years ORT in Canada has been led by Mr. Lyone Heppner, Dorothy Shoichet, and Ruth Druxerman.

Funds for ORT work have come from Australia. It includes membership dues as well as an allocation to be used in projects connected with refugees.

Chapter XVI

New Horizons

It was only after World War II that ORT began systematic work in countries outside the traditional Ashkenazic communities. The world had shrunk after the Holocaust and Jewish communities everywhere had become "One World." The needs in some of the Jewish communities of Africa and Asia were overwhelming.

In Moslem and Other Lands

Even before the war was over, the ORT Emergency Committee in New York had been considering the possibilities of activity in North Africa where Jewish people had been living before it became a Roman province. It had discussed such an initiative with *Alliance Israelite Universelle*, which had experience in the area (see Chapter XI).

Jews of the area had for centuries been working predominantly as peddlers and semi-skilled artisans; with no facilities available for acquiring modern skills they were at the bottom rung of society, without hope of bettering their social and economic status. ORT went into the area fully

304

aware of the awesome dimension of the problems and of the obstacles that might arise in years to come.

French North Africa was the first area to be liberated by the Allies, in 1942. It was several years before ORT began to conduct programs among the Jews of Algeria, Morocco, and Tunisia. Like those of other Jewish agencies, these activities were hampered by the political and military situation in the area.

Algeria—From Earliest Contact to the End

In 1943, the ORT Emergency Committee in New York, as a pilot project, had made a small grant to a school in Algiers, with the proviso that the Geneva office approve the action. Algeria was then an organic part of France, its territory including three French departments. While the Jews of Algeria, French citizens since the 1870 Cremieux decree, were legally in a different position from their co-religionists of Morocco and Tunisia, they were overwhelmingly in need of vocational education geared to the younger generation.[1]

Educational opportunities in Algeria had in fact been liquidated during the Pétain regime by the abrogation of the Cremieux decree in 1940, with the result that Jewish youths lost some five years of schooling.

Beginning in 1947, ORT brought its programs to three centers of Algeria—Algiers, Oran, and Constantine. Its schools provided training in 17 skills from stenography and typewriting for girls to plumbing and mechanics for boys. Algerian central and municipal authorities supported these programs[2] which were maintained for some 13 years.

In the late 1950's, the political situation in Algeria underwent a radical change. Algerian nationalists were demanding independence, while the French in Algeria, some of them third-and-fourth-generation Algerian-born, wished to preserve what in fact was a semi-colonial regime.

Civil war engulfed Algeria, and Algerian Jews became frequent victims of the fighting on both sides. Jewish property was destroyed. The great synagogue of Algiers, built by Napoleon III and situated in the Casbah, one of the most beautiful prayer houses in the city, was looted in 1960.

In 1961, Algeria became independent. This event signaled the end of this ancient Jewish community. Fearing for their future they left along with Frenchmen, some for Israel, but most for France, where they swelled the enrollments of the hospitable ORT schools. Thus ended the ORT program in Algeria.

Tunisia and Morocco

Unlike Algeria, Tunisia and Morocco were French protectorates. ORT programs in Tunisia began in 1950. Elie Nataf was President of the local ORT organization. On his death, he was replaced by Albert Bessis, who remained at the helm until his death in 1972.

Administratively, ORT activities have been under the direction of A. Berlant. Later, David Alberstein took over the direction. Given conditions in Tunisia the program was significant in bringing modern technology to the youth of the community. During the mid-1950's instruction was provided to some 1,100 students.

In 1956, after prolonged negotiations, France recognized Tunisian independence. Although the new constitution guaranteed the rights of religious minorities, there was deep concern in Jewish circles about the future of a community in a country in process of joining the Arab League and with the clear intent of participating in the fight against Israel. Emigration to Israel and France continued, but the training offered by ORT was much sought after and appreciated by the remaining Jewish community.

In 1959-60, the Ariana School, near Tunis, had 473 pupils and graduates were doing well in the job market. Some 735 young men and women were enrolled in the apprenticeship program. Admission to ORT-*Alliance* schools was also sought by non-Jews.

For some years there had been tension between Tunisia and France. The Bizerte incident of 1962, following which the naval base was handed over to Tunisia, shook the country. Despite subsequent improvement in French-Tunisian relations, there was no peace of mind for the Jews. Emigration accelerated. Out of a 1955 population of 120,000, by the mid-1960's, only some 15,000 Jews remained in the country, a disproportionately large number of them older persons. In 1972, the last ORT school in Tunis was closed.

The economic status of the large majority of the Jewish population in Morocco was depressed. Poverty was so deep as to make every day a battle for survival. Restricted to ghettos, their condition resembled life in the Middle Ages. Relief, medical services, and, above all, vocational training for the younger generation were needed.[3]

The vocational training center established by ORT in Casablanca for the abandoned children of the *Mellah* was the beginning of an important program headed by Moroccan ORT President Senouf.

The center, organized in cooperation with *Alliance Israelite Universelle*, was inaugurated in November, 1948, with ORT managing the vocational part and *Alliance* responsible for general education. Within several months about 600 pupils were in dressmaking and machine work courses.

With the establishment of the State of Israel there was an exodus of Jews out of Morocco. Nevertheless, ORT maintained its program, proceeding on the theory that skills were needed by both those who remained and those who would be going to a new life in Israel.

With the departure of large numbers of Jews, local communities, with a population of about 250,000 in the early 1950's, disintegrated. The 1975 population of some 30,000 was mainly concentrated in Casablanca. Many Moroccan students went to Europe, where they completed their studies in ORT schools in Montreuil, Villiers le Bel, and Strasbourg. Some graduates were admitted to the Anieres Institute. In 1950, enrollment in all programs was about 1,000; in 1957, it reached some 1,330, and in 1962, more than 2,200. But the tide was irreversible.

At its peak, ORT courses were being conducted in Casablanca, Marrakesh, Tetuan, and Sefrou. The network was gradually reduced, some programs being liquidated and others consolidated. In 1975, Moroccan ORT consisted of an apprenticeship service in Casablanca, a school in Ain-Seba for 254 boys and a school for 156 girls in Val d'Anfa. Both schools had dormitory facilities. The Ain-Seba boys school was given up as too huge for the number enrolled. A new school on a reduced scale was built in 1977. Emigration reduced enrollment to about 900 in the late 1970's.

One school deserves special mention—the Institute for Deaf Children created in 1957 in collaboration with *Alliance Israelite Universelle*. In 1975, in addition to general subjects, 24 children here received manual training by a deaf teacher. Creative education workshops in other community schools, the few still functioning, included 173 students in Marrakesh, Fez, and Meknes.

Throughout, in cooperation with OSE, ORT provided assistance not only to its students, but to their families. Among other agencies that have contributed, Women's American ORT has sent clothing, shoes, and other personal articles to students in addition to funds for social and medical purposes.

At the time of writing, ORT continues its work in Morocco, and seems set to do so for some time. Its program plays a vital role in the more or less stabilized community, providing education and skills to Jewish youth looking for social advancement.

Iran

The Jewish community of Iran, numbering some 80,000 in the 1950's, consisted mainly of families blessed with many children, but without even minimal means of subsistence. More than 25 per cent were children between the ages of six and 16. Poverty and disease were rampant. Some ten per cent of Jewish children suffered from trachoma and skin diseases.

One of the most effective organizations working in Iran in the field of education was *Alliance Israelite Universelle* which, through its schools and former pupils, had a considerable impact on Jewish community life. *Otzar Hatorah,* a religious agency, although it entered the scene rather late, was influential in some sectors. Vocational education, however, was practically non-existent.

ORT's program in Iran began in 1950, but it was some time before a stable committee was formed in Teheran under Morteza Senehi and Moussa Taub. In the mid-1960's, Abraham Rad assumed the chairmanship of ORT-Iran, leading successful fund-raising efforts. A modest beginning was made with the establishment of workshops in masonry and carpentry for the 120 Iraqi and Kurdish Jewish refugees awaiting emigration to Israel.

The need was such, however, that in 1951, only a year after the initial move, more than 1,000 students were receiving training in 16 trade schools and workshops in Teheran, Shiraz, and Isfahan. The program included two years' schooling in mechanics, electrical installation, and dressmaking for 361 students, and workshops and courses of seven to 14 months for 579. In addition, pre-apprenticeship training in woodwork and embroidery for 70 young men and women was provided.

It was a time of departures for Israel. In an effort to stabilize the program, an understanding was reached with *Aliyah* that no trainees would be admitted to *Aliyah* who had not completed their studies. There was cooperation with many Jewish agencies in Teheran, particularly JDC, which conducted a program of social assistance that included ORT students.

A significant aspect of the ORT program in Iran was a concerted indoctrination of the Jewish people to the need of a radical change in their way of life. The emphasis was on modern occupations, possession of a craft that would not only make possible employment but impart quality to Jewish life in a community where large numbers were peddlers unwilling to move out of the traditional pattern of transient and petty trading.

Training courses for young people up to the age of 25 and for graduates of *Alliance* and *Otzar Hatorah* schools were introduced. Some were conducted in cooperation with *Alliance*. Following a visit by Mrs. Ludwig Kaphan and Nathan Gould of Women's American ORT, Iranian activities were included in the Women's American ORT "Guardianship Program," which provided a stimulus to the local women's ORT group.

ORT assisted graduates in finding jobs or other outlets for their acquired skills. In the early fifties, graduates were established in workshops and loans were provided for acquisition of equipment.[4] Although this type of assistance was on a relatively small scale, it was important in the early years of the program when the underdeveloped local industry was not in a position to absorb skilled manpower.

As the programs grew, there were dozens of such small undertakings which, while they did not materially change the situation, were important in a community on the verge of radical transformation. By the sixties, on the basis of oil revenues, the country was developing at an accelerated tempo of modernization under seven-and five-year plans. Prospects improved for ORT graduates. Suddenly, they were among the technical elite. They now easily found employment at good wages in private and state enterprises. Those who went to Israel took with them skills that would be useful there.

ORT-Iran gained importance at the national level as an organization that had introduced modern techniques into vocational education, besides pioneering in new areas of specialization.

The ORT Junior Technical College provided a course in refrigeration, the first such course available in the country. A school for girls introduced an innovative English-Persian secretarial course for girls. ORT diplomas were recognized as qualifying a student for continuing studies at an engineering college.

Class in office skills in the ORT School for Girls in
Bombay, India, 1974.

Girls' School of the ORT Vocational Center in Teheran, Iran, 1969.

Hebrew class in the ORT Vocational complex in Teheran, Iran, 1973.
(Photo by Leni Sonnenfeld)

Teheran ORT School for Boys, 1973. (Photo by Leni Sonnenfeld)

Electronics laboratory in Teheran ORT installation, 1973. (Photo by Leni Sonnenfeld)

Trade school for girls in Casablanca.

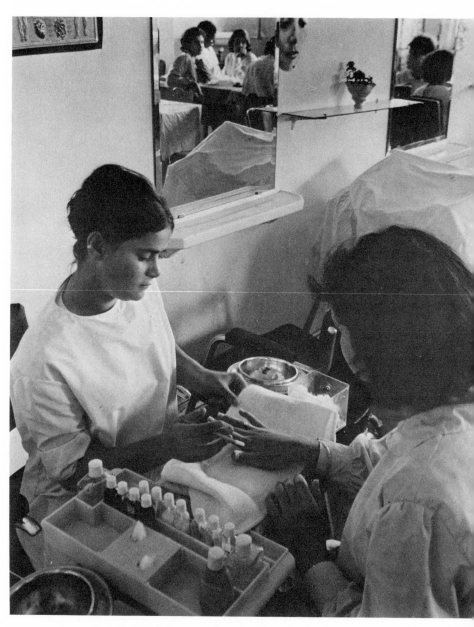

Beauty culture class in ORT Casablanca school, 1956.

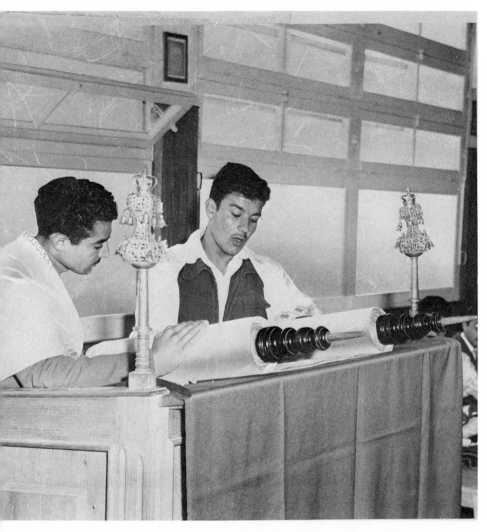

Sabbath services in the Miriam Earle Synagogue, donated by Women's
American ORT, in the Ain-Seba ORT School, Casablanca, 1968.

ORT School for Automechanics in Tunis, 1959.

The ORT School in Tunis, 1963.

African trainees from Guinea and Mali at the Central ORT Institute in Switzerland, 1965. (Photo by Jean Mohr)

As a result of these successful efforts, ORT decided to substantially enlarge the Teheran school. In 1961, with the aid of Women's American ORT, a dormitory building was added, making it possible for students from the provinces to matriculate.

In 1967, ORT enlarged further by establishing a Center for Basic Education, the aim of which was to provide abandoned ghetto children and dropouts with opportunities for a productive life.

Under the supervision of Mrs. Parvine Motamed, the ORT-Iran Director, continuous measures have been taken to improve the quality of training, bringing the Teheran School to the level of the best of technical schools. David Lhayani, the technical director of ORT-Iran, a graduate of the Anieres Institute, has systematically reviewed teaching methods, introduced a modern audio-visual system, and endeavored to adapt the latest educational techniques to ORT schools. The government recognized the importance of the school by granting it a continuing subvention.

Much is being done to foster Jewish education and teachers have been brought to Iran from Israel through the good offices of the Jewish Agency. Various *Shabbat* evening activities arranged by ORT have helped in stimulating interest in Jewish concerns, including religious awareness, among the detached youth.

In the late 1970's, the regime in Iran was under the concerted attack of various opposition groups, including a powerful drive of Islamic forces directed by Ayatollah Khomeini from his exile in France. The growing political unrest was having an increasing effect on the old Jewish community there.

For the Bene Israel of India

The wildest dreams of Bramson and Syngalowski would not have gone so far as to envision the spread of functional ORT activities to India and Ethiopia. In both countries there existed problems about claims on the part of some groups of Jews to their Jewishness.

In India, the small Jewish community, consisting largely of Bene Israel, was stirred by the rebirth of Israel and many began to leave the country.[5] Exodus notwithstanding, ORT initiated a program in India in 1961 in collaboration with JDC. At the beginning, differences of opinion within the community as to the site of a proposed school had to be resolved. In 1962, the ORT-India Polytechnic was created on the grounds of the Sir Elly Kadoori School in Bombay. Graduates receive certificates of qualification for other than white-collar jobs.

Ten years after its initiation, ORT-India was providing training to some 130 boys and 120 girls, the latter by benefit of a grant from the Danish government. Boys received training in mechanics and drafting, girls in secretarial skills and hairdressing.

In addition, ORT conducted manual training at the Sir Jacob Sassoon High School for some 170 boys and girls. While a small undertaking, because of emigration, the program, under the leadership of Gerhard Gabriel, goes beyond the immediate goals of vocational training, encouraging, through Jewish studies, intensification of the Jewish way of life.[6] ORT camps, organized to coincide with *Sukkot* and *Simchat Torah*, particularly those in Cochin—an area of a very old Jewish community—deserve special mention.

Among the Falashas of Ethiopia

Following a request from President Yitzchak Ben-Zvi of Israel, the World ORT Union Executive Committee, in the late 1950's, decided to send a mission to the Gondar region of Ethiopia to study the needs and possibilities of vocational work among the Falashas.[7]

Prof. Norman Bentwich, for a long time interested in the fate of the Falashas, later returned to the idea. He visited Ethiopia in the 1960's. However, already earlier, Robin Gilbert of the ORT staff and Hermann Guggenheim went to Ethiopia where they surveyed the situation of the Falashas in the Gondar region of the country. It was not until the 1970's, however, that a limited ORT program was initiated among the Falashas.

Some 28,000 Falashas not only suffered from discrimination, disease, and poverty in their own country, but had to endure the suspicious attitude of fellow Jews who doubted the Falasha claim to Jewishness. Dispersed throughout several hundred villages with few medical or educational facilities, centuries backward in their way of life, the Falashas needed help to prevent their physical disappearance. Most of them work the soil which belongs to the non-Falashas or are blacksmiths, weavers, and potters.

While *Aliyah* might have provided a solution, there was initial hesitation in Israel because of doubts about the Jewish status of the Falashas. Ethiopia was also one of the few countries in Africa with which Israel maintained ties (although without diplomatic recognition) and since the Ethiopian government was opposed to emigration, Israel was reluctant to give priority to the emigration of Falashas to Israel. Under these conditions, only a few hundred Falashas managed to emigrate to Israel.

In 1973, the Sephardic Chief Rabbi officially recognized the Falashas as Jews and, in 1975, the Israeli Government extended to Falashas the benefits of the Law of Return. But in the absence of diplomatic relations with Ethiopia, the Law of Return had little effect.

After the revolution in 1974 that overthrew the imperial regime of Hailie Selassie, and amid the violence and civil war between the new government and its enemies on the left and the dispossessed landowners on the right, and a variety of secessionist movements, the Falasha situation worsened. The hostility between the government and the rebels spread to the province of Gondar, where half of the Falashas in North Ethiopia reside, and to Tigre and Wollo. Many Falashas fled their homes and fell victim to bandits; some were killed, and children were abducted for ransom.[8] ORT's goal has been to help the Falashas under any circumstances.

With the abatement of civil violence, Jewish social services coordinated by JDC-ORT from Geneva, but mainly the responsibility of ORT, provided help to Falashas in the area of community development at the most basic level, including farming, vocational training, medical services, and general and religious education. Simon Guedj of the World ORT Union Executive Staff was the man in charge of the operation.

In 1977, ORT received authorization from the Ethiopian government to work in Gondar province. The only Jewish agency permitted to work in Ethiopia, ORT obtained this permission on condition that it extend its efforts to all inhabitants of the area, including non-Falashas living there. Haille Selassie had made the same point to the ORT delegates in the late 1950's. While this was, perhaps, not the best solution, it was not the first time that Jewish organizations had been confronted with such a situation. During World War II, some Jewish relief activities in the Soviet Union were conducted in this way.

In developing its activities to improve the living conditions of the Falasha population, regardless of long-term plans, ORT had to take account of the conditions of life among the Falashas. Falasha children customarily assist in farm work and tend cattle. Families are dispersed over large areas and children must often walk long distances to and from school.

A few schools situated in remote areas were temporarily closed. Nevertheless, the program in 1977 included 19 schools with over 1,400 pupils and 73 teachers. Assistance and training were extended to religious leaders, the *Kohanim*, and there was a program for training Hebrew teachers. In addition, synagogues were built or repaired in 10 Falasha villages.[9] This activity was conducted on behalf of the JDC.

A health center was established in Ambober and Tedda, and teams of medical aides travel to distant villages with Falasha populations. Special attention was given to Falasha artisans, who received technical and financial assistance under a revolving fund. Credit was extended to Falashas to provide for seed, tools, and livestock.

A plan was developed whereby, on every school compound, land, if available, is used for vegetable gardens cared for by pupils. The Ministry of Education has been enthusiastic about these projects and has approved them in all schools of the district. It will be recalled that the idea of such gardens, in somewhat different form, had been a part of ORT programs in Eastern Europe in the 1920's.

The programs in Ethiopia have been financed by grants from the governments of Canada, Holland, Germany, and the United States. JDC provided funds for religious purposes.

As these lines are being written there are increasing press and radio reports of clashes between the armed forces of the government and the opposition, and of intensified hostilities with Arab-supported Eritrea. The ORT leadership is sensitive that these events may have a serious impact on its programs in Ethiopia. Still, in the midst of chaos and uncertainty, the ORT connection to the distant Falashas is, in fact, continuing.

TECHNICAL ASSISTANCE
IN THE "THIRD WORLD"

In 1960, the Agency for International Development (AID) of the United States Department of State approached ORT with the suggestion that it apply its specialized experience in developing manpower skills to modernizing the nations of the "Third World." This was a new field for ORT that would take it out of its natural framework of activities on behalf of Jewish populations and into the sphere of international economics.

It was a problem of fundamental principle. ORT had for years accepted non-Jewish students in its schools; but there is a vast difference between non-Jewish students in an ORT school and undertaking a project dealing with the needs of an indigenous population in countries without Jews. After much reflection and debate at the 1960 ORT Congress in

London, at which some leaders expressed doubts as to the wisdom of ORT's going beyond the Jewish field, it was concluded that the humanitarian aspects of the proposed initiative could not be ignored. ORT had no moral basis to respond negatively to a request to lend its experience to others, with the proviso that nothing be done to deplete personnel and ORT experts from the basic program. On that premise it was agreed to undertake a number of projects.

The decision having been taken, Max A. Braude devoted his energies to extending this new field of ORT work. He assumed overall responsibility for it, assisted, in Geneva, first by Charles Levinson and, later, by Eugene Abrams, who headed the ORT Department of Technical Assistance. Since the U.S. Government cannot proceed in areas of technical assistance unless projects are implemented by an American agency, American ORT played a large role in many of these undertakings. In addition to purely technical aspects involved in obtaining government grants, knowledge of established procedures was called for. Paul Bernick was especially active in the American phase of the program. In Canada, Germany, Israel, and Sweden, local ORT people dealt with their respective governments.

ORT technical assistance programs, undertaken at the request of the U.S. Government, began in 1961 with a survey of vocational needs in eight sub-Saharan African countries. Since then, such programs have grown in scope, diversity, and geographic distribution.

The ORT effort involves three basic services: (a) evaluation of manpower needs to help governmental bodies or the private sector to plan development; (b) designing specific technical training programs; and (c) implementing the programs.

Broad Implications

This broadening of ORT activities is, more than anything else, indicative of change in ORT, both in its programs and its character. All the projects undertaken have required a high level of technological, political, and pedagogical "know-how," and a sophisticated capacity for technical organization. Post-World War II ORT possessed both. Its experience in North Africa, India, and Iran, the familiarity of its international staff with a wide variety of languages, and, not least, the spirit of courageous exploration, characteristic of the latter-day ORT, have been invaluable assets.

ORT technical assistance is now undertaken on a contractual basis with the United States, Switzerland, Denmark, Canada, Sweden, and West Germany. There are other projects with a number of international agencies, including the European Economic Community, the United National Development Program, and, most important, the World Bank.

ORT enjoys consultant status with specialized agencies of the United Nations and is registered as a technical assistance resource with, among others, the British Overseas Ministry. It has acted as a non-political organization engaged in technical assistance on a non-profit basis. Funding has come from the governments of beneficiary countries, governments of other countries, private industry, and voluntary agencies working in the field.

Duration of projects has ranged from several months to several years. Programs have been carried out in more than 30 countries on three continents and have covered fields as varied as water supply, road maintenance, bank management, hospital personnel, teaching techniques, and agricultural training centers.

Among the countries involved have been Afghanistan, Bangladesh, Botswana, Burundi, Cameroon, Chad, Gabon, Ghana, Guinea, Ivory Coast, Kenya, Madagascar, Mali, Mauretania, Nepal, Niger, Nigeria, Rwanda, Senegal, Swaziland, Tanzania, Upper Volta, and Zaire. Projects of technical assistance were also conducted in Israel. It is estimated that the total funds expended to date have amounted to several tens of millions of dollars.

In conducting the technical assistance program, ORT is performing a major social service, bringing new techniques to underdeveloped areas.[10]

ORT Enrollment by Country and Type of Training—1977

Country[1]	Enrollment	Teaching Staff	Vocational and Technical Schools	In Community Schools[2]	Apprenticeship	Adult Services
Argentina	4,690	112	1,083	3,547		60
Brazil	1,005	44	269	660		76
Chile	931	90	931			
Colombia	140			140		
France	6,966	281	2,985		902	3,079
India	650	26	325	316		9
Iran	1,198	72	1,020	148		30
Israel	55,503	2,248	35,987		5,484	14,032
Italy	8,080	75	543	1,429		6,108[3]
Mexico	355			355		
Morocco	941	36	516	187	173	65
Paraguay	97			97		
Peru	450			450		
Uruguay	1,309	74	404			905
U.S.A.	349	17				349
Venezuela	1,178	6		1,178		
Switzerland Central Institute	146	12	108			38
Total	83,968	3,093	44,171	8,487	6,557	24,751

Explanatory Notes

1. To this listing should be added scholarship programs for Jewish youth in Greece, scholarship and guidance programs for Jewish youth in South Africa and other unlisted services, as well as technical assistance projects in Cameroon, Guinea, Mali, Niger, Nigeria, Upper Volta, Zaire and other countries.

2. ORT programs in Jewish community day schools introducing updated courses in the sciences, industrial arts and orientation for careers and work.

3. Majority are Soviet Jewish refugees in transit enrolled in ORT English language and orientation programs.

Source: *ORT Year Book*, World ORT Union Edition. New York, 1978.

Chapter XVII

Israel-on a Nationwide Scale

ORT started its programs in Israel in 1949. For decades before, however, it had been present in Palestine, not as a functioning organization but through its many alumni. Graduates of ORT schools in Poland, Rumania, and Lithuania, they had gone there on *Aliyah* and were among the builders, both in the kibbutzim and the private sector, of the State of Israel.

With DP emigration continuing in 1948 and 1949, ORT was obliged, under its agreement with IRO and various DP committees, to transfer workshop equipment and supplies to Palestine following the departure of DPs for that country.[1] Already in 1946, before the creation of the new state, the World ORT Union had established in Tel Aviv, under the chairmanship of Yehuda Beham, a Tool and Supply Corporation to provide artisans with machines and tools, costs to be reimbursed by recipients in small installments.

Working in close cooperation with governmental and public bodies, the Corporation provided machinery to the new immigrants so they could earn a living. The Corporation also supplied machines to the Kibbutzim and Kvutzot, often promoting the establishment of a workshop in a given trade.

It was an important contribution to the developing economy. For example, as of 1953 over 150 Kibbutzim and Kvutzot benefited from this service. Some 4000 machines were put at the disposal of families with about 12,000 members.

Syngalowski came to the new Jewish state in November, 1948, remaining until April, 1949. He was known to have a non-Zionist outlook, and ORT itself was generally viewed as essentially a Diaspora movement. Nor were trade schools altogether novel in Israel.

The powerful Israeli labor organization, Histadrut, had a network of *Amal* vocational schools in Israel. There were also some long-established trade schools operated by municipalities, by WIZO, by Hadassah and by youth organizations that looked upon ORT as a competitor. Some resistance to ORT might therefore have been expected. But this was 1948 and the Jewish state was fighting for survival.

Syngalowski met with President Weizmann, Prime Minister Ben-Gurion, Zalman Shazar (a future President of Israel and friendly to ORT), and many others, most of whom he had known for a long time. He convinced them that as a non-political organization ORT had a contribution to make to the economy and social fabric of the country.

First Steps

A modest program was initiated in 1949 which from the beginning was predicated on the idea of creating the highest standard of training that the country needed if it was to industrialize and develop a diversified economy. ORT therefore would not work in areas already developed in Israel, but would open up possibilities for training in skills still undeveloped.

By the time Syngalowski's visit ended in April, 1949, 18 ORT units had been established; by the end of 1949, 23 units were serving 686 students in Jerusalem, Tel Aviv, and other cities.[2]

From the beginning there was some interesting experimentation. In a project conducted jointly with Yeshiva Torah Umlacha, at Kfar Abraham, students were trained in machine shop and mechanics after their morning Talmudic studies.

Under an agreement with the Israeli Defense Ministry, ORT was soon engaged in vocational training of discharged soldiers and war invalids referred by the Rehabilitation Department of the Israeli army. A large building was placed at the disposal of ORT, and the Defense Ministry assumed 40 per cent of the costs. The ORT training center for ex-servicemen also accepted civilians, particularly newly arrived DPs. A large number of the instructors employed at the center were ORT graduates from Europe.

During his stay, Syngalowski arranged for the organization of an Israel ORT committee, to which he had attracted a group of lay leaders interested in the development of skilled labor, among them Joseph Shapiro, the energetic activist of ORT-Israel and later a Vice-President of the Central Board of the World ORT Union. In 1954, on Beham's death, he took over the chairmanship of ORT-Israel's Executive Committee.

Dr. Wirklich, a former high Israeli official, took over administration for a short period. He was succeeded by Jacob Oleiski, who had settled in Israel after leaving Germany and visiting the United States and other countries.

There were difficulties involved in working in a society in the process of building and receiving waves of immigrants of diverse cultural background. One was to find housing adapted to the needs of the schools. There was not only the problem of raising the necessary funds, but of locating and delivering materials, most of which had to be imported from abroad, causing troublesome delays.

As if these were not enough, from the outset most of the schools were operated jointly with other agencies and ORT by itself could do little to hasten the completion of buildings. Nevertheless, by the end of December, 1950, ORT-Israel had schools and workshops in Jerusalem, Ben-Sheman, Jaffa, Ain-Charod, Givatayim, Kfar Abraham, Kfar Monash, Ramleh, Safed, Rechovot, Kfar Ganim, Holon, Tel Aviv, and Ramath-Gan.

Most were under a four-year curriculum. Some workshops offered training from two to three months and others up to 18 months. Under Oleiski's dynamic direction, ORT expanded dramatically. ORT schools accommodated their pupils under a program whereby three months of schooling alternated with three months on a job. The 1950 enrollment in all ORT schools in Israel was 1,228.

New People in a New Nation

From the beginning, ORT efforts were geared to the needs of the successive waves of immigrants: DPs and Jews from North Africa, Asia, and Eastern Europe. This predetermined to a degree the scope and rate of growth of the schools. With DP immigration coming to an end, it would appear that ORT might soon have been able to devote its efforts to programs for a stable population, but this was not the case.[3]

"THE SECOND ISRAEL"

The creation of the Jewish state exerted a strong messianic appeal among Jews in Africa, and thousands were on the move to Israel.[4] Jews from Cyrenaica (Libya) migrated to Israel. In the mid- and late 1950's, emigration from North Africa, particularly Egypt and Morocco, brought tens of thousands of Jews to Israel.

Jews from Asia followed. Although there was some emigration to the West, particularly of Algerians who were French citizens, emigration to Israel continued.

By the 1970's, of some 500,000 to 600,000 Jews in North Africa, only 45,000 remained, and of 330,000 Jews in Arab countries of the Middle East, only 10,000 remained.

The influx of Jews from African and Asian countries soon

created a split community. On one side were those of privileged Western background, and on the other the underprivileged. Although the children of Asian and African origin constituted 50 per cent or more of the school-age population, only a small percentage took advantage of schooling beyond primary grades and their presence in schools of higher education was tiny.

Half the population of Israel felt that they did not share equally in opportunities provided by the construction of new social and economic conditions in a modern Israel. This state of affairs created not only economic problems, but problems of social status. Jews from the underdeveloped countries lacked the positive self-image that would provide the individual and the community with the ingredients Israel needed if it was to develop into a unified Jewish society.[5]

EVOLUTION OF SCHOOL RESPONSIBILITIES

From the first, the state had provided primary education for children in schools based on eight years of elementary schooling. Education was free and compulsory for children aged five to 14. A later reform introduced comprehensive schools providing for six years of elementary, three years of junior high, and three years of high school education—in other words, free education through the twelfth grade.

Comprehensive schools included vocational education and, in fact, in the late 1970's more than half of Israel's school children of high school age opted for vocational programs.

Introduction of a national education program of this magnitude called for mobilization of all the energies of government down to the lowest echelon. In these efforts, with substantial priority accorded to the vocational sector, the UJA-Israel Education Fund contributed substantially. The new program was in many ways reminiscent of Harvard President James B. Conant's idea of a comprehensive school giving graduates what Conant called "marketable skills." Marketable skills, of course, was what ORT was all about.

Part of the National Fabric

With the number of students in vocational schools growing daily, it was obvious that ORT schools would have to be integrated with the Israeli education system. When ORT began to broaden its programs, it therefore endeavored to adjust them to the needs of the country and integrate them into the existing educational structure.

Much effort was devoted by ORT to improving the quality of technical programs. Modern teaching methods, including programmed instruction, which was particularly needed since the vocational education system had been little aware of advances in the field, were introduced. Refresher courses introduced teachers to modern teaching methods. Instructors participated in seminars in Geneva, and some were sent abroad for further training.

Graduates of the Anieres Institute were especially welcomed. In 1975, 33 graduates of the Anieres Institute were employed in ORT schools in Israel in administrative and teaching positions. A special department of publications was established to provide manuals and other materials for teachers and students. Modern teaching methods were developed based on experience acquired in the United States and other countries.

ORT schools in Israel differ fundamentally from those in other countries. The difference is not only of standards or quality. Other ORT schools have achieved high standards. The difference is that outside of Israel, ORT schools offer technical training to a relatively small number of students—more in some countries, less in others, depending largely on the community from which students are drawn, representing a limited effort in a specialized field. In Israel they are a substantial and organic part of the educational system of the country.

Were it not for ORT, the state would have to create an equivalent network of schools. Vocational education in Israel fulfills many functions beyond providing skilled labor for industry. It serves as an instrumentality for the alleviation, through enhancement of the status of the underprivileged, of a serious social problem in the deeply divided society.

In 1948, students in all vocational schools in Israel numbered 1,500 to 2,000. By 1975, the number had risen to 69,000[6] with hundreds of institutions. Sixty-five per cent of ORT vocational courses are in mechanics, electricity, and electronics, but, in addition, more than 30 trades are taught in such diverse fields as hotel services, hairdressing, interior decoration, chemistry, and tourism. Because it regards ORT educational standards highly, the Ministry of Education has invited ORT representatives to serve on various professional committees.

Many ORT schools in Israel are organized in cooperation and partnership with municipalities, local councils, religious bodies, *yeshivot*, and factories. While cooperating agencies in some instances provide buildings, overall direction of the schools is the responsibility of ORT, although in some cases the cooperating agency shares in management.

In addition to ORT schools proper, there are schools linked to ORT, and others that have vocational programs initiated and conducted by ORT. In the course of its work, ORT has also cooperated in numerous projects of the Jewish Colonization Association.

Program Building Blocks

The ORT system is organized roughly in six categories:

(1) Four-year courses in technical vocational high schools;

(2) Three-year apprenticeship courses in factories;

(3) Industrial schools connected with factories, where training is of three to four years' duration and students are paid salaries for assigned jobs;

(4) Two-year technical junior colleges;

(5) Comprehensive six-year programs covering the seventh to twelfth grades;

(6) Training courses for adults.

Except for industrial schools cooperating with plants, and apprenticeship programs, which are under the Ministry of Labor, ORT schools are under the jurisdiction of the Ministry of Education. Programs are intended essentially to serve the needs of the state; curricula reflect the continuous process of industrialization, particularly in the defense field, where plans had to be revised after the Yom Kippur war to take into consideration the newly gained experience.

Some ORT schools provide training in maintenance of aircraft—a service as applicable to civilian aviation as it is to the military. Other schools train maritime personnel. ORT has pioneered in the study of plastics, hydraulics, and numerical control, all of great importance to the industrial life of the country.

ORT has been successful in developing a system of junior technical colleges and other kinds of post-secondary education. Uniquely, this level of studies is not housed in separate buildings but rather together with and as an optional continuation of high school.

In 1975, post-secondary levels were in operation in the following schools: Syngalowski Center, Givatayim Technicum, Natanya Lvovitch Center, Jerusalem, Kiryat Bialik, and Ashdod. There are some limitations on the number of 18-to 19-year olds who wish to continue their education after high school. Acceptance is based on quotas established by the military.

The scope and diversity of ORT-Israel programs may be seen in table 15 (pages 336 and 337).

Mention should be made of schools that have attained a special status. The Syngalowski Memorial Center, established in 1958, in whose funding Women's American ORT was pivotal, was the first modern vocational education institution in Israel. It is considered an excellent, "tough" school. Its diplomas are highly regarded and other schools view it as a model institution.

TABLE 15

The ORT Network in Israel, 1977

Locality	Junior High Schools (Middle Schools)	High Schools	Yeshiva and Other Religious Schools	Industrial Schools and Classes	Apprentice-ship Programs	Colleges and Other Post-Secondary Institutions	Adult Programs	Total
Affula		841						841
Ashdod		309				53		362
Ashkelon		700		113	555			1,368
Bat Yam		1,236						1,236
Benyamina		254	107					361
Bet-Eyl				169				169
Bnei Brak		325						325
Chof Hasharon		401						401
Eilat					277			277
Ein Harod	200	387						587
Ein Harohesh		10						10
Gam Yavne			266					266
Givatayim		1,556				839		2,395
Haifa	92	484		344	1,429			2,349
Hazor	126	66	482					674
Herzlia		419						419
Holon		1,694		384				2,078
Iusfiya		214						214
Jerusalem	1,792	2,264		618	988	513	48	6,223
Julius				242	50			292
Kfar Abraham		270						270
Kfar Habad			498					498

								Total
Kfar Saba		928				99		1,027
Kyriat Bialik	1,537	975				204		2,716
Kyriat Gat					564			564
Kyriat Tivon	426	204						630
Lydda		883		227	40			1,150
Meiron			242					242
Nathanya		2,164				318	17	2,499
Nazareth		447						447
Ramat Gan		2,770						2,770
Rehovot		731	107					838
Sdeh Eliyahu			160					160
Shaar Hanegev				65				65
Shafir			791					791
Tel Aviv		2,109		685	1,581	1,176	13,967	19,518
Tel Nof				180				180
Tel Yeruham				9				9
Yavneh				168				168
Zrifin				114				114
Totals	4,173	22,641	2,653	3,318	5,484	3,202	14,032	55,503

Source: Table taken from the ORT Year Book, World ORT Union Edition. New York, 1978.

One of the earliest ORT schools in Israel, founded in 1949, in
partnership with a religious institution in Kfar Avraham.

A workshop in the ORT Vocational School of ORT-Mizrachi in Kfar
Avraham.

Photo of the first graduation class from one of the earliest ORT schools in Israel, in 1953.

Main building of the Syngalowski ORT Center in Tel Aviv, built by Women's American ORT. (Photo by Leni Sonnenfeld)

Opening day at the Syngalowski ORT Center in 1964.

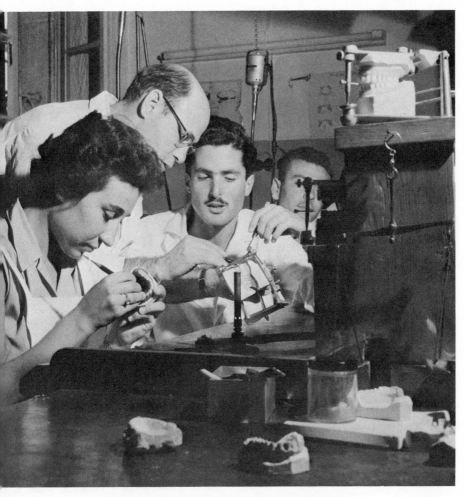

Adult course for dental technicians in Jerusalem.

ORT College in Chemical Technology in Beersheba, 1965.

John F. Kennedy ORT Apprenticeship Center in Jerusalem, 1971.
(Photo by Leni Sonnenfeld)

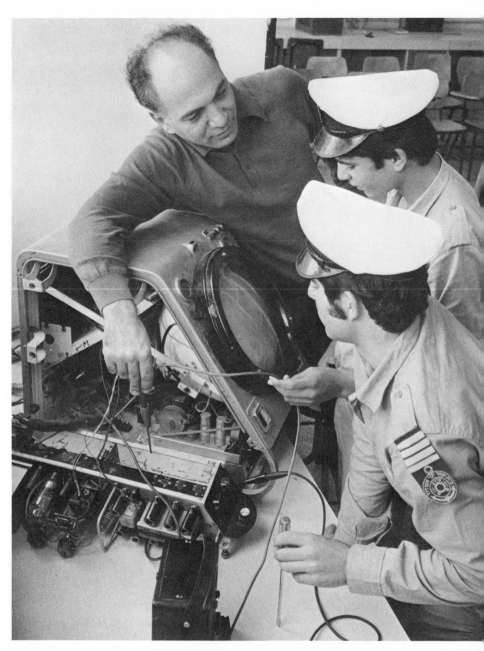

ORT School in maritime skills in Ashdod, 1973.

Hotel trades school in the ORT center in Nathanya, 1975.

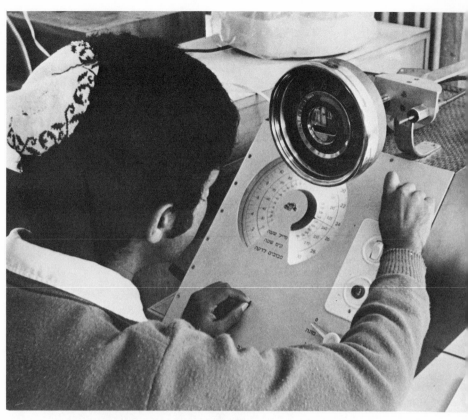

Instrument laboratory at the ORT Technical College in Nathanya,
Israel.

At the inauguration of the ORT School for Engineering on the Hebrew
University campus, Jerusalem, 1976.

Section of the ORT School of Engineering in Jerusalem.

The Moshinski Pedagogical Center in Tel Aviv, funded by a gift from the Moshinski family of Mexico, has maintained a high level in its seminars and courses for teachers as well as in the preparation of text materials and audio-visual aids. Located in a building on the Syngalowski Memorial Center campus, it has concentrated on pedagogical projects. ORT-Israel is now able to train its own teachers—not a small achievement.

A major addition to the ORT network is the Engineering School in Jerusalem. Opened in 1976 and appropriately situated on the Givat Ram campus of Hebrew University, it provides training for technical engineers.

Its new modern building was made possible largely through gifts from the late Leonard Cohen, Women's American ORT, Canadian ORT, and many donors from the USA, Great Britain, and other countries.

A new departure in ORT programming, the school symbolizes ORT's movement from trade training for manual labor to technical education leading to a practical engineering degree—the culmination of a revolution that has been in process in ORT education since World War II. The school was planned for a student body of 2,500, with a faculty shared with Hebrew University.

It includes a program of teacher training in technical subjects conducted in cooperation with the Hebrew University School of Education. While ORT circles everywhere have approved the creation of the Engineering School, not all are happy about the new orientation toward more sophisticated training.

The Institute of Combined Vocational Training includes correspondence courses in literally scores of subjects, including Judaism and preparation for matriculation. The Hofberger School for the Deaf is operated in cooperation with the Tel Aviv municipality and the Ministry of Education. They are exemplary institutions with small enrollments, geared to satisfy the special needs of their students.

The Maritime School at Ashdod, where an electronics-technician class was set up in the mid-1970's, has been another important addition to the ORT system.

National Objectives

The ORT programs could not have achieved their success without the close cooperation of the Israeli government. The 1964 agreement with Jerusalem to double the capacity of ORT vocational high schools, was entered into by Braude with Zalman Aranne, Minister of Education. This goal was achieved in 1969. The Braude-Aranne agreement signified that the Israeli Ministry accepted responsibility for each new student added to the ORT network. As a consequence, the Israeli government met more than 80 per cent of the ORT-Israel budget.

In the last ten years, ORT in Israel has had to assist in the absorption of over 100,000 Jewish immigrants from Russia. The task has involved, among other things, tutoring of Soviet newcomers in preparation for examinations to qualify for higher studies at Israeli universities. A special course for newly arrived Soviet teachers was initiated in Jerusalem, in addition to other courses, to facilitate the integration of immigrant Soviet technicians and teachers into Israeli life, and into the faculties of ORT schools.

Pace of Expansion

Between 1950 and 1955, ORT-Israel provided training for some 9,000 persons. Between 1955 and 1959, this number rose to 18,000. In 1967, student enrollment stood at 26,700. Six years later, in 1973, the network was serving 44,205.

The number of students has continued to grow. In 1977, ORT schools in Israel had 55,503 students and a faculty of 2,248 distributed among 88 ORT schools. On October 3, 1973, three days before the Yom Kippur war, ORT President Chaim Herzog officiated, together with Minister of Labor Yosef Almogi, at graduation exercises for the one-hundred-thousandth ORT student.

Enrollment of students from economically impoverished classes of the population has grown along with the general growth in enrollment.[7] In 1974, pupils of Oriental origin represented some 60 per cent of total enrollment. To facilitate the integration of this group, dormitories have been provided in several schools, including the Rogosin Maritime School in Ashdod and the Lvovich Center in Nathanya. Dormitories are also maintained in religious schools and *yeshivot*.

In 1975, ORT schools were training 3,399 Moslem, Christians, and Druse students, including 336 in two schools for non-Jewish students in Nazareth and Iusifia. The four schools in East Jerusalem had 2,481 Arab students; 413 were studying in the Harcarmel Apprenticeship Center in Haifa; 169 were in various ORT schools together with Jewish students.[8]

ORT is the principal system in vocational and technical education in Israel. Budget figures are revealing. In 1955, 55 per cent of the ORT-Israel budget came from the World ORT Union; by 1959, more than 50 per cent came from local sources, and by the late 1970's local contributions represented 88 per cent of the budget, a figure indicative of Israel's perception of ORT's worth to the nation.

New Men

After the death of Joseph Shapiro in 1964, E. Lewin-Epstein took over the chairmansip of ORT-Israel. In 1968, General Chaim Herzog, son of the late Chief Rabbi of Israel, a lawyer and noted military analyst, was elected Chairman of the ORT-Israel Executive Committee. Herzog was later elected a Vice-President of the Central Board of the World ORT Union and Vice-Chairman of its Executive Committee. In 1975, when Herzog became Israeli Ambassador to the United Nations, the chairmanship of the ORT-Israel Executive Committee passed to Uziel Steinberg.

In 1967, Oleiski retired after decades of service. Joseph Harmatz, Comptroller of ORT since 1960 and Deputy General Director since 1965, replaced him as Director General in

Israel. Harmatz, of Lithuanian origin, had spent the years of the occupation in the Jewish underground in Vilna. He was one of the leading men of *Bricha* to Palestine.

It was through his imagination and persistence that the Jerusalem Engineering School became a reality. He must be credited with having brought ORT-Israel to its present high status. His Deputy Director is Michael Avitzour.

In no country, including Tsarist Russia, its birthplace, has ORT achieved the status that it has in Israel. Here, all objective conditions—national, political, and social—have coalesced to create a great base for ORT development, which is as it should be.[9]

Chapter XVIII

Facing Its Second Century

The reader is again reminded that this history of ORT is not intended to be an all inclusive display of facts, reflecting every ORT effort. Such an attempt at inclusiveness would require four or five volumes. The historian has to select and, in selecting, to use his judgment, one that obviously is not always shared by others. He must distinguish between passing, perhaps momentarily important, events and enduring trends. This is true with respect to general events no less than with regard to developments and changes within ORT.

ORT is a child of the Jewish Enlightenment, born when the second and third generations of enlightened Russian Jews had begun to apply their ideas to the Jewish Pale of Settlement (see Chapters I and II). But neither the Tsarist functionaries nor the well-meaning Jewish merchants, rabbis, and writers could come up with a practical plan for the Jews of a backward Russia.

By the time the idea of encouraging crafts and agriculture among the Jews had become a realistic project, Russia was already deep in the process of industrialization and Russian Jews had begun to be moved by the ideas of the Enlightenment, brought to Russia from Germany.

The Roots of ORT

Haskalah was not the only way to survival in a world in the process of change. For the Jews to survive they had not only to change external patterns and acquire secular education, they had to change the whole socio-economic structure of the Ghetto. Was this feasible in a capitalist society under Tsarist conditions?

Progressive Jewish circles of 20th-century Tsarist Russia were divided in their response to this fundamental question. Some were pessimists, denying *golus*, others insisted that much could be done even under unfavorable conditions. All, however, insisted on the need to change Jewish social patterns and, as a means of doing so, called for proletarianization, productivization—that is, work with one's hands.

In ideological terms, one side was too uncompromising in its denial of *golus*, and the other perhaps too vague in formulating its goals. The interesting outcome of this debate, which went on in Russia, Poland, and elsewhere, is that both sides mirrored the fashionable Russian slogans of the day and did not—perhaps could not—foresee the revolutionary change in technological structures that was to come only decades later.

The introduction of automation, electronics, numerical control, and similar technologies made possible the gradual "technolization" (perhaps a better term than "productivization," which implies manual labor) among the Jews, which now proceeded with little hindrance.

It might not have been possible to make workers out of a majority of Jews in Tsarist Russia, but now new technical professions became possible for them everywhere. (We shall not discuss here the case of Soviet Jews, although in Soviet Russia, too, the newest technical professions have played a role.) Thus, modernization has become an ally of ORT and, indeed, has provided both a reverse justification of its traditional position and a continuing framework for its ongoing efforts.

Place in History

As these lines are being written, the ORT movement is entering its one-hundredth year of existence. The event is important not only in the history of ORT. It may in truth be said that without a knowledge of ORT, its beginnings, and its growth, a large segment of the history of Jewish life in Eastern Europe and, indeed, of the history of the Jewish people the world over, would be missing.

While ORT is mentioned in various Jewish studies, there has been little in-depth investigation of the ORT concept and its unique contribution to Jewish life. What is ORT? Where does it belong historically? Is it an organization created by some people of good will oriented toward labor and determined to provide Jewish youths and adults with occupational skills, or is it, as Syngalowski wrote, a Jewish movement of large social perspective?

We shall not analyze the concept of a "movement" except to say that neither Syngalowski nor, in more recent times, Nathan Gould, has presented a systematic formulation of his thinking. Syngalowski turned inward and looked toward the needs of the Jewish people, but his thinking was focused on the patterns of Eastern European Jewry.

His concept of ORT-emancipation through work and social and economic integration followed that of Bakst. There was a fundamental difference, however, between the two men's understanding of work. For Bakst, manual labor was a necessary part but only a part of a healthy social engagement; for Syngalowski it was something more. He believed that one must live by labor in order to live fully. [1]

It is ironic that Syngalowski's thinking, colored as it was by his socialist views, should, in its own way, uphold the basic approach of the moderate, if not conservative, Bakst. (See Chapters I, II, IV). For Syngalowski, therefore, ORT was an organic part of the Jewish struggle to achieve full emancipation and become part of a new, just society.

ORT as Concept

In this sense, ORT was larger than the ORT organization; it was a movement, organized by the intelligentsia and maintained by the Jewish people. It followed that the ORT movement must continue until such time as its goals are fully realized.

Gould, by placing ORT within the framework of contemporary Jewish life and new technological development, defines ORT endeavors in somewhat different terms. He acknowledges the centrality of Israel. If we may compress his thinking, without doing it full justice, he views the broader objectives of ORT from his vantage point; that is, working as he does in the United States, he believes that emancipation, at least in some areas, has already been achieved and that what is necessary now is to maintain momentum, without losing sight of the larger social concepts that Jews share with their non-Jewish fellows.[2] This is, indeed, a simplification, but it defines an important issue.

Syngalowski saw the Jew as an alienated, marginal man, ill at ease in Christian society and in need of radical social and psychological change. Gould apparently sees the Jew as already well into social adjustment but needing to maintain his efforts in order to achieve his social goals. Hence, Gould sees ORT as a movement bridging Jewish and non-Jewish concerns (see Chapter IX).

We have perhaps schematized the positions of the two men. Theirs has been a descriptive approach; both have taken for granted the basic characteristics of the Jewish situation as they see it and the need to control Jewish social reality. Although Syngalowski looked from the inside out, and Gould looks from the outside in, both have recognized that the changes desired for the Jewish people lie in the direction of work—thus seeing the ORT movement as an objective expression of Jewish needs.

An Engine of Change

ORT has spread its work throughout the world, and not only the Jewish world, and has taken firm root in many countries where social and economic conditions are light years removed from those of Tsarist Russia. Its functional framework now includes health care, language courses, Judaic studies, and activities that might be considered outside its primary functions. Along with the sophisticated contemporary technical programs has come a profound change in the attitude of the Jewish middle class toward their children's occupational future and an acceptance of the new ORT occupational ideas. Hundreds of thousands of Jewish men and women, youths and adults, have been trained and taught skills, and many thousands of them have been given opportunities for social advancement, a significant accomplishment in a society increasingly dominated by symbolic images and problems of status.[3]

Although the initiative in the creation of ORT came from the top, in a relatively short time it found a spontaneous response among the Jewish people. Thus did ideas postulated by a small group in St. Petersburg a hundred years ago become part and parcel of the interests and concerns of the people themselves. The beneficiaries have ceased to be passive recipients of ORT efforts and in many ways have become participants who have contributed to the content of its work.

The cross-fertilization of ideas and experience resulting from this phenomenon has been of great significance to both the center and periphery. It would be no exaggeration to say that the constant interaction between the ORT organization, its professional staff, and the involved communities has been and continues to be one of the most important factors in ORT's survival. As ORT grows, the younger generation of professional managers and instructors is tempted to see in their schools, with their computers and modern machinery, systems of vocational training that are surely among the best, an end in itself. ORT does impart technical education, but it represents something more.

From the reports and other presentations of the men who have led ORT in the last quarter of a century—Haber, Mayer, Braude, and others—we see that while they have continuously called for constant updating, they have at the same time pointed to the need to remember the concepts of the founders.

In a way they warn against the temptation to adopt the "now" vision, and assert the need for an awareness of inherited Jewish values that presided at the birth of the movement and has continued to govern it. It would seem that this is what ORT must have in mind as it enters its second century of devotion to Jewish needs.

Notes

For the convenience of the reader, we shall use the modern system of spelling and transliteration of foreign names, places, and terms. Thus, we will use "Tsar," not "Czar," "Aleksandr," not "Alexander," and "Nikolaii" not "Nikolai." In many instances, however, it has been necessary to retain the old spellings in order to make identification easier. There is also an additional problem with transliteration of various names. Baron Gintsburg (to use the Russian way), one of the founders of ORT, was known abroad as Gunzburg but some members of his family active in ORT spelled their name as Guinsbourg. Jaszunski of the Polish ORT was spelled in some ORT material as Jaschunsky; also, Sliozberg or Sliosberg. Naturally these variations will be clarified in the index.

All dates prior to February, 1918, are according to the Old Russian calendar.

There will therefore be some inconsistencies in the text with respect to spellings and dates, but it is hoped that the reader will be able to overcome this difficulty.

There will be a glossary of foreign words and terms used in the volume.

Chapter I: The Setting

1. Richard Pipes, in "Catherine II and the Jews" *(Soviet Jewish Affairs,* 1975, Vol. 5, No. 2) criticizes Jewish historiography for its excessive ethnocentricity. He views the measures enacted by Catherine II as an effort to treat Jews favorably. He concedes, however, the discriminatory character of some features of the 1794 law. John D. Klier, writing in *Slavic Review* (September, 1976), attempts to soften the role played by anti-Semitism and prejudice under Catherine II.

2. Leon Shapiro, *History of the Jews in Russia and Poland, by S. Dubnow, with a Biographical Essay, New Introduction, and Outline of the History of Russian and Soviet Jewry, 1912-1974.* New York: Ktav Publishing House, 1975, Vol. II, pp. 154ff; G. Sliozberg, *Dela Minuvshikh Dneii.* Paris, 1933.

3. Nota Shklower, active in efforts to ameliorate conditions in the Pale, died in St. Petersburg in 1804. His descendants were known under the family name of Notkin. In the last year of his life he opposed the Derzhavin project, some parts of which were based on ideas dear to him.

4. In 1791, Ber Isaac-Berr, a friend of Robespierre and a leading member of the Jewish community of Nancy, inspired by the recent decree emancipating French Jews, addressed an appeal to the Jews of France inviting them to enter manual professions, thus creating a Jewish working class. Berr, while calling for vocational pursuits, also made other suggestions in the spirit of Mendelsohnian enlightenment, then in full swing in Germany. Some writers, among them Dr. Vladimir Halperin, stress the importance of the role of Ber Isaac-Berr in preparing the ideological background of future ORT activities. Halperin points out that Heinrich Heine, Edward Ganz, and Moses Moser, members of the *Verein für Kultur und Wissenschaft des Judentums,* were enthusiastic about the idea of developing crafts and agriculture among Jews. See: V. Halperin, "Le Travail vu par un Juif," in *Rencontre-Chrétiens et Juifs,* No. 10, 1969, Paris; S. M. Dubnow, *Emansipatsia Evreev Vremia Frantsuzkoii Revolutsii, 1780-1791 g.* Knigoizdatelstvo Pravda, Warsaw, 1906. See also, Simon Schwarzfuchs, *Les Juifs de France,* Editions Albin Michel, Paris, 1975. See also B. Weinryb, *Jewish Vocational Education.* New York: Jewish Teachers Seminary Press, 1948. Earlier, a booklet by an "anonymous citizen" proposed farming, among other activities, as a proper occupation for Jews. A Polish deputy, Butrymowich, issued a version of this in the late 1780's.

5. The idea of introducing Jews to agriculture and physical labor current among the Tsarist bureaucracy was essentially concerned with a kind of compulsory enlightenment which, in the minds of some among them, would lead enlightened Jews to convert to Greek Orthodoxy. An 1804 law offered certain benefits and exemption from the double tax to Jews going into agriculture. The first chapter of the 1804 law bears the title "On Enlightenment," but it was coupled with decreed expulsions of Jews from the villages and a prohibition against the keeping of taverns, inns, and other establishments by Jews. In 1817 a special decree offered land, civil equality, and tax benefits to the Jews of Russia if they would convert to the

Greek Orthodox faith. In connection with the Congress of the Holy Alliance at Aix-la-Chapelle, Lewis Way, a British missionary, in 1818 presented a memorandum to Aleksandr I on the Jewish situation. In addition to civil equality for Jews, Way suggested the development of a Jewish peasantry and vocational education. Nikolaii Novosiltsev, Imperial Commissioner attached to the provisional government of Warsaw (the Polish kingdom under Russia established after the Vienna Congress and which existed from 1815-1830), who was friendly to the Jews, in a project submitted in 1817 also suggested promotion of agricultural and crafts occupations among Polish Jews. Later, in the 1840s, new shortlived efforts were made to encourage Jewish agricultural activities in Siberia. A Jewish peasantry appeared in South-Russia near Ekaterinoslav (now Dnepropetrovsk), in Bessarabia, in Lithuania, and in White Russia.

6. See: S. Dubnow, *World History of the Jewish People* (in Yiddish). New York: Elias Laub Publishing Co., 1948; Salo W. Baron, *A Social and Religious History of the Jews*. Philadelphia: Jewish Publication Society of America, Vols. II, III, and IV. (This work is now in its 17th volume.) The question of the economic position of the Jewish community in the medieval period and later is highly complex. The many factors creating the Jewish socioeconomic structure, including the impact of the Jewish religious framework, cannot be discussed here. See: Simon Federbush, *The Jewish Concept of Labor*. New York: Torah Culture Department of the Jewish Agency and Hapoel Hamizrachi of America. See also Salo W. Baron, Arcadius Kahan and others, *Economic History of the Jews*, edited by Nachum Gross. New York: Schocken Books, 1975; Mark Wischnitzer, *A History of Jewish Craft and Guilds*. New York: Jonathan David Publishers, 1965.

Chapter II: A Backward Glance

1. I prefer not to use the word "shtetl" because in some writings it has a sociological connotation that appears to me to be not clearly defined and thus often confuses the reader.

2. See: Shapiro, *op. cit.*

3. F. I. Dan, *Proiskhozhdenie Bolshevisma*. New York: Novaia Demokratia, 1946; George Vernadsky, *A History of Russia*. New York: New Home Library, 1944. N. M. Druzhinin, *Russkaia derevnia na perelome 1861-1880 g.g. (The Russian Village at the Turning Point)*. Moscow: Izdatelstvo Nauka, 1978.

4. See: Shapiro, *op. cit.*; Salo W. Baron, *The Russian Jews under Tsars and Soviets*. New York: Macmillan Publishing Co., 1976; "ORT Inquiry," as quoted by J. Lestschinsky in *Kniga o Russkom Evreiistve. 1860-1917*. New York: Union of Russian Jews, 1960.

5. Some Russian writers of the period were sympathetic to the Jewish situation. Among the most notable in this connection are Aleksandr Herzen (1812-1870), Nikolaii Chernyshevskii (1828-1889), Nikolaii Dob-

roliubov (1836-1861), representing the left wing of the Russian intelligentsia; Leo Tolstoy (1828-1910), Vladimir Soloviev (1853-1900), and Mikhail Saltykov-Shchedrin (1826-1889); Nikolaii Pirogov (1810-1881), a physician and educational administrator.

6. Pavel Akselrod (1850-1928), a Menshevik leader, who joined the Populist movement in 1872 and was later one of the founders of Russian Marxism, referred to this situation in his piece, "O Sadachakh Evreiisko-sotsialisticheskoii intelligentsii." Among the early Jewish revolutionaries in the Populist movement were Aron Zundelevich, Vladimir Iokhelson, and Mark Nathanson.

7. See: Shapiro, *op. cit.*

8. See: Gregory Aronson in *80 Years of ORT*. Geneva: ORT Union, 1960.

9. A Russian-Jewish press appeared in the 1860s: *Rasvet* in 1860 in Odessa and, later, in St. Petersburg; *Den* in 1869 in Odessa; *Russkii Evreii* in 1879 in St. Petersburg; *Voskhod* in 1881 in St. Petersburg. There may have been a difference of emphasis with respect to social goals as between the Russian-Jewish and Hebrew-Yiddish press.

10. See: David Patterson, *The Hebrew Novel in Czarist Russia*. Edinburgh: At the University Press, 1964; Samuel Niger, "Yiddish Literature in the Past 200 Years," in *The Jewish People Past and Present*. New York: Jewish Encyclopedic Handbooks (CYCO), 1952, Vol. III.

11. See: Iulii Gessen, in *Evreiiskaiia Entsiklopediia*, St. Petersburg, Vol. 3, pp. 698-702; G. B. Sliozberg, Baron G. O. Gintsburg [Russian spelling], *Ego Zhizn i Deiatelnost*. Paris: Committee Honoring the Memory of Baron G. O. Gintsburg in Connection with the Celebration of the 100th Anniversary of His Birth, 1933. Louis Grinberg, in *Jews in Russia* (New Haven: Yale University Press, 1965), writes: "It was due to his [Bakst's] efforts that S. Poliakov, whose adviser he was on Jewish matters, established and subsidized the organization to encourage agriculture and artisanship among Jews which later became known as ORT." See also Circular letter of the Conference for the Fund in the name of Bakst. *Otchet, Obshchestva remeslennago i zemledelcheskago truda sredi evreev v Rossii za 1909 god. Prilozhennie III*, p. 46 and following.

12. Sliosberg, in *Baron G. O. Gintsburg. . . ., op. cit.*, states that "Owing to his [Gintsburg's] efforts, the government permitted the collection of funds." See also piece on Gunzburg in *Evreiiskaia Entsiklopediia*.

13. See: *Kratkii ocherk istorii vozniknoveniia obshchestva remesl. i. zemled. truda sredi evreev v Rossii i deiatelnosti vremennago komiteta. Prilozhenie k otchetu obshchestva za 1907 god*. St. Petersburg, 1908. Hereafter we shall designate all annual reports of the Society as *Otchet*, indicating the appropriate year.

14. The Russian text of the "private" letter can be found in *Otchet* for 1907.

15. *Ibid.*, pp. 27ff, a short outline of the history of the Society (ORT), as presented to the first General Assembly, December 3, 1906, by Iakov Gal-

pern. Out of 12,457 donations, 11,448 sent from 1 to 25 rubles; 756 from 25 to 100; 250 from 100 to 5,000; and 3 from 10,000 to 25,000.

16. The Russian text of the rules will be found in the volume. The title of the society to be created was *Obshchestvo remeslennago i zemledelcheskago truda sredi evreev v Rossii*, or ORT, which is composed of the initials of the Russian words indicating the character of the Society. Later, in Europe and in the U.S.A., an effort was made to adapt the abbreviated Russian title to its English and French equivalents, i.e., Organization for Rehabilitation Through Training, and *Organisation Réhabilitation Travail*—in short, ORT.

17. See: *Protokoly Zasedanii vremennago Komiteta po obrazovaniiu obshchestva remesl. i zemledel. truda sredi evreev Rossii v pamiat dvadzatipiatiletiia tsarstvovaniia imperatora Aleksandra II*, St. Petersburg, 1882. Hereafter we shall use the abbreviation ORT.

18. *Ibid.*, pp. 2, 5.

19. The rabbinical schools of Zhitomir and Vilna, created in 1847, were the nurseries of the Enlightenment. Both were closed by the authorities in 1873.

20. Mikhail Katkov (1818-1887). Although a disciple of the liberal writer Belinsky in his youth, he became a nationalist and reactionary and had great influence on the government. Katkov was the author of the slogan "returning home" (*vozvrashchenie domoii*), meaning that Russia should return to its own Russian ways instead of imitating the West. Bakst believed that "returning home" was compatible with a fair attitude toward the Jews of Russia.

21. See: *Otchet za 1908 god*. The so-called Palen Commission, or High Commission for the Revision of Current Laws concerning the Jews, was created in 1883. Count Palen succeeded to the chairmanship after the death of the first chairman, Makov. The Commission included, in addition to representatives of various government departments, Jewish experts.

22. See: Sliozberg, *op. cit.*

23. *Ibid.*

24. An interesting story is reported of a Russian Minister of the Interior telling an assemblage of high state functionaries that, when student riots erupted in St. Petersburg, he had stopped them by threatening to banish Baron Gunzburg from the city. The point of the story is the assumed solidarity among Jews of various social classes and political persuasions. See: Hans Rogger, "Russian Ministers and the Jewish Question 1881-1917," *Slavic Studies*, Vol. XIII. Berkeley: University of California Press, 1975.

25. There were to be changes in the attitude of the Russian Jewish intelligentsia so that, in a sense, even assimilationist propaganda in some Jewish periodicals focusing on Jewish needs had an intrinsically positive Jewish aspect. See: Aronson, *80 Years of ORT, op. cit.* quoting I. Zinberg, *History of the Jewish Press*.

Chapter III: First Steps

1. The Jewish Crown School (*Evreiiskoe Uchilishche*) was introduced by Nikolaii I in 1844 by a ukase on "The Education of Jewish Youth." In a secret memo addressed to the Minister of Public Instruction it was indicated that the training of Jewish children should endeavor to bring them closer to the Christian population and eradicate the "prejudices of the Talmud." Before that time, however, some Jewish schools had been opened by *maskilim*, including one in Odessa, one in Kishinev, and one in Riga.

2. See: *Protokoly zasedanii vremennago komiteta . . ., op. cit.*, pp. 2, 3.

3. *Ibid.*

4. Vesoler became an honorary member of the Society in 1911.

5. The volume of work during this initial period is reflected in Table I in the text.

6. See: *Protokoly. . . ., op. cit.*

7. Two types of vocational education existed in Imperial Russia: preparation in vocational, technical, and industrial art schools; and supplementary preparation for individuals already in handicrafts in once-a-week evening classes and special workshops. By 1910, there were in Russia 18 trade schools for men under the sponsorship of ORT and ICA (Jewish Colonization Association). See: *Evreiiskaia Entsiklopediia*, Vol. XIII.

8. See: *Russkii Evrei* for 1879 and 1880; also *Rassvet* for 1879, particularly with respect to agricultural work. For the period after 1880, see *Voskhod*. Gregory Aronson, in his article "Genesis of ORT," quotes a piece by M. Margulis that appeared in *Rassvet* of October 18, 1879, in which Margulis proposed obtaining from the authorities permission to organize a society for the establishment of vocational and agricultural schools. Aronson also quotes an article in *Rassvet* of December 18, 1880, in which the connection between the ORT initiative in 1880 and an 1869 project in Kovno (Kaunas) was pointed out. At the time, a large number of Jews on their way to the West found themselves in Kovno where circumstances compelled them to remain, at least temporarily. Jews in neighboring Germany, through a local Kovno committee organized by local elements, raised funds to help Russian Jews. As indicated in the text of this chapter, the idea of creating an agency to deal with economic problems in the same way as the Society for the Diffusion of Enlightenment was intended to deal with matters of education was in the air. The Kovno committee, located as it was in provincial Kovno, must have been a local project for dealing with a particular situation. Historical sources of the period do not indicate a direct connection between Rabbi Jacob Ruelf's Relief Committee (also referred to by Aronson), the Kovno project, and ORT. (See Aronson's article in *Eighty Years of ORT*. Geneva: ORT Union, 1960; an article on Rabbi Ruelf in *Evreiiskaia Entsiklopediia*, Vol. XIII; and Ruelf's *Mein Reise nach Kovno* [1869] and *Drei Tage in Judisch Russland* [1882].

9. Among the members of *People's Will* were some Jews. In the group that participated in the actual assassination was a Jewish woman, Hesia Helfman, but she played only a secondary role.

10. The Pale of Settlement consisted of 25 provinces (*gubernias*) in Lithuania, White Russia, southwestern Russia, southern Russia, and Poland.

11. See: Jacob Lestschinsky, "The Jew in Czarist Russia," *ORT Economic Bulletin*, Vol. II, No. 1, Jan.-Feb. 1941.

12. The 1897 census showed the following occupational distribution of Russian Jews:

Industry-handicraft	36.3
Commerce-insurance	31.0
Day laborers, servants	11.5
Professions	4.7
Communications and transportation	3.0
Agriculture	2.4
Without gainful occupation	7.6
Military	3.5

In addition to the 7.6 per cent without gainful employment, a substantial percentage of individuals reported as in commerce and insurance were in fact, according to local *Kehila* information, unable to earn a living. Some 25 per cent of the Jewish population was in need of public assistance provided by *Kehila* agencies and private contributions. An economic survey conducted by a group of students in the important Jewish city of Odessa in 1900 showed 8,435 Jewish families in need of assistance. The sample covered by the survey included 48,539 persons, about 32 per cent of the total Jewish population of Odessa. The survey indicated that some families for personal reasons did not wish to avail themselves of public charity, and that some 6,000 other families were living at the edge of poverty. Of the 2,980 Jews who died in Odessa in 1899, 1,890 received burial provided for by public charity, and 625 were provided burial at a minimum rate; only 465 had the full cost of burial paid for by relatives. About 68 per cent of the needy Jews lived in the so-called Moldavanka district, which has been brilliantly described by Babel in his stories. To appreciate the significance of these figures it should be borne in mind that some 82 per cent of those recorded as needy in the survey came originally from areas outside Odessa. (See: *Knizhki Voskhoda*, St. Petersburg, May 1901.)

13. See: *Protokoly Zasedanii Vr. Komiteta* 1880-1882 and 1884-1889.

14. Lesnoi Institute was a school for higher learning at the university level whose diplomas were highly valued.

15. Some financial and statistical data available from early sources will throw some light on how the activities developed. Allocation and disbursements of funds during the first 21 months of the Committee's activity are shown in the following table.

Allocations and Disbursements by the
Provisional Committee
November 4, 1880—August 1, 1882

		Allocated	*Disbursed* *
		(in rubles)	
1.	Transfer of artisans	13,820.00	12,045.00
2.	Local subsidies to artisans	1,537.95	1,537.95
3.	Subsidies to vocational schools, including vocational training in folk-schools, Talmud Torahs, etc.	3,626.70	2,276.70
4.	Grants to students in specialized vocational schools (railroad, agricultural, gardening, etc.)	440.00	397.00
5.	Subsidies to farmers	6,865.00	1,965.00
		26,289.65	18,221.65

*Amounts disbursed are smaller than amounts allocated because release of grants was sometimes in installments or after a certain date pending actual departure of a beneficiary or the beginning of a new program.

16. Some of the subsidies to schools were to vocational schools under private Jewish sponsorship.

17. This amount includes payments to master-artisans for training of apprentices.

18. There may be slight differences in the actual number of individuals assisted, since in certain cases overall amounts were allocated for specific purposes, while actual distribution of funds was made locally. It was not possible to ascertain the names of all beneficiaries.

19. See: *Protokoly Zasedanii*, 1882-1884, pp. 52, 72. Mark Antokolskii (1842-1902) was a distinguished Russian Jewish sculptor whose works were exhibited at several Russian museums. Kadushin, later a well-known Russian Jewish master of graphic arts, continued his art work well into the 20th century.

20. In 1895, Pobedonostsev expressed concern that the Jews were exercising a dangerous influence over the religious lives of their non-Jewish servants.

21. The ICA (Jewish Colonization Association) was founded in 1891 in London by Baron M. Hirsh to promote agricultural settlement of Eastern European Jews in Argentina. The plan included settling some 3,000,000 Russian Jews there. Later, ICA extended its activities to include Palestine and other countries. One of the interesting efforts undertaken by ICA was a survey of the economic situation of Russian Jewry during the period from June, 1898, to the end of 1899, which covered some 1,400 localities containing Jewish settlements. The results were published in 1904. During the early period, ICA extended financial support to designated ORT proj-

ects in Russia. Leon Bramson who, from 1899, was the executive of ICA in Russia, participated actively in this work. This cooperation between the two organizations continued during certain periods in Russia and in other countries.

22. Shapiro, *Dubnow, op. cit.*, Vol. III.

23. *Ibid.*

24. *Otchet za 1907 god. Prilozhenie*, p. 39.

25. Shapiro, *Dubnow, op. cit.*

26. Under the new law, approval by the authorities was not required for certain types of associations, but only registration.

27. *Otchet za 1907 god. Idem*, p. 38.

Chapter IV: The Great Debate

1. This attitude survived World War I and the war's aftermath. There is a curious example of it in a book (*Evreiiskii Mir*) published in New York in 1943, devoted to the memory of Leon Bramson. Dr. Julius Brutskus, a Jewish activist at the beginning of the century, future leader of OSE (see note 2), and a historian of Russian Jewry, recalling the beginnings of ORT, wrote: "Years ago, in the early 80's, ORT was the repository of great hope [for the Jewish people—LS]. Sometime later, it froze under the administration of an old and odd character, Prof. M. (*sic*) Bakst. For a long period of time, Bramson, who tried to do something to change the situation, used to take us to Bakst's apartment for all kinds of conversations and negotiations. However, the old man was absolutely inflexible and continued to hold the society in a state of *anabiosis* up to the moment of the Russian revolution [1905—LS]. Only then did he give up and accept to introduce reforms."

In his youth, Dr. Brutskus had been among the "young Turks," and his recollection of events is tainted by the hostility that surrounded Bakst, a phenomenon that occurs frequently among memoirists recollecting political and social events. Dr. Brutskus even used an incorrect initial for Bakst's given name. The statement that Bakst yielded on reforms only at the moment of the 1905 revolution is also inaccurate as, unfortunately, Bakst passed away in 1904. Brutskus probably remembered the anti-Bakst attitudes of his friends of old, but he is absolutely wrong about the timing of events and the participants in them. Among the editors of the *Evreiiskii Mir* were writers, including Gregory Aronson, who were still, after more than forty years, influenced by the Russian Jewish impressions of their youth and "remembered" things of the past accordingly. Some of Bakst's friends in ORT sought to establish a fund in his memory, but they were unsuccessful in obtaining support for it. The ORT report for 1908 (p. 52) noted: "Such lack of response on the part of the members . . . unwittingly attracts attention."

2. OSE (*Obshchestvo Zdravookhraneniia Evreev*) was created in Russia in 1912 as a society for improving the health of Russian Jews. It was later also active outside of Russia. Brutskus was a leading figure in OSE and in cooperative OSE-ORT actions; he was also a lifelong Zionist, who at the same time, and until his death, maintained a liberal position with respect to Russian politics.

3. The problem of proletarianization of the Jewish masses was widely discussed in the Jewish press of that period. Ber Borochov (1881-1917), one of the most influential leaders of the Poale-Zion movement, who had spent time in the United States, developed a complex theory which he considered Marxist. He believed that it was impossible for the Jewish proletariat to develop fully under the conditions of the Diaspora in which it was forced by existing conditions into secondary occupations. In order to develop its own normal class struggle and achieve an advanced position leading to socialism, it must return to its own land, Palestine, where, under normal conditions, it would achieve the social revolution.

4. Toward the end of the 19th century some 600,000 Russian Jews were gainfully employed in industry and agriculture. "A simple increase in numbers will not ameliorate the economic situation of the Jewish masses. . . . The task of the organization [ORT—LS] should tend toward creation of conditions under which the productive work would assure sufficient income. . . . Only then would an increase of the cadres of Jewish productive population be possible in large numbers, and this population will not be forced, as is the case now, to migrate in masses abroad." (*Otchet* for 1907, pp. 43ff.)

5. In the Kishinev pogrom, which occurred on April 19 and 20, 1903, 47 died and some 600 were wounded. The pogrom was organized by Tsarist officials following a campaign of hate conducted by a local journalist, Krushevan, in his newspaper, *Bessarabets*, on the pretext of an invented ritual murder story.

6. Only 12 responses were received in St. Petersburg.

7. The conference was held in Vilna at the end of December, 1908. G. Sliosberg and S. Meerson represented ORT. In the course of the four-day meeting the discussion concerned problems of the vocational schools, including the need of materials in Yiddish and the introduction of training in non-traditional Jewish trades.

8. See letter of J. Frumkin addressed to Sussya Goldmann dated May 1, 1961, in ORT History Archives.

9. See *Otchet* for 1909.

10. The Second Congress of Artisans (January, 1911), organized by the Society for Russian Industry, included as participants 102 Jewish delegates (28 from St. Petersburg and 74 from other cities). Among the questions under discussion was the problem of Sabbath observance (rest days) by Jewish artisans.

11. See *Otchet* for 1912, *god.*, p. 10. E. Khaikin suggested a return to

individual assistance since, according to him, ORT was not in a position to promote large general projects requiring substantial outlays.

12. Piotr Stolypin (1862-1911), Minister of the Interior, who became president of the Council of Ministers in July, 1906, introduced a repressive regime of courts-martial and punitive expeditions against revolutionaries. After the second Duma he reduced both the franchises and representation of nationalities. Aggressive nationalism and emergency legislation were his guidelines. He was assassinated in September, 1911 at the Kiev opera by Dmitri Bogrov, a revolutionary and agent of the secret police.

13. See *Otchet* up to and including 1914, and *Otchet po uchilishcham i electrotekhnicheskim kursam za 1909 i 1910 god*. Leon Frenkiel, at that time head of the Vilna vocational school, was assigned to prepare a program of courses which later was approved by the educational authorities of the Vilna region.

The courses began in January, 1910. The academic schedule included geometry, technical design, electro-technical studies, and practical work. Among the supporters of the project was the municipality of Vilna. As of October, 1910, there were 42 students enrolled, and as of January, 1911, 39.

The courses required a substantial budget, a large part of it for the acquisition of equipment. For this purpose, ORT extended a one-time grant of 3,000 rubles and an annual subsidy of 1,650 rubles. Frenkiel became the head of the project. Later, in Germany and France, he was still closely associated with ORT throughout the Nazi occupation and after the liberation of France. See also Jack Rader, *By the Skill of Their Hands. The Story of ORT*, Geneva, 1970.

14. The number in each instance includes members of local divisions and individuals who had made contributions of no less than 50 rubles before the establishment of ORT. This was in accordance with Article 11 of the ORT Bylaws.

15. In 1911, Mendel Beilis was charged with having murdered a Christian boy in order to use his blood for Jewish ritual purposes. The celebrated trial in Kiev ended with the acquittal of Beilis in 1913.

16. At this time ORT headquarters were located in Petrograd, on Iamskaia Street No. 16.

17. According to the rules, the executive head of ORT was at the same time an elected member of the directing committee (*chlen deloproizvoditel*). The successors of Bakst on the Provisional Committee were I. Berger, M. Bomze, L. Bramson, and M. Gurevitch, the latter replacing Bramson in May, 1915. After Poliakov in the Provisional Committee, Baron Horace Gunzburg was elected the first president of ORT, serving from 1906 to 1909. He was succeeded, after an interval, by J. Galpern (1910-1914). Upon Galpern's death, and again after an interval, G. Sliosberg became president (1915).

18. The bibliography was issued as a supplement to *Voskhod* and is known as the *Ukazatel*.

19. In 1917 the Trudoviks joined the Popular Socialists. Among the leaders of the united group was Aleksander Kerensky.

20. Gregory Aronson, in his book *Idisch-Russische Intelliguentz*, Buenos Aires, 1962, has a short essay on Bramson.

Chapter V: Years of Turmoil

1. See: Shapiro, *History of the Jews in Russia and Poland, by S. Dubnow, op. cit* See also Abraham G. Duker, *Jews in the World War: A Brief Historical Sketch* in Contemporary Jewish Records, Vol. II, No. 5; September-October 1939, New York.

2. EKO (*Evreiiskoe Kolonizationnoe Obshchestvo*, the Russian name of ICA).

3. "ORT and ICA," in *Vestnik, op. cit.*, pp. 10-12.

4. See *Otchet* for 1914.

5. Shapiro, *History . . . by S. Dubnow, op. cit.*

6. A group of ORT members expressed a desire to participate in the efforts to help Jewish refugees through work by assessing themselves the sum of 10 to 20 per cent of their rent. By the end of 1914, 103 members of the group had collected 6,405 rubles 50 kopeks.

7. EKOPO—*Evreiiskii Komitet Pomoshchi Zhertvam Voiny*. Jewish Relief Committee for War Victims, organized at the beginning of the war at St. Petersburg.

8. *Retch*, No. 216 (Aug. 8 [21], 1915).
   No. 221 (Aug. 13 [26], 1915).

9. *Retch*, No. 212 (Aug. 4 [17], 1915).

10. These are the old names of the cities. Some were given new names by the Soviets.

11. A "thick" periodical was the Russian way of identifying a serious publication with its own outlook. *Vestnik Trudovoi Pomoshchi*, No. 10, 1916, St. Petersburg, pp. 21, 22, 23. The magazine carried advertisements, including some for the radical periodical *Delo*, in the publication of which A. Potresov, the well-known social-democratic theoretician and founder of the Marxist Union for the Liberation of Workers, participated; for *Letopis*, a periodical published by Maxim Gorky; and similar publications. Bakst would hardly have tolerated this type of advertisement in an ORT publication.

12. *Otchet za 1915 god.*

13. See: *Vestnik Trudovoi Pomoshchi*, No. 2, Petrograd, January, 1916, pp. 79, 80.

14. See: *Société de Propagation du Travail Industriel et Agricole Parmi les Juifs (ORT), 1880-1920*, Paris, 1921.

15. *Evreiiskii Mir, op. cit.*, pp. 24-25.

16. *Otchet za 1913 god.*

17. Aronson, in his *Idisch-Russische Intelliguentz, op. cit.*, stated that Bramson left the Committee "by accident," implying that it was his turn to step down. This is inaccurate, as is clearly indicated in *Vestnik, op. cit.*, p. 10, 1916.

18. N. Sviatitski, a Socialist-Revolutionary who later went over to the Bolsheviks, states that Bramson assisted in the organization of an illegal S. R. printing shop (*Katorga i Ssylka*, Vol. I, 1931).

19. Aronson, *Idisch-Russische Intelliguentz, ibid.*

20. Shapiro, *History . . . by S. Dubnow, op. cit.*

21. *Novy Put*, No. 13-15, Moscow, April 23, 1917.

22. Shapiro, *History . . . by S. Dubnow, op. cit.*

23. The Socialist-Revolutionary party (S.R.) was formed through unification of various Populist groups. It emphasized the role of the Russian peasantry and preached democratic socialism. It advocated "socialization" of the land.

24. *Evreiiskii Mir., op. cit.* Bramson and Lvovich reported on their mission to the first Congress of ORT in 1921 in Berlin. In Paris, Bramson opened an office in the Pension Sevigny, Sevigny Place, the first ORT address abroad.

Chapter VI: New Beginnings

1. Lvovich, in *Evreiiskii Mir, op. cit.*, noted that "connections [with Russian ORT] toward the end of 1919 were broken." Even within Russia it was difficult to deal with Petrograd from Kiev and Odessa, where Bramson was.

2. The Russian habit of addressing colleagues and friends by their first names and patronymics was followed in both France and Germany.

3. The report, in Yiddish, is among the materials in the archives of ORT World Union in Geneva. See also *Baricht funm Farband ORT*, January, 1923-January, 1926, Berlin, 1926.

4. See: *Eighty Years of ORT, op. cit.*

5. It was common knowledge that during the February (March) revolution, Bramson, under the chaotic conditions in Petrograd, was able to secure the necessary means, including food supplies, for the functioning of the Petrograd Soviet, where he represented the Trudoviks. R. Abramovitch, the Menshevik leader, has related that the members of the Soviet and their families would have died of hunger had it not been for Bramson and his managerial talents. See: Aronson, *Idisch-Russische Intelliguentz, op. cit.*

6. *Misnagid* (plural, *Misnagdim*), an opponent of the Hasidic movement.

The *Misnagdim*, chiefly from the northwestern part of Russia, emphasized the way of the law and the necessity of "dry" learning, and were critical of the "enthusiasm" introduced by the Hasidim in their prayers and life style.

7. See article by Lvovich in *Evreiiskii Mir, op. cit.*, p. 26.

8. Vilna, between 1918 and 1920, was ruled, in turn, by Lithuania, Russia, and Poland. In 1922, the Polish Diet voted to join Vilna to Poland. In 1939, Vilna was given to Lithuania by the invading Germans and Soviets. See: *Obshchestvo . . . ORT*, 1880-1920, Paris, 1921.

9. See: C. H. Feigin, "Souvenirs," in ORT History Archives, and Jacob Oleiski, "ORT in Lithuania," also in the ORT History Archives.

10. See: *Société de Propagation du Travail Industriel et Agricole Parmi les Juifs (ORT), 1880-1920*, Paris, 1921, p. 11. The limited scope of the work of the Bureau may be seen from the following figures:

Machinery and Tools Purchased by the ORT
Purchase Bureau for Use in Eastern European
Countries, 1920-1923*

Trade	Machines	Small Tools, Parts, etc.
Tailoring	131	10,230
Shoemaking and leatherworking	144	7,992
Smithing, lock- smithing and electrical	121	5,447
Carpentry	37	13,415
Sockmaking	146	102
Binding	22	—
Weaving	—	683
Other	270**	—

* Includes both Paris and Berlin Bureaus.
**Includes some unclassified parts and small tools.

Some supplies were also acquired locally in Warsaw, Kovno, Vienna, and Lodz. See: S. F. Blum, "Ort—Fifty Years of Jewish Relief in Eastern Europe," in *Ort Economic Review*, Vol. V, No. 2. New York, December, 1945.

11. *Protokoly Sasedanii Pravleniia, 1921-1922*, ORT, Berlin.

12. Bramson, when not traveling on a mission, devoted himself to everyday details, including technical aspects of local ORT schools. See correspondence re Vilna Technikum in ORT archives at YIVO, New York; also: Aronson, *Notes of the ORT Secretary* (unpublished), and S. Goldmann, *A Sheaf of Memoirs*. Geneva: ORT Union, 1965.

Chapter VII: Consolidation and Expansion

1. See: *Baricht*, 1923, *op. cit*. We may surmise that ORT in Russia was denied permission to send a delegate abroad. (ORT in Soviet Russia will be discussed in a separate chapter.)

2. The offices of the Reconstruction Fund were located in London at 79b Belsize Park Gardens, in Paris at 9 bis rue Vineuse, in Berlin at Bleibtreustrasse 34/35.

3. Agro-Joint (American-Jewish Joint Agricultural Corporation) was founded in the United States in 1924. It dealt with the Jewish agricultural colonies in the USSR. It was controlled by JDC, which held all its stock. Joseph A. Rosen was its first president.

4. The extent of the work of the Corporation in 1924-1926 may be seen in the table below.

Year	Number of Machines	Cost
1924–September	33	$ 2,108.20
October	—	—
November	—	—
December	14	828.05
1925–January	35	1,811.35
February	99	2,083.00
March	51	1,425.25
April	48	1,482.15
May	201	2,098.90
June	33	2,562.95
July	12	5,361.60
August	13	3,763.60
September	11	1,558.90
October	39	2,941.65
November	6	340.90
December	45	3,486.10
1926–January	30	3,001.00
February	62	7,388.10
March	34	11,529.10
	766	$53,770.80

In 1928, 1,223 machines were sent to beneficiaries, including Russian beneficiaries.

5. The declaration of Polish independence had been celebrated, in November, 1918, by the Poles and especially by Polish legionnaires, with a

bloody pogrom in the Jewish areas of Lvov (Lemberg). According to some Polish sources, this was a "natural" reaction to the position of neutrality taken by the Jews in the conflict over Ukrainian and Polish claims in Galicia. In Vilna, where Poles accused the Jews of harboring secret pro-Soviet sympathies, Jews were murdered. Among the Vilna victims was the talented young Jewish writer, A. Waiter.

6. See: *Obshchii obzor deiatelnosti, 1926-1928*, Berlin.

7. For a general survey, see: George Gliksman, *L'Aspect Economique de la Question Juive en Pologne*. Paris: Aux Editions Rieder, 1929. Also: I. Schipper, "The Problem of the Productivization of the Jewish Masses," in Jubilee issue *Hajnt* (in Yiddish), Warsaw, 1928.

8. See: *Baricht, op. cit.*

9. See: *Baricht, ibid.*

10. JDC assistance fell from $244,336 in 1923 to $64,984 in 1924. In 1925, when it decided to work directly through its own representatives, JDC also significantly reduced its grants.

11. See: *Baricht, op. cit.* p. 120.

12. The amount disbursed there in 1923, 1924, and 1925 was about $11,000, a considerable amount at that time in Rumania, where the official rate of exchange of leis to the dollar was 194 in 1923, 204 in 1924, and 215 in 1925.

13. See: *Baricht, op. cit.*

14. An accounting system was developed that reflected the resources of the Center and also estimated local income, thus providing a more complete picture of funds that could be budgeted for various programs.

15. Emigdirect was created to assist Jewish emigrants. Its central office was at that time in Berlin. The united campaign with OSE began in 1926. In 1927 the united campaign was expanded, particularly in Holland, Sweden, Switzerland, Czechoslovakia, and South Africa.

16. These figures are given for illustrative purposes only. See: *Obshchii obzor deiatelnosti, 1926–1928, op. cit.*, and official ORT budgets without administrative expenses quoted in S. Blum, *ORT: Fifty Years of Jewish Relief in Eastern Europe, op. cit.*

Chapter VIII: ORT in the Soviet Union

1. See: Shapiro, *History of the Jews in Russia and Poland by S. Dubnow, op. cit.* Lenin fought the Jewish Bundists who, according to him, wanted to establish "a spiritual mood hostile to assimilation, the mood of the ghetto." (*Iskra*, No. 5, October 22, 1903.) Stalin, in his *Marxism and the*

National Question (1913), still the bible in the USSR, spoke of the Jews as "a nation without a future and whose present existence [as a nation] is yet to be proven."

2. Shortly after its establishment EVKOM became a Department (*Evot-del*) in the Commissariat for Nationalities. It was abolished in 1919 and its functions, if not its ideas, were taken over by *Evsektsiia*.

3. See: *Société de Propagation du Travail . . . parmi les Juifs, op. cit.*

4. *Ibid.*

5. NEP was proclaimed by Lenin in March, 1921, following the Kronstadt revolt, when the garrison of the naval base at Kronstadt rebelled against Communist oppression and called for the granting of real rights to the Soviets to deal with the intolerable conditions brought about by the October revolution. Their slogan was "Soviets without Bolsheviks." Trotsky and Tukhachevsky led a military attack against the uprising.

NEP aimed at the easing of state controls, encouragement of some private initiative, increase of productivity, and other measures. The all-out industrialization in the second half of the 1920's, followed by the all-out collectivization of peasant farming, signified the end of NEP.

6. See: Solomon Schwartz, *The Jews in the Soviet Union*. Syracuse, N.Y.: Syracuse University Press, 1951.

7. See: *Protokoly pravleniia* (minutes of August 15, 1921, Berlin).

8. *Ibid.*, July 11, 1922.

9. *Ibid.*, 1923 and 1924.

10. A. Syngalowski, "Sixty-five Years of ORT," and G. Aronson, in *80 Years of ORT, op. cit.*

11. A movement, "Changing of Landmarks" (*Smena Vekh*), arose among Russian emigres. Many Smena-Vekhovtsevs returned to Soviet Russia, where one of its ideologues, N. Ustrialov, was killed. See: Robert C. Williams, *Culture in Exile: Russian Emigres in Germany* (1881-1941). Cornell University Press, 1972. David Bergelson (1884-1952) was one of the great Yiddish writers. After his conversion to Communism he wrote in the socialist-realist style yet will remain forever in the annals of Yiddish literature.

12. See: Aronson, *Idisch-Russiche Intelliguentz, op. cit.*, Aronson was friendly with Syngalowski whom he admired. He felt that Syngalowski's short-lived interest in "the left" should be recorded. See also discussions regarding the Russian program in materials in ORT archives.

13. *Tribuna Evreiiskoi Sovetskoi Obshchestvennosti*, No. 10, Moscow, June 15, 1928.

14. Leon Trotsky, *The Revolution Betrayed*. Garden City, New York: Doubleday, Doran Company, 1937.

15. The number of Soviet Jews indicating a desire to engage in farming

reached substantial proportions. The following are registration figures of KOMZET as of July 1, 1925:

Region	No. of Families	No. of Individuals
Kiev	3,431	
Chernigov	1,116	
Volynsk	3,722	
Odessa	3,335	
Don	249	
Ekaterinoslav	815	
Podolsk	1,495	
Poltava	835	
Total, 8 regions of Ukraine	14,998	73,000
Smolensk, 7 towns	147	
Pskov, 7 districts	211	
Gomel	665	
Belorussia, 10 regions	6,836	39,161
Total	22,857	112,161

These figures are quoted by U. Golde, "The Results of Registration of Jewish Population," in *Evreiiskii Krestianin* (in Russian), Vol. 1, OZET, Moscow, 1925. There are some typographical errors in the original Russian table, but these are of no importance here. See: Baron, *The Russian Jews . . ., op. cit.*; Shapiro, *History of the Jews . . . Dubnow, op. cit.*; S. Borowoy, *Jewish Agricultural Colonization in Tsarist Russia* (in Russian), Moscow, 1928; and *Evrei v. S.S.R.*, No. IV, OZET, Moscow, 1929. By 1929-1930 Jews in agriculture numbered about 300,000; after that time the number declined. L. Zinger, in *Dos Banaite Folk: Tsifern un Faktn vegen Idn in F.S.S.R.*, (Verlag Emes, Moscow, 1941), indicated 392,500 Jews in agriculture in 1939. In connection with this figure, some definition of terms is called for; for example, is a white-collar employee working in a *kolkhoz* engaged in agriculture?

16. See: *Statisticheskie Materialy*, No. 7, Moscow, 1930, and *Biuleten Statisticheskikh-economicheskikh Materialov*, No. 1, KOMZET, January, 1931.

17. American Jews participated in these endeavors mainly through Agro-Joint, the largest agency in the field, which invested some $20,000,000 in Jewish land projects in the Soviet Union. ICA was also very active in the field. Interestingly, the ORT man in Odessa, A. Weinstein, in a letter dated October 16, 1928, suggested that the ORT Union avoid sending "ORT guests" to the Soviet Union, since the depressed mood and the situation of the colonists would impress them unfavorably.

18. Figures based on reports in the files of ORT History Archives. They would appear to give an adequate picture of the situation.

19. L. Zinger, *Evreiiskoe Naselenie v. Sovetskom Soiuze Gos. Soc. Econ. i-vo*, Moscow, 1932; also his "Idn Proletarier in F.S.S.R.," in *Emes*, Moscow, 1933.

20. Reports of Soviet ORT (ORT Soiuz) for 1931-1934 (in Yiddish and Russian).

21. *Tribuna Evreiiskoi Obshchestvennosti* No. 12, Moscow, 1928, reported that the Presidium of Soviet ORT decided to participate in industrial work in Birobidzhan.

ORT-supported Industrial Enterprises
in Birobidzhan, 1935-1936*

Place	Type of Enterprise	No. of Workers
1. Birobidzhan	Plywood	227
2. Birobidzhan	Furniture	400
3. Birobidzhan	Sawmill	70
4. Birakan	Marble	100
5. Birobidzhan	Cedar Oil	25
6. Birofeld	Tiles	30
7. **	Woodwork	10
8. **	Toys	30
9. **	Baskets	20
10. Birakan	Haberdashery (artel)	35
11. **	Haberdashery (artel)	40

Rapport du Comité Executif de la Direction Centrale de l'Union ORT, Paris, September, 1936. Prepared by I. Koralnik.

**Information not available.

Not all of these projects were completed. It was expected that when reaching full capacity they would provide employment for some 1,000 Jewish families. On the ORT discussion concerning Birobidzhan, see *Protokoly Zasedanii Pravleniia ORT'A* (in Russian), 1934.

22. See: *Protokoly Zasedanii Pravleniia ORT'A*, 1934, and *Proces Verbal Réunion Plénière de l'Administration Centrale,* Paris, 1934; also, Schwartz, *The Jews in the Soviet Union, op. cit.*

23. Machines and Raw Materials Supplied by Soviet ORT to Enterprises and Artels Outside Birobidzhan, 1935-1936: (Table on the following page.)

24. *Gulag*—Russian acronym for Chief Administration of Camps. See: A. Solzhenitsyn, *The Gulag Archipelago.* New York: Harper & Row, 1974.

25. Before its liquidation, ORT in Moscow had a staff of 45, including specialized technicians and executives, among them Bromberg, assistant to Tsegelnitski; Frumkin, head of the supply department; and Zhukov, head of the locksmithing shop. As far as is known, they survived the closing of ORT. The ORT offices were located on Zhdanov Street, and its shops on Ostapenko Street. After the liquidation the ORT offices housed a taxi-drivers' club. (See letter of Arkady Pukhovitsky, a former assistant to the ORT chief engineer, dated November 29, 1976. Pukhovitsky came to the United States in 1976.)

Name	City	Type of Production	No. of Workers
Avtovias	Moscow	Stocking factory	459
Kooptextil	Bar	Weaving factory	300
Krasnyi Metalist	Bobruisk	Metals	205
Chekkardpriadsukno	Boguslav	Weaving factory	90
Samodeiatelnost	Dnepropetr.	Stocking factory	200
Promderevo	Zhitomir	Furniture	118
Lingerie "OZET"	Kiev	Lingerie	181
Promkust	Kiev	Stocking factory	120
Kombinat. Ukr. Kr. Krest	Kiev	Stocking factory	60
Kombinat Koopinssoiusa	Kiev	Jersey	185
Chervonny Tkasch	Kamenets-Pod.	Weaving factory	130
Uchprokombinat	Kamenets-Pod.	Chemical factory	38
Obiedinennyi Trud	Loshvitsa	Stockings	45
Lubodiag	Lubny	Stockings	70
Chervonnyi Tkasch	Novgorod-Sew.	Weaving	100
Chulochnyi Trikozhnik	Poltava	Stockings	337
Koopkust	Poltava	Stockings	120
Uchebnyi Kombinat	Proskurov	Furniture	42
Promkombinat	Priluki	Weaving	160
Rosa Luxemburg	Roslavl	Textile	291
Krimozet	Simferopol	Stockings	117
Udarnik	Slutsk	Textile	136
Chulochnik	Smolensk	Stockings	151
Slavtextil	Slavuta	Weaving	158
Chervonnyi Botschkar	Smela	Barrels	70
Grusozet	Tiflis	Woodwork	30
Standard	Khislavichi	Stockings	227
Shveinik Oktiabria	Svisloch	Clothing	80
Trud	Khislavichi	Shoes	50
Krasnyi Truzhenik	Khislavichi	Lingerie	30
Lesokooperator	Khabno	Sawmill	60
XI. Let Oktiabr. Revol.	Chernevtsy	Stockings	96
Promkombinat	Chornyi Ostr.	Stockings	130
Promkomtextil	Chernigov	Stockings	75
III God Piatiletki	Shumiatichi	Lingerie	30

Source: *Rapport du Comité Executif de la Direction Centrale de l'Union ORT,* Paris, September, 1936. Prepared by I. Koralnik.

26. See correspondence in connection with the liquidation, particularly the letter to Moscow dated August 24, 1938, in ORT History Archives. The amount requested, $264,317.09, included $192,729.60 for imports for agricultural projects and $71,587.49 for imports for industrial projects.

27. See correspondence in ORT History Archives. ORT archives in Odessa, the Crimea, and Birobidzhan were deposited with local archival agencies. The Moscow archives, 73 large crates weighing more than three

tons, were deposited in the Main Archival Office on October Street, Moscow.

28. Nikolai Ezhov was head of the secret police in 1936-1938, during the worst of the Stalin terror years. He was downgraded in 1938 and after serving for short periods in secondary positions, perished in one of the purges.

Chapter IX: Midpassage: Fifty Years of ORT

1. *Eighty Years of ORT, op. cit.*

2. See minutes of the meeting of *Pravlenie*, January 29-31, 1922, Berlin.

3. See ORT reports covering the Russian period, particularly the years immediately preceding World War I. The average vocational school provided for 35 hours of training out of a total schedule of 46 hours.

4. The discussions of educational matters reflected an earlier debate in Russian circles following the reforms introduced under Aleksandr II. An ICA survey showed that in the period covering roughly the 1890s, in the 25 *gubernias* (regions) of the Pale there were 500,986 Jewish artisans (259,396 master artisans, 140,528 assistant artisans, and 101,062 apprentices, the latter representing 20 per cent of the total). At the same time, only 600 youths were undergoing training in vocational schools. In 1907 the number of pupils in 37 schools (20 for boys and 17 for girls) providing vocational training amounted to 2,391 (1,311 boys and 1080 girls). Comparing the number of youths in training in shops and the number in schools, it is clear that the role of the latter, while important, was limited.

5. There were also some Jewish socialist groups that, in addition to territorialist demands, were also demanding various forms of local autonomy.

6. See: S. Goldmann in *Recueil présente a l'occasion du dixième anniversaire de la mort du Dr. Aron Syngalowski, 1956-1966*, U. M. ORT, Geneva.

7. *Ibid.*

8. See: G. Aronson, *Zapiski Sekretaria ORT'a*, in ORT History Archives. Aronson knew the ORT leaders well, having been active in ORT in Gomel and Vitebsk. After his exile from Soviet Russia because of his Menshevik connections he was received by the ORT people in Berlin as an old colleague and ORT activist. See also: A. Syngalowski, "Distress and Knowledge: A Dialogue on Vital Jewish Questions," in *Progressive Outlook*, Johannesburg, South Africa, May-June, 1936.

9. The colloquium was devoted to a study of changes in ORT activities under the impact of modern technology and the changed conditions of Jewish life.

10. See materials prepared for the celebration of the fiftieth anniversary in the ORT History Archives (in Russian). See also: Minutes of *Pravlenie*,

March 14, 1930. Zylberfarb repeatedly offered to prepare a piece on "ORT Ideology." He wanted particularly to do the piece for the publication planned for the celebration of the fiftieth anniversary.

Chapter X: The Thirties—A Decade of Crisis

1. Refugee statistics are a complex matter. The figures given in our text are estimates sufficient for our purposes. See: Gerald Reitlinger, *The Final Solution*. New York: Beechhurst Press, 1953; Leon Shapiro and Boris Sapir, "Jewish Population of the World," in *American Jewish Yearbook*, Vol. 50, 1948-1949. Werner Rosenstock, "Exodus 1933-1939. A survey of Jewish Emigration from Germany." *Yearbook* #1, Leo Baeck Institute, London, 1956.

2. A special agreement had been arrived at between the Jewish Agency and the Germans under which Jews could transfer money and property to Palestine in the form of export of German goods. This agreement, known as the *Haavarah*, permitted many German refugees to save at least part of their property. It was estimated that between 1933 and 1937 the total amount taken out of Germany under *Haavarah* came to some £4,500,000.

3. National Socialist German Workers Party, the full title of the Hitler party. On November 6, 1932, the NSDAP received 33 per cent of the vote (it had received 37 per cent in 1930), the Socialists 20 per cent, and the Communists 17 per cent.

4. On the night of November 9-10, 1938, on the pretext of retaliation for the assassination by Herschel Grynspan of Ernest von Rath, an employee of the German Consulate in Paris, the Nazi authorities organized a wholesale pogrom during which some 400 synagogues in German-held lands were destroyed by fire.

5. See: Minutes of meeting of ORT Executive Committee, January 8, 1934, Paris.

6. See: ORT History Archives, particularly a memorandum, dated October 19, 1977, of Dr. Arthur Feige, former teacher at the Berlin school who was among ORT personnel who did not receive visas for England, and an official document of ORT-Berlin dated April 17, 1941.

7. See: *Rapport du Comité Executif (1935-1936), rédige par I. Koralnik*, Secretary General of the ORT Union, Paris, September, 1936.

8. *Consistoire des Israelites de France*, a religious association, had a membership mainly of old settled French Jews. The *Fédération des Sociétés Juives de France* coordinated the activities mostly of Jews of East European origin.

9. See: Minutes of a meeting of Parisian members of the Executive Committee, November 11, 1933.

10. See: Report on the 50th anniversary of ORT-France, prepared by F. Schrager, dated September 23, 1971, in ORT History Archives.

11. In our preparation of the text on British ORT use was made, in addition to reports and various documents, of a draft of *The History of British ORT*, by Cecily Zimmerman, dated 1976 (London). Mrs. Zimmerman, for many years the organizing secretary of British ORT, and now retired, was good enough to meet with this writer and discuss some questions in connection with ORT work in England.

12. It was estimated that the rate of increase among the Polish Jewish population was about ten per 1,000, and that emigration, in the long run, corresponded approximately to the natural annual increase of 30,000.

13. Address by Jaszunski at the International Conference of ORT held in Paris, August 25, 1937.

14. Samuel Milman, an old-time communal leader and ORT activist from Lodz, who for decades had been a municipal counselor of Lodz, in a conversation with the writer in January, 1979, emphasized the innovative character of this program.

15. In 1935-1936, in addition to the ORT schools there were also vocational schools supported by ICA which had 2,644 pupils.

16. See: *Jewish Reconstruction Work, 1930-1936*, ORT Union, Paris.

17. See: *L'Histoire de l'ORT en Roumanie, 1931-1949*, unsigned manuscript in ORT History Archives.

18. Due to territorial changes following World War I, the Rumanian Jewish communal structure was a complex one, retaining the prewar character of its constituent parts. Dr. Filderman was chairman and Aureliu Weiss vice-chairman of the ORT Executive Committee.

19. The history of Jewish credit cooperation is described in detail by Moshe Ussoskin in *Struggle for Survival*. Jerusalem Academic Press, 1975.

20. See: *Mir Wern Poerim* (in Yiddish), ORT-Lithuania, 1935. For a general picture, see: *ORT Kalendar 1937* (in Yiddish), published by ORT-Lithuania.

21. Figures taken from ORT Union financial statements for 1930-1939.

22. The table on the next page shows ORT vocational programs as of January, 1937.

Chapter XI: World War II and the Catastrophe

1. Sussya Goldmann, in *From Congress to Congress* (ORT Union, Geneva, July, 1965), relates an amusing incident about the ORT move to Vichy that reveals something about Bramson the man of ORT and Bramson the man. In September, 1939, after the general mobilization, when ORT was preparing to leave Paris, Bramson instructed his staff to call the Ministry of Communications to arrange for rail transportation of ORT

ORT Vocational Training Projects
January, 1937

Country	Day Schools and Technicum	Workshop for Adults	Upgrading and Other Courses	Other Institu-tions	Total
Poland					
Institutions	18	28	20	—	66
Trainees	1,824	1,386	1,369	—	4,579
Rumania					
Institutions	14	10	1	6	31
Trainees	1,002	401	14	262	1,679
Lithuania					
Institutions	3	7	2	1	13
Trainees	196	275	57	—	528
Latvia					
Institutions	5	5	1	—	11
Trainees	288	136	28	—	452
France					
Institutions	—	12	1	—	13
Trainees	—	368	12	—	380
Bulgaria					
Institutions	3	1	—	—	4
Trainees	70	15	—	—	85*
Germany					
Institutions	1	1	—	—	2
Trainees	101	13	—	—	114
TOTAL					
Institutions	44	64	25	7	140
Trainees	3,481	2,594	1,480	262	7,817

*Error in original table corrected.

ᴀrchives out of the city. When his secretary told him that all rail facilities were reserved for the troops, Bramson said, "Well, in that case please tell [the Ministry] that the President of ORT demands it." The staff, knowing Bramson, and knowing also that there was no way out, simply told Bramson that the Ministry switchboard did not answer.

2. Emanuel Ringelblum, *Ksovim fun Geto*, Vol. I, II, Idisz Buch, Warszawa, 1961. See also Rachel Gourman, "In the Ghetto of Warsaw," in *Material and Memoirs*, ORT, Geneva, 1955; B. Mark, *Der Oifshtand in Warshever Geto*, Idisz Buch, Warszawa, 1963.

3. See: Lucy S. Davidowicz, *The War Against the Jews, 1933-1945*. New York: Holt, Rinehart & Winston, 1975.

4. *Ibid.*

5. See: Isaiah Trunk, *Judenrat*. New York: Macmillan, 1972.

6. *Ibid.*

7. See selected reports on ORT work in Poland from 1939 to 1943 in *80 Years of ORT, op. cit.*; D. Klementinowski, *Lebn un Umkum fun Bialostoker Geto*, New York, 1946; M. Dworzecki, "Jerushalaim D'Lite," in *Kamf un Umkum*, Paris, 1948.

8. For reasons of clarity we use the prewar Jewish population of about 400,000. As indicated in the text, due to territorial changes during the war the Jewish population of Hungary increased substantially. The losses of Jewish population suffered at the hands of the Nazis should be established on the basis of the 1939 population within the 1939 territorial borders.

9. The description of the situation in Lithuania is based on Oleiski's report in the ORT History Archives.

10. See: P. Minc Alexander, *In di Yorn fun Idishn Umkum un Widershtand in Frankreich*. Buenos Aires: Editorial, 1957. With reference to ORT work in camps, see: Vladimir Akivisson in *ORT Economic Review*, No. 4-5, 1941. See also *ORT Sous l'Occupation en France*, Geneva 1947—with respect to the relationships between ORT and U.G.I.F. (Union Générale des Israelites de France) created by the authorities as the central organization for the French Jews.

11. See: Cecily Zimmerman, *op. cit.* In 1959 one of the former pupils of the ORT school formed a committee to assist ORT in Israel.

12. See: David Kranzler, *Japanese, Nazis, and Jews*. New York: *Yeshiva University Press*, 1976.

13. See minutes of Emergency Committee for World ORT Affairs, May 19, 1942, and minutes through 1946.

14. Organization established in 1860 by a group of French Jews. Among its aims were defense of civil and religious liberties of Jews and promotion of educational opportunities.

15. See minutes of Emergency Committee for World ORT Affairs of March 15, 1945.

16. Boudin letter to Lvovich dated May 13, 1946. Later in a memo addressed to Julius Hochman dated June 29, 1945, in connection with the so-called American proposals, Boudin wrote that "the problem of a proper finance and accounting system is an exclusively American demand."

17. The reports were published in a 230-page double issue of *ORT Economic Review*, June-September, 1948. In them, Boudin makes his case with thoroughness and an array of supporting documents, including exchanges of letters between himself, Walinsky, Sard, and the European ORT activists. ORT leaders, believing the reports were exaggerated and presented only one side of the story, withdrew the issue from publication. Only a few copies are still in existence.

18. With the aim of diffusing the concentration of power held by Syn-

galowski and Lvovich, the ORT Union appointed a Committee of Five to meet monthly to deal with pressing ORT matters. Among the five members was Admiral Louis Cahn, known for his administrative ability. It was expected that Walinsky would be the executive secretary of the Committee, but he was not elected to that post, apparently because of the opposition of the Europeans.

19. One of the hidden problems in the dispute was also the desire on the part of some members of the ORT ruling body to "Westernize" the leadership and get rid of the "Russian leftovers," meaning those around Syngalowski. See: *ORT Economic Review, op. cit.*, pp. 88, 89, 246.

Chapter XII: The American Anchor

1. See S. Dubnow, *World History of the Jewish People* (Yiddish), *op. cit.*

2. JDC was organized in 1914 by the American Jewish Relief Committee, representing mainly upper- and middle-class Jewish circles. It was later joined by the Central Relief Committee formed by Orthodox groups and the People's Relief Committee set up by Jewish labor. (See: Boris Sapir and Leon Shapiro, *The Joint Distribution Committee in Jewish Life in Israel of Tomorrow*, edited by Leo Jung. New York: Herald Square Press, 1949.)

3. See: *Notes on Origins of ORT in America–The Earliest Days*, in ORT History Archives. It is not accidental that from the earliest days, P. Block, manager of the Socialist Yiddish *Daily Forward*, was the director of ORT in the United States. In 1929-1930, Panken resigned the Chairmanship of the organization and it was agreed that H. S. Cullman would succeed him. Later, however, he strongly objected that Cullman, a "bourgeois," should take over. As a result, Murray Levine was elected President and the "Forward" group was very unhappy. See memo by L. Boudin to Julius Hochman, dated June 29, 1948, in the ORT History Archives.

4. It was incorporated on November 5, 1924, as the American Society for the Promotion of Trades and Agriculture among the Jews-ORT.

5. Figures quoted in A. B. Tart, "25 Years of ORT in the U.S.A.," in *ORT Economic Review*, December, 1947.

6. See: Jehuda Bauer, *My Brother's Keeper, the History of AJDC, 1929-1939*. Philadelphia: Jewish Publication Society, 1974.

7. In some years ORT received less than the $2,000,000 contracted for, since its programs, particularly in the immediate postwar years, did not absorb all the funds due. In addition, JDC funded some ORT programs locally, for instance, students' meals and clothing.

8. See: Memorandum of Agreement between JDC and ORT entered into January 20, 1947, in New York. Prior to the ORT-JDC agreement, the total ORT collection, i.e., from the 1920's to 1947, amounted to some $6,000,000. See memo by L. Boudin of June 29, 1948 in the ORT History Archives, *op. cit.*

9. See: *10th Anniversary Journal, American and European Friends of ORT and the ORT Trade School*, and Jack Rader, *op. cit*. It is important to record that already in the early 1940's ORT organized vocational courses at the Yeshiva Torah—Umlachah, where the majority of the students came from Transylvania.

Chapter XIII: The Survivors

1. See: Leon Shapiro and Boris Sapir, "The Jewish Population of the World," in *American Jewish Year Book*, No. 50, 1948-1949.

2. For a definition of "displaced person" see: "International Refugee Organization," in *Year Book of the United Nations, 1946-47*, New York, 1947. See: "Report on the Progress of Repatriation, Resettlement and Immigration of Refugees and Displaced Persons," United Nations Economic and Social Council. E/816, June, 1948.

3. See: D. Kranzler, *Japanese, Nazis and Jews, The Jewish Refugee Community in Shanghai, 1938-1945, op. cit*.

4. See: Leon Shapiro and Boris Sapir, *op. cit*., and A. S. Hyman in *American Jewish Year Book*, No. 51, 1950.

5. *Three Years of ORT Activities*, 1946-1949, Geneva and Paris, 1949.

6. Central Committee of Liberated Jews in the British Zone, Germany, 1945-1947.

7. Dr. Z. Grinberg, "ORT's Great Task in the D.P. Camps," in *ORT Economic Review*, March-June, 1946.

8. Following a survey made by Earl Harrison, special representative of President Truman, Jewish DPs, in view of their suffering under the Nazis, were given special advantages. There were also advisers on Jewish affairs at the headquarters of the theater commander. The first such adviser was Judge Simon H. Rifkind. In 1948, before he became active in American ORT, Dr. William Haber was one of the advisers. In the spring of 1947, the Jewish DPs were distributed as follows:

	Number	Population	Per cent of total
Camps	63	103,000	67.0
Hachsharoth	39	3,600	2.5
Communities	139	43,700	25.3
Children's centers	14	4,100	2.8
Hospitals and sanatariums	48	3,500	2.4
TOTAL	303	157,900	100.0

9. See pieces by Gringaus and Keller in *ORT Economic Review*, No. 6-9, 1948.

10. According to 1948 data, the occupational distribution, in percentages, in the DP countries was as follows:

Trade group	Germany (U.S. Zone)	Austria	Italy
Needle trade	46	50	46
Metal trade	10	6	5
Electrical trade	7	17	5
Mech. service and hand trade	12	13	8
Building trade	6	6	10
Agriculture	—	—	4
Miscellaneous	19	8	22
	100	100	100

Quoted in Gringaus, *op. cit.*

11. Jack Rader, *op. cit.*, cites 22,620 enrolled in ORT DP courses by the end of 1947. Rader obviously had in mind individuals in training, graduates, and those who left the courses.

12. See: Leon Frenkiel, "ORT in Germany," in *ORT Economic Review*, No. 6-9, 1948.

13. These conservative estimates are based on official data published in reports of the World ORT Union. In considering these figures it should be borne in mind that the Jewish DPs were a transient population and that statistics in the DP camps were difficult to gather. There is no way to unravel some of the information. Sussya Goldmann, in "ORT in the Post War Period, 1945-1960" (*80 Years of ORT, op. cit.*), writes about 80,000 who were helped by ORT. Vladimir Halperin in his article "Les Efforts de Réconstruction Juive après le Hourban" in *D'Auschwitz à Israel après la Liberation*" (Paris: C.D.J.C., 1968), gives a total of 85,000 in ORT DP programs, probably counting all who registered whether they graduated or left without completing their training. Rader, *op. cit.*, uses a figure of about 80,000. In this connection it should be noted that at the beginning of ORT's DP program it was difficult to attract Jewish DPs to a course requiring a year since it was unthinkable for a Jewish DP to consider staying a year in Germany. Some ORT courses were therefore scheduled for three or six months. The situation changed later, but, in any case, a three-month course, whatever its value, cannot be compared to a full-time vocational program. A World ORT Union report covering the peak period July 1946-June 1949 gives the following picture:

	Adm.	Partly trained	Grad.	Status June 1949
Germany	30,023	22,704	9,254	2,838
Austria	4,036	2,186	1,451	669
Italy	5,419	2,035	1,575	1,809
TOTAL	39,478	26,925	12,280	5,316
China	826	502	1,075	33

List of Training Centers by Location:

Austria

Vienna   Ebelsberg   Steyr   Salzburg   Hallein   Wels

Germany (American Zone)

Bensheim	Neunberg
Frankfurt	Passau
Lampertsheim	Passau
Marburg	Regensburg
Offenbach	Weiden
Wiesbaden	Bad Worishofen
Eschwege	Landsberg
Kassel	Lechfeld
Backnang	Neu Ulm
Heidenheim	Feldafing
Schwab.-Hall	Fohrenwald
Stuttgart	Gauting
Ulm	Aschau
Wasserfing	Bad Aiblg
Ansbach	Bayr. Gmain
Bamberg	Gabersee
Furth	Munich
Windsheim	Reichenhall
Amberg	Traunstein
Deggendorf	
Eggenfelden	

British Zone

Belsen   Berlin   Hamburg   Hanover

Italy

Bari	Barletta	Fermo	Florence	Genoa
Grotta-	Jesi	Livorno	Merano	Milan
Ferrata	Tagani	Pisa	Rome	Turin
				Trani

Chapter XIV: After the Nazi Scourge

1. See: S. Dubnow, *World History of the Jewish People* (Yiddish), Vol. X, pp. 399-406.

2. See: Frederick Harbison and Charles A. Mayers, *Education, Manpower and Economic Growth*. New York: McGraw-Hill, 1964.

3. It should be noted that in the case of universities enormous pressure and decades of work are usually necessary to effect a change in the curriculum of an undergraduate or graduate school.

4. V. Halperin, in his article in *D'Auschwitz à Israel, op. cit.*, gives a figure of 3,071 without indicating its source.

5. There were debates at various Jewish conferences during World War I. In one, held February 7-9, 1916, in Petrograd, much time was devoted to the problem of technical education of children and adults. See: *Vestnik Trudovoi Pomoshchi sredi evreev* No. 3-4, February-March, 1916. During the Tsarist era it had been practically impossible to create the needed pedagogical conditions. With this in mind, ORT endeavored to enlist trainees in various evening courses where they could receive additional instruction in general subjects. ORT groups also organized an artisan museum where students could familiarize themselves with new equipment, designs, and other technical materials.

6. See: *Bulletin téchnique et pedagogique #39 special: seminaire sur le 20e anniversaire de l'Institut Central, ORT Geneve,* 1969. See also, *Ziele und Program des Zentraler ORT Institute zur Ausbildung von Gewertelehrern in Anieres,* ORT Union Hauptbureau, Geneva, 1948. See also, ORT reports issued in Geneva through 1978.

7. Now First Vice President of the World ORT Union, Appleton emphasized the difficulties of such an undertaking, particularly under ever-changing social conditions.

8. The World ORT Union budget consists of two essential parts: (a) funds coming to the Union from the U.S. (JDC, WAO, AOF) and other countries, including South Africa, Canada, England, Switzerland, Latin America, Scandinavia, and a few other countries; (b) local contributions to local ORT operations from government and municipal bodies, communities, membership dues, tuition fees, and other sources. Some funds in both categories are sometimes earmarked for specific projects. The figures given in Table 11 represent estimates which later are adjusted in the light of actual income and expenditures. They are sufficient to illustrate the trend. A part of the increase is due to inflation, and even more, in the last few years, to the drastic devaluation of the dollar, in which ORT budgets are determined.

Chapter XV: Renewal and Growth

1. See minutes of New York ORT Emergency Committee of July 5, 1944.

2. Poland had the distinction of being the locale of the first postwar anti-Jewish pogrom, which occurred in Kielce on July 4, 1946.

3. See report on the Chorin-Halperin mission to Poland of September 10-25, 1957.

4. See: *Folkssztyme,* Warsaw, February 5, 1959; also, Leon Shapiro in *American Jewish Year Book* No. 61, 1961.

5. The Rumanian section of the World Jewish Congress in 1942 issued the following statistical picture of the occupational distribution of Rumanian Jews:

Occupation	Number	%
Artisans and workers	39629	36.6
Comm. office workers	31334	28.9
Business and Industry	21181	19.6
Professions and Univ.	5379	5.0
Rel. Teachers, Clergy	3394	3.1
Various	7355	6.8
	108,272	100.0

6. The territory between the Dnestr and Bug, taken from Russia, which was administered by the Rumanians under the fascist government of Antonescu. It became a dumping ground for deported Rumanian Jews.

7. See: Introduction by Judge Meiss in *Bulletin d'Information*, ORT Francais, December, 1946. See also, J. Lubetzki, *La Condition de Juifs en France sous l'Occupation Allemande*, C.D.J.C., Paris, 1945, and Leon Shapiro, "A Review of Lubetzki's Study," in *Jewish Social Studies*, Vol. III, New York, July, 1946. When the Vichy government introduced the so-called "*Statut Juif*," which abrogated the rights of French Jews, the Chief Rabbi of France, Issaie Schwartz, protested this abomination in a letter dated October 27, 1940, addressed to the Chief of State and members of the government.

8. During the occupation, the 1870 Cremieux decree was abrogated by Vichy. For a discussion of the legal and social status of the Jews in French North Africa see Michael Ansky, *Les Juifs d'Algerie*, Edition du Centre, Paris, 1950; André Chouraqui, *La Condition de l'Israelite Marocain*, Presse du Livre Francais, Paris, 1950, and Maurice Eisenback, *Les Juifs de l'Afrique du Nord*, Imprimérie du Lycee, Algiers, 1936. See also, *ORT Francais, son Activité en 1950*.

9. See minutes of New York ORT Emergency Committee of June 23, 1943 and September 16, 1943.

10. See: Cecily Zimmerman, *op. cit.*

11. See: Cecily Zimmerman, *ibid*. In the course of the author's visit to London in July 1977, he was privileged to meet with both Mrs. Mowshovitch and Mr. Wolff, who gave him the benefit of their thorough familiarity with ORT efforts in Great Britain.

12. British ORT contributions include amounts given by ORT, Women's ORT, and special allocations for the Jerusalem Engineering School.

13. See annual reports of ORT activities.

14. See: *ORT-Idies* No. 4, February, 1944, New York. See also, *ORT Economic Review*, Vol. III, No. 2, 3-4 1942, New York.

15. Use was made of the story of ORT in Brazil, mainly in Rio de Janeiro, prepared by Vice Chairman of ORT, Brazil, Salomon Serebrenick in cooperation with Samuel Malamud, the Chairman. The author is indebted to Mr. Malamud for sending him this material.

16. See: *ORT-Idies, op. cit.*

17. *Ibid.*

18. *Ibid.*

19. See: Paul Bernick, "Impressions of the South American Journey," American ORT Federation, New York, undated. Bernick's visit occurred in 1971. See also, Jacob Shatzky, *Communidades Judias en Latino America.* Buenos Aires: American Jewish Committee, 1952; Boris Sapir, *The Jewish Community in Cuba, Settlement and Growth.* New York: Jewish Teachers' Seminary and People's University, 1948.

Chapter XVI: New Horizons

1. See reports on ORT activities of 1948, 1951, 1952, 1957.

2. See report of M. Braude to the Executive Committee, 1959, 1960, and *Assises du Judaisme Algerien*, March 12-13, 1959, Algiers.

3. See September, 1955, report of F. Schrager, *Vegn unzere Meglichkaitn un Oisgabn in Morocco.*

4. These loans were made out of the D. Lvovich Fund established in memory of D. Lvovich.

5. Bene Israel, about 15,000 in 1948. Some are descendants of intermarriages, creating problems of Jewish status. Of late, the Sephardic rabbis have looked with favor on their integration into the Jewish community. See: S. W. Baron, *A Social and Religious History of the Jews*, Vol. III. Philadelphia: The Jewish Publication Society of America, 1957; and Solomon Grayzel, *A History of the Jews.* Philadelphia: The Jewish Publication Society of America, 1957.

6. See: *ORT-India Purim Magazine*, undated.

7. See report by Robin Gilbert made to the American JDC Executive Staff Conference, March 20, 1959; also report of World ORT Union for 1962, Central Office, Geneva. Ben-Zvi, second President of Israel, devoted much of his research and writing to the Oriental Jews. See letter by President Ben-Zvi to M. Braude, May 27, 1957 (in Hebrew). Modern research on the Falashas is attributable to Jacques Faitlovitch who visited Ethiopia in 1904-1905. See, among his writings, "Notes d'un Voyage chez les Falachas. Rapport présente à M. le Baron Edmond de Rothschild." Paris, 1905.

8. It was reported that 38 Falashas were killed and 18 sold into slavery.

See: *Overseas Reports*, Council of Jewish Federations and Welfare Fund, New York, January, 1979.

9. See memos and reports in AOF files dealing with ORT work in Ethiopia, particularly with respect to religious activities, dated September, 1978.

10. For general data and statistics by country see reports of the World ORT Union, ORT Union, Geneva, 1946-1978. See also, M. Braude's reports to the Executive Committee.

Chapter XVII: Israel–On a Nationwide Scale

1. Paragraph 19 of the ORT memorandum to the IRO dated December 3, 1947, states: "In accordance with promises ORT has made to the DP organizations, ORT is to have the possibility to transfer its vocational training workshops, together with the remaining ORT supplies and equipment, to Palestine or to other receiving countries as the population and the students which ORT was assisting emigrate to such countries." In a reply to this memorandum, PCIRO, on December 24, 1947, stated: "It is understood that the right of ORT to transfer supplies, equipment, and other properties to Palestine or other receiving countries, as referred to in Paragraph 19 of your letter, is limited to properties to which, at the time of the proposed transfer, ORT is absolutely entitled in its own right or over which it has an absolute right of disposition, the removal of which will not contravene any regulation of the governing authorities of the territory in which such properties are located."

2. In a message to the American ORT convention held in New York in May, 1949, President Weizmann expressed his happiness with the progress of ORT in Israel. Paul Bernick, in a conversation, remembered having gone to Weizmann's suite in the Waldorf-Astoria to obtain the message.

3. See Braude's reports to the Executive Committee, 1957, 1958, 1959.

4. See: Leon Shapiro, "A Glimpse of the Mahgreb," in *The American Zionist*, Vol. 44, No. 7, February 15, 1954.

5. See: Abraham S. Hyman, *Education in Israel–a Survey*. New York: Israeli Education Fund, undated.

6. See: Joshua Fliedel, *Changes in the System of Occupational High Schools in Israel in 1960-1975*. Study submitted to Tel Aviv University, March, 1977.

7. See: Herzog address at American ORT Federation dinner, January 26, 1974, in files of American ORT Federation.

8. *Ibid*.

9. For ORT in Israel, see also minutes of the Executive Committee, ORT-Israel, for the period June 7, 1949, to December 25, 1951 (in Hebrew).

Chapter XVIII: Facing Its Second Century

1. See: *Récueil présente à l'occasion du dixième anniversaire de la mort du Dr. Aron Syngalowski, 1956-1966*, UMO, Geneva.

2. Nathan Gould, "ORT as a Movement in Jewish Life," Women's American ORT position paper, New York, 1968. For Women's American ORT involvement in general affairs, see Kenneth B. Hoyt, *Women's American ORT and Career Education*, U.S. Department of Health, Education and Welfare, Office of Education, U.S. Government Printing Office, Washington, D.C., 1978.

3. See more particularly reports on ORT in Latin America where ORT's participation in the local day schools was changing the character of Jewish education there.

GLOSSARY

Aliyah—immigration to Palestine and later to Israel

Artel—small scale groups of workers or artisans collectively engaged in an industrial or agricultural project.

Benelux—an economic Union involving Belgium, the Netherlands, and Luxembourg.

Bezprizornye—children left behind by families exiled or otherwise destroyed by the Soviets and numbering in hundreds of thousands.

Bricha—illegal immigration to Palestine during the period of World War II.

Conseil National de Résistance—The underground coordinating body of the French Resistance during the Nazi occupation.

Duma—A legislative parliament which existed in Russia from 1906 through 1917.

Evsekovets—a member or a follower of the *Evsektziia*.

Gezeig—Yiddish word for machines and/or instruments.

Golus—Diaspora

Gubernia—an administrative territorial unit in pre-Bolshevik Russia

Haidamaks—Ukrainian rebels who rose in the 17th century against their Polish landlords, and who organized merciless anti-Jewish pogroms.

Hovevei-Zion—proponents of Jewish colonization in Palestine in the 1880's. Spread through Tsarist Russia, particularly after the pogroms of the 1880's.

Khaper—from the Yiddish word *Khapn,* to catch. Men who, under Nikolai I, delivered to the authorities the imposed quota of young Jewish boys for military service.

Kohanim (Kohen)—decendants of Aaron—priests.

Kolkhoz—a Soviet collectivized peasant economic unit.

Kramola—a Russian word for sedition

Kulak—a well to-do peasant

Landsmanschaft—society of former residents of towns located in the old country.

Lesnoi Institute—a school at the university level preparing for careers in forestry.

Ligue des Droits de l'Homme—the major civil rights organization in France, traditionally reflecting the leftist sector of French society.

Lishentsy—from the Russian work *lishat',* to be stripped of (in this case) rights.

Loan Kassa—a credit help society

Luftmench—a Jew without occupation or gainful employment

Maskil—an enlightened Jew, following the Western ways.

Mellah—Jewish quarter of the city in Morocco

Merchants of the First Guild—In Tsarist Russia merchants were distributed among various catagories. Jewish merchants of the First Guild belonged to the top group and benefitted from all the rights given to non-Jews.

Narodnichestvo—a Russian social movement, involving intelligentsia and sons of upper classes going to the people (*narod* in Russian) to bring enlightenment and revolutionary ideas to the masses.

Otchet—a Russian word meaning report

Pan—landowner in Polish

Purim—a holiday commemorating the defeat of Haman, as recorded in the book of Esther.

Rachmones—pity, charitable attitude

Shtadlan—a Hebrew term designating a Jew who represented Jewish interests before the authorities. *Shtadlonim* were often self-appointed rich Jews.

Sviataia Druzhina (Sacred League)—an extremely nationalist anti-Semitic secret group organized in Russia after the assassination of Alexandr II.

Tsar Chesed v'Emes—righteous Tsar

Tsar Osvoboditel—Aleksandr II, who freed the peasant serfs. From the word *svoboda* - freedom.

Uchilishche—a Russian term for a school or a college

Yidgezkom—abbreviation of *Yiddisher Gezelshaftlicher Komitet.*

Zemstvo—rural self-government in Tsarist Russia.

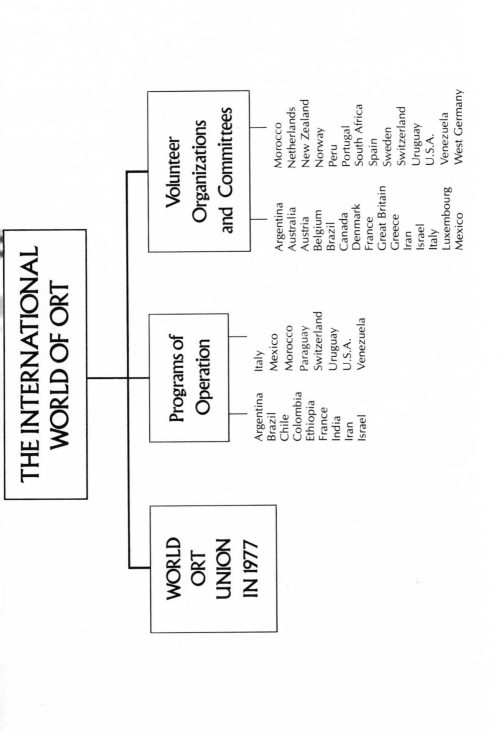

THE INTERNATIONAL WORLD OF ORT

WORLD ORT UNION IN 1977

Programs of Operation

Argentina	Italy
Brazil	Mexico
Chile	Morocco
Colombia	Paraguay
Ethiopia	Switzerland
France	Uruguay
India	U.S.A.
Iran	Venezuela
Israel	

Volunteer Organizations and Committees

Argentina	Morocco
Australia	Netherlands
Austria	New Zealand
Belgium	Norway
Brazil	Peru
Canada	Portugal
Denmark	South Africa
France	Spain
Great Britain	Sweden
Greece	Switzerland
Iran	Uruguay
Israel	U.S.A.
Italy	Venezuela
Luxembourg	West Germany
Mexico	

Greece
40 Rue Du Stade
Athens 132
Hon. Dir.—Nissim Alcalay

India
P.O. Box 16233
Bombay 400010
Chm.—Gerhard L. Gabriel
Dir.—Joseph Guedj

Iran
P.O. Box 1525
Teheran
Pres.—Nejat Gabbay
Dir.—Mrs. Parvine Moatamed

Israel
39 Shderot David Hamelech
P.O. Box 16087
Tel Aviv, Israel 64954
Pres.—Chaim Herzog
Dir.—Joseph Harmatz

Italy
Via S. Francesco di Sales 5
00165 Rome
Pres.—Dr. Ing. Bruno Jarach
Dir.—Ferrucio Sonnino

Via Sally Mayer 4
20146 Milan
Chm.—Dr. Eugenio Mortara
Dir.—Ing. Izidor Alkalay

Luxembourg
26 Rue Glesener
Luxembourg
Pres.—Dr. Simon Hertz

Mexico
ORT Femenina de Mexico
Mariano Escobedo 331-6
Mexico 5, D.F.
Pres.—Mrs. Julia Retchkiman
Sec.—Helen Gutverg

Morocco
11, rue Eleonore Fournier
Casablanca
Chm.—David Amar
Dir.—Joseph Amar

Netherlands
4 Weesperplein
Amsterdam
Chm.—B.A.M. Vorst

Norway
Norwegian ORT Committee
c/o Norwegian Refugee Council
Professor Dahlgt. 1
Oslo 3
Pres.—Hans Cappelen
Sec.—H.P. Boe

Peru
Pezet 961/401/S.I.
Lima
Chm.—Izak Wallach

Portugal
c/o Narciso G. Arié
Rua Alexandre Herculano 11,40
Lisbon
Chm.—Narciso G. Arié

South Africa
P.O. Box 5883
93 Iris Road, Norwood
Johannesburg 2001
Chm.—Richard Goldstone

Sweden
Foreningen Svenska ORT
Odengatan 81
113 22 Stockholm
Chm.—Ivar Philipson
Exec. Sec.—Mr. David
    Kopniwsky

Switzerland
3, Rue de Varembe
1211 Geneva 20
Acting Pres.—Mrs. Jacqueline
    Maus

United States
817 Broadway
New York, N.Y. 10003
Pres.—Harold Friedman
Exec. Dir.—Paul Bernick

Uruguay
Cuareim 1457
Montevideo
Dir.—Bernardo Blejmar

Venezuela
Apartado Aereo 6606
Caracas 101
Chm.—Emerico Lanes
Sec.—Mrs. Sara P. de Sharifker

Index

401